Retreat from Power

VOLUME ONE: 1906–1939

RETREAT FROM POWER

Studies in
Britain's Foreign Policy
of the
Twentieth Century

VOLUME ONE
1906–1939

Edited by
DAVID DILKS

Professor of International History
University of Leeds

© David Dilks, Norman Hillmer, Michael Howard
Norton Medlicott, Colin Strang, Philip Taylor,
Keith Wilson 1981

First published 1981 by
THE MACMILLAN PRESS LTD
London and Basingstoke
Associated companies in Delhi Dublin
Hong Kong Johannesburg Lagos Melbourne
New York Singapore and Tokyo

Printed in Great Britain by
J. W. Arrowsmith Ltd, Bristol

British Library Cataloguing in Publication Data

Retreat from power.
  Vol. 1: 1906–1939
   1. Great Britain – Foreign relations – 20th century
  I. Dilks, David
  327.41   DA566.7

  ISBN 0–333–29909–9
  ISBN 0–333–28910–2 Pbk

Contents

Preface   vii

Introduction   1
    DAVID DILKS

BRITISH POWER IN THE EUROPEAN BALANCE,   21
1906–14
    KEITH WILSON

2 PUBLICITY AND DIPLOMACY: THE IMPACT OF   42
THE FIRST WORLD WAR UPON FOREIGN OFFICE
ATTITUDES TOWARDS THE PRESS
    PHILIP TAYLOR

3 THE FOREIGN OFFICE, THE DOMINIONS AND THE   64
DIPLOMATIC UNITY OF THE EMPIRE, 1925–29
    NORMAN HILLMER

4 BRITAIN AND GERMANY: THE SEARCH FOR   78
AGREEMENT, 1930–37
    NORTON MEDLICOTT

5 BRITISH MILITARY PREPARATIONS FOR THE   102
SECOND WORLD WAR
    MICHAEL HOWARD

6 THE HOARE–LAVAL PACT RECONSIDERED   118
    NORTON MEDLICOTT

7 APPEASEMENT AND 'INTELLIGENCE'   139
    DAVID DILKS

8 THE MOSCOW NEGOTIATIONS, 1939   170
    THE LATE LORD STRANG

Notes and References   187

List of Contributors   203

Index   204

The illustration on the front of the book shows some of the key figures involved in British foreign policy between 1906 and 1939: Lord Grey of Fallodon, Mr Antony Eden, Sir Samuel Hoare, Sir Robert Vansittart, Lord Halifax and Mr Neville Chamberlain. The photographs are reproduced by kind permission of the BBC Hulton Picture Library.

Preface

ALL the papers in this volume, and in its companion, relate to the period of Britain's decline as a great power. That is not to say that each author tells a story of unrelieved failure or unbroken retreat. Nevertheless, the broad theme of the volume is provided by the inability or unwillingness of the British to match their resources to their risks. Some of the papers deal with such large questions as Britain's contribution to the European balance before the First World War, or her military planning and relations with Germany in the 1930s; some with celebrated episodes like the Hoare–Laval pact and the fruitless negotiations at Moscow in 1939 between the Soviet Union, Britain and France; others with issues which have so far received comparatively little attention.

Although the late Lord Strang's article on the Moscow negotiations was composed more than ten years ago, it remains the best compressed account, and – because none of the other participants in the political discussions has written of them – retains a documentary value of its own. In providing footnote references for that paper, as in so much else, I have had the invaluable advice of Professor W. N. Medlicott. His own article on Britain and Germany has long been out of print and is reproduced here by kind permission of the Athlone Press. None of the other essays has been published previously; all are based upon seminars or lectures given here, and it is a source of particular pleasure that three of the contributors to these volumes, Professors Margaret Gowing, Michael Howard and Norton Medlicott, are honorary graduates of the University.

I should like to acknowledge with gratitude the help of Miss Katherine Riley, Mr John Davies, Mrs Joy Farquharson and Mrs Rona Ure in the searching out of references and preparation of the typescript.

School of History
The University of Leeds

DAVID DILKS
9 January 1980

Introduction

DAVID DILKS

IN the great days of the empire eighty or a hundred years ago, we are
sometimes told, the British ruled the world and through the Royal Navy
enforced peace; exported their talent and goods chiefly to British
territories overseas; were grand enough to afford a policy of 'splendid
isolation'; and even pursued with consistency a policy intended to
prevent the domination of Europe by a single power or alliance. Each of
these beliefs is apt to mislead; their combined effect is to magnify the
height of Britain's power and thus the depth of her fall. Undeniably, the
fall has been swift and serious; but we may measure it more accurately
by remembering that, far from being a period of profound peace, the
nineteenth century was a time of frequent wars, some large and some
small. The pax britannica did not prevail uninterruptedly over large
parts of the world. For the acquisition and retention of the empire, the
British fought often. In contests which could be determined by sea
power, Great Britain could usually prevail, could (as Lord Salisbury
characteristically expressed it) gain her way by squadrons and tall talk.
In disputes where sea power could play a considerable role, but not
necessarily a determining one, the British found themselves with a
substantial influence if they cared to exercise it, though not always with
the deciding voice; the crisis which culminated in the Congress of Berlin
in 1878 is a case in point. But in numerous other issues, especially in
Europe, the British found themselves virtually impotent in this century
of their supposed dominance; for the most important weakness of
Britain's international position at the end of the nineteenth century, as
in 1914 and 1939, was that in relation to her risks, she maintained a
small army.

The reasons for which British statesmen wished to retain mastery at
sea are clear enough; the invasion of the British Isles would be

impossible, the seaborne trade upon which the country depended would be sustained, the sprawl of territories constituting the British empire could be reached in safety. Hence the anxiety with which ministers viewed some of the extensions of that empire in the last quarter of the century. Hence the keenness of the British not to share a land frontier with a first class power. They had already one such frontier, it is true, between Canada and the United States. Since it was over 3000 miles long, with no hope of local defence, the British could only pray earnestly that the United States would not be seized by a renewed zeal for expansion. The Indian subcontinent, on the other hand, provided a source of ceaseless anxiety as Russia's frontier in Central Asia moved southwards. Hence the British determination to preserve a buffer, embracing Tibet and south-eastern Persia but above all Afghanistan. At the end of the nineteenth century and early in the twentieth, war against Russia was regarded as more probable than any other. That, rather than the defence of the Low Countries, was deemed the chief task of the British and Indian armies.

'Splendid isolation' did not mean freedom from commitment. On the contrary, no great power was more heavily engaged. Nor did it mean that Britain was detached from the rest of the world, for her interests were more widely scattered than those of any other power. In practice, Great Britain was pledged to defend her empire, parts of which lay in every continent but Europe, and some territories – for instance, sheik-doms in the Persian Gulf, Egypt, the Sudan – which were not enfolded within it. As for Europe, it was not the invariable practice of the British government to support the weaker side. After the defeat of France in 1871 and the establishment of the alliance with Austria, there was no doubt that Germany and her allies were stronger than potential rivals. Nevertheless, the British frequently aligned themselves with Germany. There were two main reasons: first, Germany was judged to be a satisfied power, and there seemed no immediate prospect that she would try to dominate the rest of Europe; secondly, Britain found herself constantly at odds outside Europe with France and Russia. Against those two powers Britain's naval building in the later nineteenth century was chiefly directed. Twice in a single year, 1898, Britain and France came close to war and already British ministers had realised how uncomfortable, rather than splendid, was the position in which they had no dependable ally. The point was promptly dem-onstrated during the Boer War, which revealed Britain's woeful weakness on land and the hearty dislike felt for her by the European powers, outweighed, mercifully for the British, by the divisions between them.

By the close of the nineteenth century, British ministers had initiated a policy of limiting the country's commitments and removing points of friction. They hoped by this means to secure immunity from major wars. Fruitless attempts were made on several occasions to come to terms with Germany; since the two powers did not have major colonial interests which clashed, or many bargains which they could strike in Europe, the material for agreement could not easily be found. Germany had no sufficient incentive to offer Britain increased security against Russia or France over African or Asian issues, nor Britain to pledge herself in Europe. On the other hand, Britain was able to reach useful settlements with the United States and then, in her only departure before 1914 from isolation properly defined (freedom from prior military commitment to an ally) a treaty with Japan.

The rise of Japan as a naval power, and growing hostility between her and Russia, implied that the British had to maintain a naval presence in the Far East capable of defending their interests against Japan; or trust to luck; or come to terms. The obligation was restricted to the Far East; Britain would not fight unless Japan were at war with two other powers; and if the contract had to be honoured, it would be done largely by the exercise of naval power and at the other end of the world. In other words, the alliance did not raise the issue of conscription which British governments dreaded on political and financial grounds alike. 'The large aggregations of human forces', Salisbury wrote on his retirement a few months later, 'which lie around our Empire seem to draw more closely together, and to assume almost unconsciously a more and more aggressive aspect. Their junction, in menacing and dangerous manner, may be deferred for many years – or may be precipitated with little notice at any moment.'[1]

The British had solid reasons, apart from apprehension about Germany, for seeking the agreements of 1904 with France and of 1907 with Russia. No British minister wished to continue quarrels with France, accord with whom would make the government of Egypt a much easier business; the French had no more desire than the British to fight when Japan attacked Russia without warning early in 1904. No doubt the fear of enormous Russian forces advancing towards India across some of the most inhospitable terrain in the world was exaggerated. Yet it was not a vision so remote as to be inconceivable, especially after the Russian railways in Central Asia moved forward. To hold India securely was the prime object of British policy. If Russia approached or crossed India's borders, if disaffection were successfully incited and the government proved incapable of upholding its authority, the basis of dominion there would be gone. All this reminds us that in international affairs the capacity to pose a credible threat may often be a factor of much importance in the formation of policy. The British had an earnest wish to escape from the dilemma in which they acknowledged that a threat to India must call for the despatch of 100,000 or even 150,000 troops – the whole of the effective army at home – and yet could not see the means of achieving it.

In beginning serious naval construction, the Germans had with commendable candour published their reasons; and in 1902 the British ambassador remarked with reluctance, 'the German Navy is professedly aimed at that of the greatest naval Power – us.'[2] British ministers of both parties began to ask why the strongest land power in Europe should spend very large sums on becoming a great naval power, when she could devote the same money more productively to her domestic purposes or (if she were fearful for her own safety, which seemed unlikely) to a further strengthening of her army.

The Anglo-French agreement of 1904 was not an alliance; it did not commit either party to belligerency or neutrality in time of war. But British apprehensions about Germany, the outbursts of ill-feeling between the two countries, the widespread mistrust of the Kaiser's motives, soon pushed Britain and France more closely together. Very few had realised how the war between Japan and Russia might end. It is said that Admiral Fisher pointed out to the Foreign Secretary the place where the Japanese fleet would most probably be destroyed. In the event, the Japanese held Russia on land, and ruined successively Russia's Far Eastern squadron and then the Baltic Fleet which limped by painful stages to the Far East only to be sunk on arrival. These events and the turbulence within Russia made an early threat to India less plausible. They also undermined for the time being the value of the Franco-Russian alliance and seemed unlikely to exercise a restraining influence on Germany.

The emperor William II said at Christmas 1904 that he was convinced England was seeking an opportunity to attack Germany; he must have had in mind a naval attack, since (as Bismarck had cuttingly put it) the British had an army which the German police could arrest. His ambassador in London, to whom this remark was made, rightly replied that no serious person in England desired a war with Germany, and the idea that England would attack Germany would only be laughed at in England. Lord Lansdowne commented that it would be 'impossible to find a sane individual in these Islands who thinks that it would be for our interest, or was likely to become our duty, to fasten a quarrel upon Germany'. On the other hand, there seemed ample evidence that the emperor was annoyed by the agreement between Britain and France; while the crisis over Morocco in 1905–6, the secret but abortive arrangement between the emperor and the czar, his reported desire to bring Germany, France and Russia together to the exclusion of Britain, caused the Foreign Secretary to write in August 1905, 'I must say that the description of the Kaiser's language and demeanour fills me with disquiet. What may not a man in such a frame of mind do next?'[3]

Such apprehensions, though not strong enough to overbear Britain's dislike of military engagements in Europe, did lead to the secret staff conversations with the French which would have been inconceivable a few years before. The outgoing Conservative Foreign Secretary, Lord Lansdowne, and his Liberal successor, Sir Edward Grey, both expressed the opinion to the German ambassador that if Germany should make an attack on France arising from the agreement of 1904, public feeling in England would be so strong that no British government could remain neutral.[4] Then the immediate crisis passed away; the Foreign Secretary confessed himself anxious to see Russia re-established as a factor in European politics; and the Russian government was willing after the defeat by Japan to accept terms not very different from those previously refused. The agreement between Britain and Russia of 1907, like that with France, was not an alliance and never converted into one. It left many causes of friction.

Most ministers conceived of the German threat in naval terms, and believed that supremacy at sea would meet Britain's main risks. The Russian disabilities not only made an agreement with that country more attainable, but even by the spring of 1906 had caused the Committee of Imperial Defence to judge that operations by Russia on a large scale against India would be 'quite beyond their power at the present time'.[5] This was just as well, since the Cabinet was already bent upon a reduction in the regular army. On the other hand, the CID did record in 1908 that so long as naval supremacy was assured against any likely combination, invasion was not practicable; whereas if command of the sea were lost, the subjection of Britain would be inevitable whatever might be the strength and organisation of the home force.

> The German Emperor is ageing me [Grey wrote just after this]; he is
> like a battleship with steam up and screws going, but with no rudder,
> and he will run into something some day and cause a catastrophe . . .
> he has the strongest army in the world and the Germans don't like
> being laughed at and are looking for somebody on whom to vent their
> temper and use their strength. After a big war a nation doesn't want
> another for a generation or more . . . now it is 38 years since
> Germany had her last war, and she is very strong and very restless,
> like a person whose boots are too small for him. I don't think there
> will be war at present, but it will be difficult to keep the peace of
> Europe for another five years.[6]

The agreements with France and Russia had not in any way
diminished Britain's determination to remain a great naval power. It
became the rule of naval policy that whatever Germany added to her
fleet should be substantially out-built by Britain. Many of the German
vessels were not designed to protect commerce or undertake defensive
action in home waters; it was believed that Germany could speed up her
naval programme; and the Foreign Secretary was accordingly among
those who insisted that ample provision must be made for a good margin
of safety against Germany in 1912–13. Justifying the increased
estimates in parliament, Grey put the point plainly enough. If Britain
alone among the great powers gave up the competition in arms and
sank into a position of inferiority, she would

> cease to count for anything amongst the nations of Europe, and we
> should be fortunate if our liberty was left, and we did not become the
> conscript appendage of some stronger Power. That is a brutal way of
> stating the case, but it is the truth . . .
>   There is no comparison between the importance of the German
> Navy to Germany, and the importance of our Navy to us. Our Navy
> is to us what their Army is to them. To have a strong Navy would
> increase their prestige, their diplomatic influence, their power of
> protecting their commerce; but it is not a matter of life and death to
> them as it is to us.[7]

This was what Tirpitz called the period of danger during which the
growing fleet of Germany might be destroyed by the British. Even

though Russia was clearly weakened, there was no sign in the period between 1906 and 1911 that Germany was willing to risk a general war. Admiral Fisher's threat that if need be the Royal Navy could 'Copenhagen' the German fleet had attained a wide currency and was no doubt taken more seriously than it should have been. Nevertheless, the threat represented a substantial fact. Unless Britain were heavily engaged elsewhere, she would presumably on the outbreak of a war use her strength at sea to cut off Germany's colonies in Africa and the Pacific and her overseas trade, including supplies of raw materials and food. The Royal Navy would prevent any German landing behind the French lines. If the British were not able to sink the German Fleet, they might confine it to port. All these consequences followed in 1914 and after.

Within the bounds of a determination to preserve naval superiority and the improved relations with France and Russia, the Cabinet did its best to avoid bad relations with Germany. The British had no ambition for territory in Europe; all attempts at a political settlement with Germany failed; and offers of a diminution or temporary suspension of naval building were turned down. As ministers repeatedly observed, Germany could not fear conquest by Britain while the British army remained so small; whereas if Germany secured control of the sea, she could (in Grey's words of 1911) 'be in London in a very short time'.[8] The First Lord of the Admiralty remarked, however, that so long as the British kept sea superiority, the enemy would be able neither to transport his forces nor to continue his trade, 'and the result of the economic pressure of the destruction of overseas trade in almost any modern state would be so serious as, I believe, to constitute something even more than a crippling blow'.[9] This was an overstatement, perhaps a natural one in representatives of a power which placed such reliance upon its navy; to some degree the error was repeated before and during the Second World War.

The Admiralty recorded each day the position of every significant German ship, whether of the German navy or of the merchant marine. This practice had been instituted well before the crisis of 1911, in which Germany's discovery of her own subjects and threatened interests, in the immediate vicinity of the only port on the western coast of Morocco which could be developed into an Atlantic naval base, was described by the Prime Minister as 'an interesting illustration of "Realpolitik"'.[10] Despite more than intermittent difficulties with Russia, the Foreign Secretary continued to believe that there was no serious prospect of war with her or France. Nor did the British wish to be dragged into some European quarrel which did not concern them. They refrained from making any binding promises.

Grey remarked in 1912, 'we arrange our foreign policy in close concert with our ship-building programme'.[11] The relative simplicity of British thinking on these subjects before the First World War strikes any student who makes the contrast with later days. The British Isles were believed safe from invasion; the parties agreed on the need to maintain a good margin of naval supremacy; all the complications introduced by the rapid development of the aeroplane lay still in the future. On the surface at least, Britain's relations with Germany in 1914 were better than for some time, a state which Tirpitz declared to have been reached the more easily because of German naval strength.

The question whether a clear British declaration would have deterred Germany in 1914, assuming that Grey had been in a position to make such a declaration, has been exhaustively debated. German military plans, about which the British were uncertain, looked for a quick victory against France. In relation to the other European powers, Britain was so weak on land that a mere announcement, or even an alliance with France, would not in all probability have produced much effect; but it is impossible to be sure, for by general consent the British empire's actual strength at sea, and potential strength in manpower, raw materials and the economic sinews of war, were great. The staff conversations with France and to a lesser extent with Russia did not bring an automatic British commitment, as the events of 1914 made plain; but they did make British neutrality less feasible.

It is widely believed that only a system of entangling alliances converted a Balkan quarrel into a great war. This is open to doubt. Perhaps states fought in 1914 not because the terms of alliance compelled it, but because their perception of their own interests indicated that course. On this reading, the alignments at the outset of war would have been much the same even if alliances between Germany and Austria, and France and Russia, had not been in force. The violation of Belgium was no doubt the occasion rather than the cause of Britain's decision to fight. In a parliamentary democracy, the occasion counts for a great deal. It clearly played a large part in tilting the balance of opinion in the Cabinet. That Grey's crucial speech should dwell both on the moral and on the practical issues was just. He asked parliament to weigh the appeal to honour; and to consider what would be Britain's position if France were beaten in a struggle for life and death, 'beaten to her knees, . . . subordinate to the will and power of one greater than herself.'

At sea, the British were well prepared. Because Japan continued to honour the alliance, there was no need to keep a large fleet east of Suez. A blockade was applied against Germany, the German fleet was confined to port for most of the war and though grievous losses to merchant shipping were sustained, they were not sufficient to starve Britain out. Nevertheless, the war exposed a failure in British foreign and defence policy. The possibility of fighting in Europe to prevent domination by Germany had been foreseen, though intermittently and faintly by most ministers. Britain had neglected to equip herself with an army related to that contingency. She had no adequate reserve of trained men. She did not have the uniforms, ammunition, rifles, artillery or even the plans for producing them. The maintenance of a much larger army would have called for agreement between the two main parties; it would have added to the burden of taxation; but by comparison with the cost of the coming struggle, the price in peacetime would have been small and the benefit in war immense.

Power was so evenly distributed between the contending alliances that despite heroic efforts, neither side could win. No accommodation could be reached. So deeply entrenched were the habits of the British that during nearly three years of murderous fighting, they still refused to introduce effective conscription. Their contribution on land was at first so modest that it was impossible to enforce an agreed strategy with France and Russia, of whose plans Britain had little knowledge. As Churchill put it to the Cabinet in 1915, 'Hitherto we have not been a military partner of sufficient status to bring our influence markedly to bear on the counsels of our Allies. We have been forced to watch the British attack at Neuve Chapelle while the French remained wholly inactive.'[12]

It is scarcely surprising that in these desperate straits the British and their allies bought support where they could. After a period of poised neutrality, Italy joined them in 1915, at the price of promises known to contradict the principle of nationality and which, worse still, the allies proved unwilling or unable to redeem in 1919. After efforts to reach a separate peace had failed, every effort was to made to hasten the decomposition of the Austro-Hungarian empire. The recreation of an

independent Poland was promised. At the end of the war, Russia
therefore ceased to have her former value to France not only because of
internal upheaval, military defeat and a proclaimed determination to
subvert other governments, but because she no longer shared a frontier
with Germany and could not bring direct pressure to bear; whereas
independent Poland provided Germany and Russia with a tempting
prize, a potent reason for hostility to the settlements, and was to be the
main sweetener and lubricant of their agreement in 1939. Perhaps the
disintegration of Austro-Hungary was inevitable in the long run;
or it may be that some looser system might have accommodated the contending nationalities. At all events, the disappearance
of the Habsburg empire meant that despite Germany's defeat in
1918, the settlement created little by way of counterpoise.

It is not meet and right for later generations to pronounce loftily
about the value or futility of others' sacrifices. There was nothing at the
time, and no convincing evidence has since been produced, to show that
the British were fundamentally wrong in their judgment of the issues at
stake; namely, that Germany might defeat France or Russia or both,
possess most of the resources of Europe, including the naval resources,
and therefore produce an imbalance of power so great that the British
could not tolerate it. In reaching this judgment, they measured by the
standards of previous wars, and had no means of imagining how long
the First World War would last, how many would be killed and
wounded and what an enormous sacrifice of economic assets would be
demanded. It is true that other countries lost more men, though
perhaps none suffered a broader swath cut through the best, most
energetic and patriotic men volunteering to go to the front. No nation
sustained greater financial damage, for in addition to upholding their
own war effort the British became the bankers of the alliance, lending
from their own resources sums which in most cases were not repaid or
(because British credit in the United States was better than that of
others) borrowing there and re-lending to allies. British holdings of
investments abroad, the income from which had been a substantial
factor in the country's economic security before the First World War,
never recovered.

The 'isolation' of the United States was a very different affair from the
'splendid isolation' of the British. Beyond the confines of the Monroe
Doctrine, which no great power aspired to challenge anyway, the
United States was genuinely free of international obligations. It is all
too easy to forget at this distance of time that innumerable and most

serious difficulties arose between the British and the Americans. In the First World War as in the Second, but to a greater degree in the former struggle, the effect of the blockade was undermined by American insistence upon the rights of neutral nations. However, the eventual arrival of America as an ally more than made good the collapse of Russia in 1917. The United States had great economic strength and reserves of manpower, though she was ill-prepared for the struggle. Her financial support was of the first importance; it is difficult to see how, without access to the American money-market and the direct help of the US government, the war could have been won. Because the United States suffered little by comparison with her European allies, she ended the war in far better fettle, wielding much political power in the later stages and at the peacemaking in Paris.

Whereas Lloyd George took good care to hold an early election and get an ample majority behind him, President Wilson could bring to the negotiations no surety that a settlement in which his influence had been so pervasive would be endorsed by the Senate and Congress. There was no choice but to deal with the American delegation on the assumption that America would ratify the treaties and be an active member of the League of Nations. Russia played no part in the peace conferences, and relatively little in the international politics of the next fifteen or even twenty years; certainly no part comparable with her importance. Because the United States took an even smaller role than Russia, except in the economic sphere, the international affairs of the inter-war years bore a peculiar character. A heavy burden devolved upon Britain and France, one which the events of the 1930s proved they could not or would not sustain.

The Covenant of the League, a most ambitious document going far beyond everything previously attempted, or anything which realistic observers have expected, for instance, from the Charter of the United Nations, purported to provide security the world over. It also laid upon each member the duty of treating an attack upon another as an act to be resisted, by diplomatic pressure and disapproval, by economic sanctions or even by force. It presumed the active membership of the great powers. Its purpose was to create an overwhelming imbalance of power against an aggressor. The embracing nature of the duties remained; the universal membership never existed. It is unlikely that the British would have accepted such obligations had it been known at the start that they would not be shared by the United States. A chasm was therefore opened from the outset between profession and likely performance.

At first glance, the allies in the summer of 1919 enjoyed ample security. Germany had been defeated and Austria–Hungary dismembered; the remnants of the Turkish empire had fallen away; Germany was to pay a large but unspecified sum in reparation. But the only cement of the victorious coalition, fear of defeat by Germany, had crumbled away. Even at the peacemaking, as had happened at the end of the Napoleonic Wars and was to happen again in 1945, old disputes revived among the allies, and new antagonisms arose. The French were deprived of the strategic security which a Rhine frontier would have brought, and also in due course of the Anglo-American guarantee which they had accepted as an alternative. The United States quickly relapsed into a sour detachment from political commitments, though it would be wrong to present that fact as an aberration; rather, it was American belligerency in 1917–18 that represented the exception to normal policy. The Americans naturally pressed the British to begin repayment of loans; the British found themselves obliged to make an agreement, but unable to obtain payment from those to whom they had lent larger sums. Anglo-French relations became, if not as rancid as those of twenty years before, scratchy and back-biting. The British, even if the war had shown that they could not afford a French defeat, refused to make any defensive alliance with France except on terms which the French would not accept.

With deep reluctance, and under strong pressure from the governments of the United States and Canada, Britain abandoned the treaty with Japan. There had been signs in preceding years, particularly when she pressed stiff demands upon China during the war, that her conduct might make it impossible for Britain to remain on close terms with the United States and simultaneously in alliance with Japan. Nevertheless, there was hardly a Prime Minister or Foreign Secretary between the wars who did not lament the loss of the tangible benefits of Japanese goodwill for the somewhat elusive favours of America. Having depended on the alliance, the British found themselves with no base in the Far East capable of maintaining a battle-fleet. Eventually it was decided to construct a great fortress at Singapore, which would command (or so it was fondly hoped) the Indian Ocean and at least the western Pacific, provide an earnest of Britain's determination to protect her interests east of Suez, enable supply lines and communications to be maintained and, in the last resort, battleships to be matched against Japan. All this turned on a number of conditions, and there was never a time, in the twenty years separating the decision to build from the capture of Singapore, when they were all fulfilled: the completion of the base itself; tranquillity in Mediterranean and home waters, or an ample margin of strength enabling a large fleet to be despatched to the Far East; sufficient support from public opinion at home; and, if at all possible, the active help of the United States.

The building of the base proceeded by fits and starts. It was begun by the Conservative government in 1923; cancelled by the first Labour government; resumed by the next Conservative government; slowed down by the next Labour government. Ten years elapsed between the decision of 1921 not to renew the alliance and the public revelation of Britain's nakedness after Japan's attack on Manchuria. Since the German navy had disappeared and war with the United States or France was hardly thinkable, the chief purpose of the Royal Navy became a possible war against Japan, or the capacity to deter Japan from action unduly damaging to British interests. Until Singapore was partially completed in 1938, the Royal Navy could not place in Far Eastern waters a fleet capable of meeting Japan on level terms; and, by then, the European and Mediterranean situation had become so menacing that despite the most obvious damage to British interests in China, the ships could not be spared.

These disasters were not foreseen early. As if their existing responsibilities were not enough, the British had acquired under mandate new territories. The commitment to a national home for the Jews, however compelling the reasons of honour and interest which inspired it, produced eventually a serious deterioration of British relations with Arab states, and even between the wars the most painful consequences in Palestine itself. From 1936, the territory was in a state of ill-subdued revolt; it is an index of the primacy of such commitments in Britain's order of duties that there were tied up in Palestine between 1936 and 1938 more troops than Britain had available for despatch to France or Belgium.

Whereas in 1914 the whole empire had been committed to war simply by the king's declaration, the sacrifices which the Dominions and India had made during the war, the enhanced sense of nationhood which sprang from it, and the commitment to the development of self-governing institutions in India, clearly meant that the old structure of empire must change. To find an acceptable relationship without transforming the empire into a hollow shell was a task to which much of the best of British statesmanship was devoted between the wars; and not without success. There were no doubt many failures of sensibility or imagination, occurring as often on the side of the Dominions as on the part of the British. Foreign Secretaries understood in varying degree that they no longer spoke for the whole empire, yet each in his turn naturally wished to have its potential power at his back. In times of peace, the white Dominions appeared a strategic liability; in time of war, they proved after 1939, as in 1914, a source of strength. It was no nice balancing of self-interest which moved them to fight in 1939; nor was cold calculation the only basis of British relations with them before then. Many British statesmen and officials felt a deep conviction that the empire represented a civilising agency of the first order, and that a failure to defend it would mean the end of Britain as a great power. This does not mean that concern for the opinion of the Dominions governed British foreign policy; but if Britain went to war while some of the Dominions remained neutral, the empire was finished as a force in international affairs. That the whole Commonwealth should have fought throughout the Second World War, and that India should have raised a large army by voluntary enlistment, constituted a capital contribution to victory.

During the 1920s, while the Far Eastern position was quiescent, Italy comparatively restrained, Germany defeated and partly occupied by the troops of the Allies, the position of the British empire was therefore one of fundamental but concealed insecurity. When the memories of sacrifice were fresh, it was hardly to be conceived that Germany could rearm within a few years. As Mr Churchill put it in 1925, 'At the worst there is a breathing space, measured by decades. Our problem is how to use this breathing space, to end the quarrel' between France and Germany. If Britain and France could join together to overawe Germany, Britain exacting as a condition of her alliance that France should cease to harry Germany, if such a union meant security in peace and victory in war, the case would be complete. However, Britain and France alone did not inspire much confidence so far as war on the continent was concerned. In writing this, Churchill undoubtedly had in mind the experience of 1914–18, when it had taken half the world to bring Germany down. He went on to argue that it was not impossible to endure the possession of the Channel ports by a victorious Germany; if Britain had sea superiority and air supremacy, she might live:

as we did in the days of Napoleon for indefinite periods, even when all
the Channel ports and all the Low Countries were in the hands of a
vast hostile military power. It should never be admitted in this
argument that England cannot, if the worst comes to the worst, stand
alone. I decline to accept as an axiom that our fate is involved in that
of France.[13]

Even with his profound study of history Churchill could not know
how closely this vision would foreshadow the situation which he himself
confronted as Prime Minister fifteen years later. The colleague whom
he addressed, Austen Chamberlain, was also looking to the future and
trying to imagine how Europe might fare in the 1950s or 1960s if
grievances were not assuaged; but instead of drawing Churchill's
conclusion, Chamberlain would have liked to make a defensive alliance
with France and then to use it as a point of departure for better relations
with Germany. He was anxious to keep Germany and Russia apart; and
realised that if the policy of broad fulfilment of the terms of 1919 was to
stand any chance of success over a long period, the German government
attempting that course must show some successes. The Cabinet refused
the defensive alliance with France; and by the Locarno arrangements of
1925 the British bound themselves to an almost mechanical application
of the old balance of power theory, whereby they would with Italy come
to the aid of the power against which aggression had taken place,
whether Germany or France. Germany had not then the strength to
attack France, and neither Chamberlain nor any other leading
statesman in Britain realised that she would gain that strength so soon.
He rightly described British policy as one of appeasement, a word which
has become much too exclusively associated with his half-brother
Neville. In practical terms, the obligation to protect Belgium and
France against German aggression did little more than recognise the
fact demonstrated in 1914. That is no doubt what Austen Chamberlain
had in mind when he approved the judgment of a later Foreign
Secretary that there was 'nothing very new in Locarno'.[14]

Successive governments made no attempt to give Locarno military
reality; that would have called for a substantial increase in the British
army, and the events of the First World War, instead of being used to
demonstrate how vital it was for Britain not to allow her strength on
land to fall hopelessly out of line with the tasks she might have to
perform, seem on the contrary to have deepened the ingrained and
ruinous British distaste for an adequate army. In Britain's conduct of

foreign policy there had therefore developed two great gaps: between
the commitment to the League and the realities of international life;
and between the Locarno undertakings and British capacity (or even
intention) to fulfil them. The deepening economic crisis after 1929
brought on the collapse of the parliamentary regime in Germany. Well
before Hitler came to power, the early withdrawal of the last allied
troops had removed the most serviceable means of placing direct
pressure upon her. Neither the French nor the British thought seriously
of a preventive war. It would not be too fanciful to say of them that
when they had the strength they lacked the will; by the time they gained
the will, they lacked the strength.

Japan's encroachments upon China reveal clearly enough the gap
between profession and performance in the League. After all, if the
Covenant were taken literally, the members had as clear a duty to
defend the integrity of remote territories – for example, Manchuria or
Abyssinia – as to protect their own vital interests near at hand. In fact,
there was no prospect that the British could uphold the Covenant
against Japan, and certainly no other power had any intention of doing
so. For all that was said at the time and has been said since, there was no
likelihood of active Russian or American help. Those vast interests in
the east, with everything which they meant for British trade and
prestige, had been existing to a large degree upon Japanese sufferance.
Even the major ports and Singapore were practically undefended and
might well capitulate before any British fleet could reach the Far East.

Here were the essential ingredients of the disaster. The loss of the
alliance with Japan, and with it the opportunity of exercising any
serious influence on Japanese policy; the conversion of alliance through
neutrality into hostility; the continuing, understandable but damaging
detachment of the United States; a marked declension of nerve and
confidence; a lack of sympathetic and intimate collaboration with
France, of the kind which might have characterised an 'exclusive
alliance' of the old diplomacy but was expressly discouraged by the new
diplomacy; distant and mistrustful relations with Russia, thought to be
militarily weak (at least for offensive purposes), avowedly hostile to the
empire and likely to fish in troubled waters; the paralysing effect of the
economic crisis and the failure to rearm on a large scale in time; and,
most important of all, the rise to supreme power of a German ruler who
knew how to exploit his opponents' weaknesses; these factors placed the
British empire in a position of the utmost danger by the later 1930s.
The coalition of 1918 was reduced in effect to Britain and France; the

potential enemies were more powerful than before 1914; the British did not have in any arm the ample superiority enjoyed by the Royal Navy in past days, or the bargaining power which that brought. The most important change lay in the Far Eastern situation. Had the British between 1935 and 1939 been able to rely upon the security of their possessions there, they would have had better hope of containing Germany and Italy. As it was, they were reduced in one crisis after another to an undignified retreat, never knowing whether the Japanese assault upon British interests might become so blatant that the bulk of the ageing fleet of capital ships would have to be sent to Singapore.

The events of 1935 and 1936 exposed the position painfully. Until then, the British and French had felt no great need of active Italian goodwill. While Germany was relatively powerless, Italy was unlikely to provide any serious danger. But with Germany openly flouting the restrictions of Versailles, and likely to seize the demilitarised zone in the Rhineland, the only physical security remaining from the settlement of 1919, Italy's help or even neutrality bore a different value. Mussolini, in choosing that time to attack Abyssinia, was exploiting the increased freedom of manoeuvre and bargaining power conferred upon him by the resurgence of Germany. The French in particular had excellent reasons, though they were incompatible with the Covenant, for purchasing his support. Outwardly, the British reacted in the opposite way. Had they felt strong enough to take the risk of war in the Mediterranean, the League might have been strengthened, Hitler restrained for a time, and Mussolini pushed off his perch. In the upshot, the two remaining great powers of the League could agree only on the surface, so that the policy pursued was neither one of determined hostility to Italy's campaign nor one of effective condonation.

In the years before the Second World War, the British found themselves forced by a growing threat from Germany, compounded in its seriousness by the aggressiveness of Japan and Italy, into a greater commitment to Europe than they would have wished. It may be that a more bold or deft foreign policy would have enabled Britain to separate her potential enemies. It is conceivable, but no more than that, that a different handling might have brought the United States or the Soviet Union to Britain's side before 1941. However, nothing less than the defeat of Nazi Germany, or the ability to bargain on more than level terms with Hitler, would have resolved the essential problem facing the British governments of the 1930s. Germany was the only power which might not only dominate Europe but even conquer the British Isles, and thus by piercing the heart put an end to the British empire. Ministers tried to seek a settlement with Germany on tolerable terms; and as the prospect became remote, took with reluctance a series of steps which tied the fate of the empire more and more closely to events in Europe. After the Rhineland crisis of 1936 came the staff conversations with France, of modest scope but with a large symbolic significance because of the conversations which were held to have committed Britain in 1914; after the Anschluss, an acceleration of rearmament; in the first Czechoslovak crisis of May 1938, a move towards commitment; on 27 September 1938, just before the Munich conference, an outright statement that if France fought, Britain would join her;[15] in the succeeding winter, at last, the decision to build up a continental army; after the German seizure of the rump of Czechoslovakia, the guarantee to Poland.

Neville Chamberlain was right to describe this as a 'tremendous departure'[16] in British foreign policy. No administration had previously given a comparable guarantee in central or eastern Europe, to frontiers for which Chamberlain's brother once said no British government would ever risk the bones of a British Grenadier. That guarantee was followed by others given to Greece, Romania and Turkey. Conscription was introduced in time of peace, a hitherto unknown event. By 1939, the British government was spending unprecedented sums upon arms. There was little choice, in a strategic situation worse than that of 1914. The Cabinet had excellent reasons for averting the contest if they could, and for postponing it if not; because foreign policy and defence policy had fallen out of line and the ground was not easily made up. The attempt to reduce enmities had been conducted from a weaker position, and less timely, than before the First World War. It was not wholly unsuccessful in the short run; the conjunction which ministers and their service advisers had dreaded, with three powers at war against Great Britain and the empire, did not occur in 1939. No reliance could be placed, however, upon the abstention of Italy or Japan.

Since Britain's war plans depended on the capacity to endure a long war, financial and economic strength had been regarded as the fourth arm of defence. Ironically, financial limits were for practical purposes abandoned in 1939 at the moment when the Cabinet had the gravest reason to fear for the economy. In January, the Chancellor of the Exchequer told his colleagues that the gold reserves had fallen by £150,000,000 in the six months before Munich. The 'settlement' had by no means staunched the flow. He remarked that recent conditions had been painfully reminiscent of those prevailing before the financial crisis of 1931. Later in the year, ministers were informed that in nine months since Munich, a further £150,000,000 had been lost to the reserves. Britain then held rather over £500,000,000 in the gold reserves, and foreign securities to the value of about £200,000,000. In the great war, Britain had borrowed heavily from private investors in the United States and from the American government; in 1939, she was debarred from either course. The Chancellor was right to judge that Britain could not finance a long war, and the Foreign Secretary to guess that if it occurred, the United States would step forth in the end to the rescue.[17]

The British government had been following in the military sphere a policy of deterrence, intending to have forces which, if not capable of defeating Germany decisively, would at least be strong enough 'to make it impossible for the other side to win except at such a cost as to make it not worth while'.[18] That policy failed. Even if it had been pursued with greater consistency and backed with greater armed strength from an earlier date, it is questionable whether it would have succeeded. There was no simple answer to the threat posed by Germany, nor was there an easy means of distinguishing what Hitler's next stroke would be. Much of the discussion is obfuscated by a failure to define terms. In many accounts, the words 'purpose', 'intention', 'plan', and 'timetable' are used almost interchangeably; but in framing a policy there is all the difference in the world between an intention or purpose, which may amount to no more than an indefinite aspiration, and a precise plan or a detailed timetable. Hitler had a general intention to make Germany an immensely powerful state in arms, increase her territory and living space, and overawe opponents; for some acts of policy he had a timetable, and for others not. Germany under his leadership was extraordinarily difficult to counter and thwart; and the strong strand of nihilism in Hitler, the willingness to bring the temple crashing around him rather than admit defeat, the instinct of the gambler to stake everything on one throw, made normal calculations of advantage foreign to him. There is no sign that he would have been willing to restrict Germany's expansion within the limits which the British were likely to tolerate.

Great Britain, the dominions and the empire thus went to war in 1939 for the same essential reason as in 1914, to prevent Germany from defeating the other powers of Europe and commanding the Low Countries, Channel ports and French coastline; perhaps naval superiority; and the human, mineral and industrial resources of the continent. That decision brought after many vicissitudes the ruin of Fascist Italy and Nazi Germany, and thereby rendered an immense service to the civilised world. It also hastened the fall of Britain as a power of the first rank.

1. British Power in the European Balance, 1906–14

KEITH WILSON

AT the beginning of 1907 Sir Eyre Crowe, then a Senior Clerk in the Foreign Office, provided the following description of the operation of the mechanism of the balance of power in Europe:

> History shows that the danger threatening the independence of this or that nation has generally arisen, at least in part, out of the momentary predominance of a neighbouring State at once militarily powerful, economically efficient, and ambitious to extend its frontiers or spread its influence, the danger being directly proportionate to the degree of its power and efficiency, and to the spontaneity or 'inevitableness' of its ambitions. The only check on the abuse of political predominance derived from such a position has always consisted in the opposition of an equally formidable rival, or of a combination of several countries forming leagues of defence. The equilibrium established by such a grouping of forces is technically known as the balance of power, and it has become almost an historical truism to identify England's secular policy with the maintenance of this balance by throwing her weight now in this scale and now in that, but ever on the side opposed to the political dictatorship of the strongest single State or group at a given time.[1]

That Great Britain was pursuing such a policy at the time, and throughout the years 1906 to 1914, is a view that has come to be generally accepted. In this view, the beginning of this policy is commonly identified with the Anglo-French Agreement of April 1904, though Gibson Bowles was the only Member of Parliament to greet it as 'a return to the older, simpler and . . . better system of the balance of power'.[2] The force of this interpretation is not diminished by the fact that officials, who enjoyed in the reformed Foreign Office a greater freedom to express their opinions, constantly and consistently employed the concept of the balance of power in their correspondence and advice. Their Chief, the Foreign Secretary himself, Sir Edward Grey, was less keen on the use of the phrase 'the balance of power'. He was anxious not to offend the sensibilities of several of his ministerial colleagues and of a large group of Liberal MPs, who held that a balance of power was not a suitable end for a Liberal Foreign Secretary to pursue. Nevertheless, it is clear that his foreign policy was discussed in Cabinet meetings in terms of the 'equilibrium' of Europe and that it was understood by his colleagues to be a balance of power policy. Lord Loreburn, one of the Radical ministers, who was not at first an assiduous attender at Cabinet meetings, was ultimately convinced that Grey's policy was a revival of 'the old Palmerstonian policy of the balance of power', and it was in all probability from Grey's own description and defence of his policy in Cabinet that this impression was derived.[3] With his representatives abroad and with the representatives in London of foreign Powers, Grey could afford to be rather more forthcoming. He told Cartwright, the Ambassador to Vienna, in January 1909, that 'the balance of power in Europe was preserved by the present grouping, and I should not think of wishing to disturb it'; in June 1909, when the German ambassador remarked that some organs of the British press were saying that friendship with Russia and France was necessary to keep Germany in check, Grey observed that 'it was a question of preventing the balance of power from being destroyed'.[4] When defending in November 1911 against attacks mainly from his own side of the House the policy he had pursued during the Agadir crisis of that summer, Grey told the House of Commons:

> The ideal of splendid isolation contemplated a balance of power in Europe to which we were not to be a party, and from which we were to be able to stand aside in the happy position of having no obligations and being able to take advantage of any difficulties which arose in Europe from friction between opposing Powers. That policy is not a possible one now.[5]

A year later, after the outcome of the First Balkan War had produced from the German government striking declarations of future support for Austria–Hungary, Haldane was sent to tell the German ambassador that 'the theory of the balance of power forms an axiom of English foreign policy and has led to the English leaning towards France and Russia'.[6] There can be no doubt that, on the eve of the outbreak of war in 1914, Crowe was correct in saying that the balance of power was 'the general principle on which our whole foreign policy has hitherto been declared to rest'.[7]

That between 1906 and 1914 Great Britain leant, as it were, towards one of the two groups of Powers in Europe – towards France and Russia rather than towards the Triple Alliance of Germany, Austria–Hungary and Italy – is not in dispute here. What is in dispute is whether this British leaning towards France and Russia can really be accounted for, as many people both at the time and subsequently have accounted for it, in terms of considerations to do with the balance of power in Europe. Were British motives really as high-minded as they were high-sounding? Were they really concerned to preserve the liberties and independence of the States of Europe? Did those responsible for the policy of associating with France and Russia really consider Britain to be a party to the balance of power in Europe? Did they really believe that Britain was a factor in that balance, that she was making such a contribution to it as to entitle them to claim that it was she who was responsible for deterring Imperial Germany from embarking upon a bid of Napoleonic proportions to secure the hegemony of the continent?

The balance of power, again according to Crowe, consisted of 'a balance of force, actual or latent'.[8] If Great Britain was to take a hand in the European game, if she was to intervene to prevent the continent from being dominated by a single Power or by a certain group of Powers, if she was to interfere with the plans so frequently ascribed to Germany, how was this to be done? What force, what might, did she have, that could be thrown into the scales? What was it that was considered to constitute the British deterrent?

In 1907 a critic of the draft of the official General Staff memorandum on the ability of the British Army to support France or Belgium against German attack complained that it had failed clearly to point out 'that our army is not big enough for the job'. Captain Ommanney added that the most important work of the General Staff in the next generation would be 'resolutely and continuously to demand that the strength of the army be fixed according to the task in front of it. This will undoubtedly require an increase in its size, and an alteration in the method by which it is raised.'⁹ Though the General Staff did not fail to raise these matters, neither of Ommanney's requirements was to be met. In March 1909 the Director of Military Operations, General Ewart, composed a memorandum on 'The Value to a Foreign Power of an Alliance with the British Empire'. This revealed that that value was much more 'latent' than 'actual'. Ewart wrote:

> the British Empire has over a million men under arms, and if they could all be utilised for a common purpose we should indeed be a considerable military power. Limitations, however, imposed by the composition of these forces, by their varying conditions of service, and by their want of organisation, neutralise the value of the greater portion of this large army. When we come to analyse its composition we find that, in any sudden emergency, at the present moment, we could not hope, at the utmost, to mobilise and put into the field at short notice for service in Europe a larger force than one Cavalry division and six divisions of all arms, with a total strength of 170,000 men.
>
> The Territorial Force is only organised for home defence; in existing circumstances it would be impossible to withdraw British troops from India; our naval stations must be held; proposals to employ our Native troops would in all probability provoke heated controversy; whilst the governments of our self-governing Dominions show as yet no disposition to guarantee the provision of contingents for Imperial service. Above and beyond all this an Imperial General Staff capable of organising and directing our vast undeveloped strength has only just been initiated.

Ewart gallantly saw 'no reason for discouragement' at the distance still to be travelled before more than one seventh of the Empire's peace establishment could be made available for common action. Many conditions, however, had to be met:

> If in the future we can all hold together; if the General Staff can work out some acceptable scheme of mutual assistance; and if our Navy can maintain our ability to cooperate; then, indeed, will our alliance be coveted by all.

As it was, the value of Great Britain as an ally in Europe, defined as he defined it – as depending on 'the strength and efficiency of the troops which we can make available for expeditionary action' – was highly problematical. When he wrote that he was satisfied that the establishment contemplated for the expeditionary force was the minimum compatible with a continuance of what he believed to be the policy of the British government in Europe, namely the maintenance of the balance of power, he was making the best of a very bad job. This is clear from the diary he kept, in which he deplored the size of the Expeditionary Force and held that if the Entente with France and Russia was to last Britain must put her military house in order, perfect her mobilisation arrangements, and increase her offensive striking power. A draft of his memorandum of March 1909 was forwarded to the Foreign Secretary.[10]

Ewart's successor as DMO, Sir Henry Wilson, had essentially the same difficulties to surmount over two years later when endeavouring to persuade a meeting of certain members of the Committee of Imperial Defence on 23 August 1911 that the whole of the British Expeditionary Force should be sent to France immediately upon the outbreak of hostilities between France and Germany. In a memorandum prepared for the meeting he admitted that England 'can only assist France to a very limited extent in promptly resisting a German invasion'. Nevertheless, the numbers of the opposing forces might be rendered so nearly equal, he contended, during the opening and early actions of a war that it was 'quite possible for the allies to win some initial successes which might prove invaluable'.[11] This was pitched rather higher at the meeting itself, at which Grey was present. 'It was quite likely', said the DMO, 'that our six divisions might prove to be the decisive factor'. This conclusion was based on his calculation of the number of through roads between Verdun and Maubeuge and the extent of front upon which a division could fight, which yielded forty German divisions against an estimated thirty-seven to thirty-nine French divisions.[12] Initial successes were all the more vital in view of Wilson's belief that

> it will tax our resources to the utmost to put and keep 6 Divisions in the field during the first six or eight weeks. After that we might be able to add some troops from India and some improvised formations from home or the Dominions, but there would not be any marked addition to our forces in France for three or four months at the earliest and even then it would not be a very serious increase.[13]

Even though, the previous December, the journalist Valentine Chirol had found the War Minister, Haldane, 'altogether lucid and convincing' in arguing that the forces of the Triple Entente and the Dual Alliance were so equally balanced that three British Army Corps would just turn the balance in favour of France,[14] it was stretching Britain's military capability to the limit to imagine that the number of divisions she would send met the General Staff's own criterion of 'decisive force at the decisive place at the decisive time'. Such a belief posited a tremendous faith in the fortunes of war. This, moreover, was not the whole story. Wilson, who was an advocate of conscription for its own sake, nevertheless privately believed that six divisions were in all probability 'fifty too few' to take to a continental war.[15] The calculations involved in reducing the disparity between eighty-four German and sixty-six French divisions to proportions that would make the British contingent decisive included the counting of the four Belgian divisions as the equivalent of four French or German divisions, and the assumptions that Austria would be half-hearted and that Russia could immobilise the whole of the Austrian army plus twenty-seven divisions of the German Army. Wilson also allocated ten German divisions to the guarding of their coasts. The picture is still not complete. Wilson had only on 20 July 1911 met the French General Staff for the first time in order to confirm the main principles of co-ordination before working them out in detail. Not until September 1911 was he told 'where the French General Staff want us to go and what their plans are'.[16] (According to Haldane, General French had been instructed that he was 'on no account' to see the French military plans, even if the French wanted to take him into their confidence during his visit to their manoeuvres in 1910.[17])

Moreover, the Committee of Imperial Defence meeting of 23 August 1911 had revealed that the Admiralty had deliberately ignored both the possibility that they might be called upon to transport the Expeditionary Force across the Channel, and their explicit instructions to arrange to do so. McKenna, who on 3 December 1908 had given a guarantee on the Admiralty's behalf that British troops could be safely transported to either French or Belgian ports, claimed in August 1911 to be hearing of this scheme for the first time, and not to have realised that the dispatch of the Army was to take place simultaneously with the mobilisation of the Fleet, which he now maintained was not possible.[18] This 'terminological inexactitude', together with his dereliction of a duty he had found it distasteful to fulfil, secured McKenna the Home Office in October 1911.

Well might Sir Henry Wilson write at the end of December 1911:

When the crisis came on us in last July–September it found us unprepared for war.
Whether we consider war from the point of view of an Expeditionary Force on the Continent of Europe, or anywhere over the seas, or whether from the point of view of the Territorial Force and Home Defence, *we are still unprepared.*[19]

It took the Balkan War scare of November 1912 to bring to a head the General Staff's 'long outstanding difficulties' in respect of the general question of the provision of ships for the transportation of the Expeditionary Force. On hearing from Cowans, the Quartermaster-General, that the Admiralty were saying they could not ship the Army in time, Wilson called this 'disgraceful' and issued an ultimatum: 'either the Admiralty must ship us or we must make the arrangements ourselves'. Though an Admiralty scheme was 'vetted' at a meeting on 1 December 1912, almost a year later the Admiralty had still not finalised the arrangements to be adopted for the admission of British transports to French ports – something the General Staff had by then been 'shouting for for a long time'; and that the Admiralty War Staff should be 'getting well forward with the question of taking up transport on mobilisation' was still 'one of the chief anxieties of the DMO'.[20] It was thus by no means a straightforward business even to arrange for the nut to be presented to the sledgehammer.

Not even Sir Henry Wilson's skill with figures could conceal what in fact he readily admitted, that the army in its present size and configuration could only constitute 'moral support' for the French, however important moral support might be.[21] If Grey, like Chirol, had been submitted, as is most probable, to Haldane's expositions of the worth of the BEF, and even found them 'lucid and convincing', then he had also been in a position to inform himself of the slow progress of the essential preliminaries. Grey himself had written in January 1906: 'I am told that 80,000 men with good guns is all we can put into the field in Europe to meet first class troops; that won't save France unless she can save herself.'[22] One wonders if the increase of 70,000 supplied by Haldane was really enough, especially as Asquith personally made it quite clear that he would allow no more than four divisions to leave Britain's shores, to cause Grey to revise this first estimate of the British Army as the prospect of conjunction with the Belgian Army caused

Churchill to revise his earlier and rather sounder estimate of 1908 in 1911.[23] Certainly there is no evidence that he did.

As for the British Navy, it was widely held in diplomatic and political circles in the summer of 1905, during the crisis over Morocco involving France and Germany, to be incapable of restoring the equilibrium between the land forces of those two countries.[24] The sentiments of even its most ardent champions would have provided cold comfort to the French. The opinion expressed by Admiral Sir A. K. Wilson, C-in-C Channel Fleet, in his 'Remarks on War Plans' of May 1907, that 'the stoppage of German trade or the capture of their ships would have little or no effect on the result (of a war between Germany and France and England combined) and if France was defeated, compensation for any injury that we had done would be extorted from our allies as one of the conditions of peace', was actually endorsed by the First Sea Lord, Fisher, than whom there was no greater navalist, unless it were Esher, in December 1908.[25] Sir Charles Ottley, a former Director of Naval Intelligence, wrote in December 1908 that since 1905 the Admiralty had held that '(in a protracted war) the mills of our sea-power (though they would grind the German industrial population slowly perhaps) would grind them "exceedingly small" – grass would sooner or later grow in the streets of Hamburg and widespread death and ruin would be inflicted.'[26] The inhabitants of Hamburg would well before then have taken up residence in Paris. Lord Esher stoutly maintained that 'the French would not be likely to deny that fear of British naval supremacy restrained and still restrains Germany from precipitating a war with France; and that naval pressure upon German trade, German commerce, and the German food supply, would be certain to influence the result of prolonged military conflict ashore'. He went on, in the course of a memorandum prepared for the consideration of a CID sub-committee on the Military Needs of the Empire, to suggest

> that the pressure which can be brought to bear upon Germany by the threat . . . of seizing her mercantile fleet . . ., by the deadly injury to her commerce, and the fear of raids, as well as by the freedom of action and moral support afforded to France, might be held to be a sufficient fulfilment of our share in the partnership between us and the French nation. In that case the British Navy might be counted as equivalent to the French Army, and if the dominating factor in preserving peace between France and Germany has been and is, not the strength of the French armies, but fear of the British fleet, the

Government and the country might hold that this represents to France the value of the *entente* in peace, whilst the fact that France would fight free from all apprehension of coastal attack, with certain use of a sea base, if required, and with complete conviction that whatever the fate of battles ashore, time and patience, even under unlikely crushing defeat, would mean – thanks to sea command – ultimate victory, is the value of the *entente* to France in war.[27]

The General Staff made short work of this in their replies, delivered the following March. They pointed out that the improvement in land communications and the enormous growth of modern European armies had greatly lessened the advantages once conferred by sea power. In their view, Germany was no more likely to withdraw any portion of her army from the decisive point on land to cope with raids than she had done in 1870 when, as Esher himself had admitted, French preponderance at sea had had no influence whatever on the fate of her armies. They concluded that 'it is a mistake to suppose that command of the sea must necessarily influence the immediate issue of a great land struggle. The battle of Trafalgar did not prevant Napoleon from winning the battles of Austerlitz and Jena and crushing Prussia and Austria.' Moreover, in their opinion as in that of Fisher and Sir A. K. Wilson:

If Germany is able in the future rapidly to secure a decisive victory by land, she will be in a position to impose an indemnity calculated to compensate her at the expense of France for any losses which we may have inflicted on her maritime and commercial interests. In fact, the greater the industrial stake which she has at sea in a struggle with the United Kingdom the more she will exact in reprisal from those who have the misfortune to be unsuccessful as our allies on land.[28]

Despite the impressive tables of statistics of Admiral Slade, the DNI, regarding the economic effect of war on German trade, credit, inflation and unemployment, the sub-committee as a whole preferred the arguments of the General Staff to the effect that reliance upon the Navy would actually do more harm than good! Having considered three methods by which armed assistance could be given by Britain to France if she were attacked by Germany, these being (a) by means of the navy alone, (b) by means of the navy and a mounted force of 12,000 men and

(c) by means of the navy and the expeditionary force of four divisions
and a cavalry division, they concluded in their Report:

> From the evidence that we have had, we are of the opinion that a
> serious situation would be created in Germany owing to the blockade
> of her ports, and that the longer the duration of the war the more
> serious the situation would become. *We do not, however, consider that such
> pressure as could be exerted by means of naval force alone would be felt
> sufficiently soon to save France in the event of that country being attacked in
> overwhelming force.* We therefore recognise the possibility that Great
> Britain's success at sea might only cause greater pressure to be
> brought to bear on France on land, and the latter country might have
> to make terms with Germany which would not be less stringent owing
> to the losses suffered by her opponent at sea.[29]

The ministers who sat on this committee and signed this Report were
the Prime Minister, Asquith (Chairman), Lord Crewe, Haldane, and
McKenna; Sir Charles Hardinge, the Permanent Under-Secretary,
represented the Foreign Office.

This verdict on the relative weight of the Navy as against that of an
Army for whose transportation facilities did not at the time exist, which
at the time was ignorant of the plan of campaign of the country to whose
rescue it therefore could go only with difficulty, and which at any time
would be able only on the most optimistic construction to make even a
putative contribution to the outcome of the struggle, was repeated in
August 1911.

As instruments with which to deter a bid on the part of another Power
for the hegemony of Europe, both the British Army and the British
Navy left much to be desired. What is striking is that ministers and high
officials who knew the true state of Britain's preparedness and
capability, and who should have known better, continued to insist that
Britain was still successfully pursuing a balance of power policy. Sir
Charles Hardinge, for instance, had expressed in February 1906 the
view that 'If it is understood by Germany that England is absolutely
"solidaire" with France, such knowledge would almost certainly deter
Germany from provoking a conflict by which Germany must lose her
entire mercantile marine and almost her whole foreign trade'.[30] In May
1909 he was still holding such views as that Britain was 'the only Power
that in the end would be able to support France and Russia in an
independent position and to enforce peace', provided she maintained

her absolute supremacy at sea and was consequently 'able to destroy in time of war German sea-borne trade',[31] despite the General Staff's demolition of them in March 1909 in the course of the proceedings of the CID sub-committee of which Hardinge was himself a member. His successor, Sir Arthur Nicolson, who rapidly became a confidant of Sir Henry Wilson, wrote in January 1911:

> I do not think that people quite recognise that, if we are to assist in preserving the balance of power in Europe and consequently the peace and the status quo, it is necessary for us to acknowledge our responsibilities, and to be prepared to afford our friends or allies, in case of necessity, some assistance of a more material and efficient kind than we are at present in a position to offer them.[32]

In May 1911, a month in which he expressed doubts as to 'whether a concerted plan of action will ever be settled', he was nevertheless maintaining that it was Britain's policy to preserve the equilibrium in Europe and that this policy must not be reversed.[33] In April 1912, after numerous conversations with Sir Henry Wilson over the previous months, he was still maintaining that 'in fact, England is really a factor of great weight either for or against peace'.[34] Goschen, the ambassador to Berlin, forwarded in March 1910 a report on the dependence of Germany on overseas traffic for supplies in time of war compiled by his Counsellor of Embassy and by the Military and Naval Attachés, the first paragraph of which read: 'We can find no evidence that the cessation of import and export by German ports would in any reasonable probability result in a shortage of the necessary articles of food for the population of Germany.' Yet in October of that year he maintained that the only thing which had prevented the Germans securing the hegemony of Europe was England's naval strength.[35] These officials would appear to have been engaged in transforming an axiom into a shibboleth or even a fetish. Indeed Goschen wrote to Grey in March 1911 that he had told the Kaiser that 'the balance of power was a fetish worshipped by the British nation and a principle which in the past it had made great sacrifices to uphold and for which it had always fought'.[36] 'The theory of the balance of power', which they complained did not appeal to the German mind, had an irresistible appeal for them.[37] The power of the theory of the balance goes far to explain what otherwise would seem at the very least remiss: that no one in the British Foreign Office should have thought the Germans perfectly capable of coming to the same conclusions regarding the effectiveness of the British Navy as those to which the CID came in 1909 and 1911 (and to which, in fact, the Germans did come); and that they should not have added these to their chronic reservations about British military strength, which they well knew were shared by the French, whom they equally well knew had serious reservations about the ability of the British Navy to save them from the German Army.[38]

Even the Radical ministers discerned the discrepancy between the proclaimed and professed ends of British foreign policy and the means of meeting them that were at her disposal. Morley, who frequently took charge of the Foreign Office during Grey's fishing expeditions, and who had the same facility as a chameleon for assuming the colouring of the background against which he operated, on one of these occasions quickly gained the impression that 'Friends and foes are beginning to ask themselves whether we are of much account in either capacity.'[39] Loreburn clearly had his doubts. He maintained that: 'If war came we could not prevent [France] from being overrun. If we are to continue the present policy we shall need to send not 150,000 men but at least half a million to be any good.'[40] His recognition that only conscription, however much he opposed it, would remedy the situation, was a comment not only upon the British Army but also upon the Navy.

What the Radical ministers did not discern was that what they took from Grey and Haldane in particular to be the ends of British policy might only be ostensible ends. Such was the gap between means and ends, however, that it does bring these ends into question. There is, moreover, a body of evidence that cannot satisfactorily be absorbed by or accommodated in the view that Britain, during the years when Sir Edward Grey was responsible for her foreign policy, was pursuing a policy designed to maintain the balance of power in Europe. If this interpretation is correct, then the least one can say is that Grey, who knew of the shortcomings of the British Army, who was familiar with the unmistakable verdicts as to the inappropriateness of a British naval contribution to a great European war passed by the CID in the sub-committee of 1908–9 and at the meeting of 23 August 1911, and who despite this knowledge and this familiarity continued to 'harp', as the Kaiser put it,[41] on the balance of power, did not trouble to undeceive a large group of his colleagues.

Just over a month before the conclusion of the Anglo-French negotiations which had begun in July 1903, Grey had voiced his appreciation of the prospect that good relations with France would offer of reducing the Two-Power Standard. He hoped that, if the friendly relations with France lasted into a less troubled period (Japan and Russia were then at war), 'no opportunity would be lost of turning that friendly spirit to practical advantage by some mutual agreement with regard to stopping the increase in the Fleets'.[42] The Anglo-French Agreement, which he inherited when he became Foreign Secretary, was welcome to him, as a member of a political party which placed a high value on economy and retrenchment, from the point of view of the elimination of a naval rival. In maintaining the Agreement, he stressed this aspect to a much greater extent than his predecessor, Lord Lansdowne, had done. At the Committee of Imperial Defence in May 1911 and in July 1912, in the House of Commons in March 1914, he stressed how 'the growth of the navies of the world generally' had affected British foreign policy. For

> if you take the total of the great European navies as they are, or will soon be, you would not be able to hold the command of the sea against them all. That has made the task of foreign policy more difficult in this respect, that it is essential that our foreign policy should be such as to make it quite certain that there are, at any rate, some nations in Europe with whom it becomes inconceivable that we should find ourselves at war.[43]

He made no secret of the fact that he was following the advice of the first Liberal First Lord of the Admiralty, Lord Tweedmouth, who told Campbell-Bannerman in November 1906 that 'good diplomacy must be trusted to secure that all the greater naval Powers should not at once be ranged against us, for we could not of course be prepared to meet such a combination'.[44]

Sticking to the Entente because it was 'the only way of retaining command of the sea'[45] had the effect of neutralising the navies of France and Russia, and of depriving Germany of the opportunity to add to her power of a smaller fleet by making naval alliances. The point here is that Grey was motivated by essentially selfish reasons of British interests. No British government wished to spend more on the maintenance of naval supremacy than was strictly necessary. Indeed one of Tweedmouth's first pronouncements to the Cabinet was that he intended to reduce the Naval Estimates by £1½ million. The elimination of naval rivals was required by 'the growth of the navies of the world generally', by 'the increase in the Fleets'. The British response to the dispositions of first France and then Russia to come to friendly terms with her was primarily in the nature of an economy measure. It was not a move in the direction of balancing power in Europe. Germany did not require naval allies in order to make a bid for the hegemony of the continent. If she did acquire a naval ally, it would increase her chances of success only in a war against Great Britain. British naval building, under the Liberals, was related above all to the possibility, at some stage in the future, of an Anglo-German war. This is why it was important even to the parsimonious Liberals to preserve the degree of naval superiority over Germany which they inherited and which, initially, they considered perfectly satisfactory.[46]

The Anglo-Russian Convention was the only feature added by Grey to the diplomatic landscape in the years of peace. There is no record, in the letters of the Prime Minister to the King, of any decision being taken in Cabinet to pursue this objective. In March 1906 the King's Private Secretary, Lord Knollys, simply received a letter from Grey declaring that an entente with Russia was 'the thing most to be desired in our foreign policy'. It would 'complete and strengthen the entente with France and add very much to the comfort and strength of our position'.[47] Four weeks later a meeting was held consisting of Grey, Haldane, Asquith, Morley, and the newly-appointed ambassador to St Petersburg, at which the matter was thoroughly discussed.[48] Grey had, nevertheless, given fair warning that he would, if appointed Foreign Secretary, seek an agreement with Russia. The sentiment he expressed in a speech on 20 October 1905, for instance, concerning the necessity of supporting France at the forthcoming Conference at Algeciras to resolve the Moroccan dispute between her and Germany, on the grounds that one did not make new friends by failing existing ones, was clearly a reference to this intention. The sentiment surfaced again at a crucial point during the Conference itself. Envisaging a breakdown of the proceedings and a Franco-German war, Grey wrote that it would be very difficult for Britain to keep out of it: 'There would . . . be a general feeling . . . that we had behaved meanly and left France in the lurch . . . Russia would not think it worth while to make a friendly arrangement with us about Asia.'[49]

It may seem that the involvement of Britain in a Franco-German war was a high price to pay for a chance to make an agreement with a Power that had recently been defeated by Japan, with a Power whose navy was at the bottom of the China Sea, a Power that was still in the throes of revolution; and that this can only be accounted for in terms of the balance of power in Europe. This impression is all the more understandable on the assumption that, after Russia's defeat by Japan and the extension of the Anglo-Japanese Alliance to cover India, the British had less reason for seeking an agreement with Russia in order to safeguard the approaches to India than they had had for many years past. This impression would, in my opinion, be false.

A number of things have to be borne in mind. It was presumed that Russia would re-establish herself as a naval power. The renewed and extended Anglo-Japanese Alliance, itself partly inspired by assumptions concerning Russia's recovery, was not considered sufficient to avert the consequences of this.[50] The Liberal Government was quickly made aware, on coming to power, of the reluctance of the General Staff and of the government of India to see Japanese troops operating on the North-West Frontier, for fear the Indians would cease to tolerate British rule if it was revealed to depend upon her oriental ally. In May 1907 the Japanese made it clear that they were equally reluctant to serve in India, and that they would confine themselves to creating a diversion on the Manchurian frontier.[51] Haldane was anxious to make economies in the Army, starting with India. Even in defeat and a state of revolution, Russia was still capable of maintaining an army of 250,000 men three thousand miles from Russia proper.[52] A study by the War Office of the military resources of the Russian empire, completed in mid-1907, stated that the number of men that the Russians could pour into Central Asia was 'practically unlimited'.[53] In recent years the Russians had so extended their system of railways as to bring them within striking distance of Kandahar and Kabul. There was no indication that this process was at an end.

Even in the first quarter of 1906 the British could not relax completely over Central Asia. It was to be expected that Russia would recover her full strength before long. The problem facing Grey and Morley was how to make permanent the situation relatively more favourable to Britain that had been created by the outcome of the Russo-Japanese war and its aftermath. An agreement with Russia was their solution to this problem. They were encouraged to adhere to this solution by the report of a sub-committee of the CID set up in January 1907 to consider the Military Requirements of the Empire as affected by the defence of India. This was chaired by Morley and included Grey, Asquith and Haldane. In May 1907 it reported tellingly in favour of 'the school who look to diplomacy rather than to arms, and hold that the foundation of our rule in India would be more securely strengthened by peace with Russia than by any success in war with Russia'. 'In default of an understanding with Russia', the process of 'insidious advance and slow absorption' on Russia's part would have to be reckoned with. Among the points made were these: that a rumour of a Russian seizure of Herat would cause a great stir amongst 'the Natives of India'; that the permanent occupation of Kabul would make it necessary for Britain 'to keep up a British force in India far exceeding the number of our present European garrison, and perhaps exceeding our capacity'; that to retain a great force of Native soldiers far from their homes for year after year, waiting on Russia's processes, would be asking more of the Indians than they had shown they were prepared to provide. Morley wrote to the Viceroy in September 1907, saying that the vital point of the report was the conclusion that the despatch of 100,000 men to India in the first year of a war was a military necessity: 'That is the fundamental argument for the Convention for we have not got the men to spare and that's the plain truth of it.'[54]

In an extensive minute dealing with some objections to his Russian policy from the Military Attaché in Persia Grey made explicit what his real priorities were:

The policy of the agreement is to begin an understanding with Russia, which may gradually lead to good relations in European Questions also and remove from her policy designs upon the Indian frontier either as an end in themselves or as a means of bringing pressure to bear upon us to overcome our opposition to her elsewhere. *If this policy succeeds India will be relieved from apprehension and strain.* If it fails we shall at any rate have secured temporarily that Russia does not get a hold of the parts of Persia, which are dangerous to us and all we shall have lost will have been the chance of preventing Russia from strengthening her hold on northern Persia: a chance which I do not believe exists except in theory . . .

Hardinge added that the dangers foreshadowed by Colonel Douglas of an advance towards India through Persia 'already exist'. An agreement with Russia was 'the only hope of staving them off effectually'. To oppose the Russian advance by adopting forward policies such as pushing British influence, telegraphs and railways into Seistan and southern Persia, lending money to the Persian government so as to bring it more and more under British control, and making every diplomatic effort at Teheran to oppose Russian influence in northern Persia, Grey argued, might actually make matters worse:

> To drop the Agreement and to adopt the forward policy would entail a certain and as I think it an intolerable increase of the military responsibilities of India and the Empire, and would provoke Russia to make it her object more than ever to worry us in Asia . . .[55]

The removal of dangers that already existed; the relief of India from apprehension and strain; the avoidance by England of the commitment of becoming a continental state in Central Asia with a common frontier with the Russian empire, and of the constant drain on her resources which the forward policies which she would otherwise have had to pursue merely in order to stand still in that region would have constituted: these were the reasons for the making and the keeping of the Agreement with Russia. It was India that Grey had it in mind to defend on the Sambre in February 1906, and by any subsequent gesture in the way of providing moral support for the French. The Anglo-Russian Agreement was devised in the interests of England's imperial position, not for the sake of the balance of power in Europe. Had the policy of an agreement with Russia not been justifiable on grounds quite separate from its necessity for the equilibrium in Europe, it is certain that Morley, who regarded the balance of power in the same way that Loreburn did, and who wrote in March 1908 that 'in entering into negotiations with the Russian government . . . His Majesty's Government were actuated not only by considerations affecting the Empire as a whole, but also, very largely, by considerations relating to India alone', would not have given the policy the backing and support which Grey recognised as being quite invaluable to its success.[56]

It is quite true that Grey did say, in February 1906, that 'an entente between Russia, France and ourselves would be absolutely secure. If it is necessary to check Germany it could then be done.'[57] It is also true that, on at least one occasion when the negotiations were faltering, Grey appealed to the Russians to 'bear in mind that larger issues than even those directly involved in these Agreements are indirectly at stake'.[58] If he was thinking of Europe, it was only in an incidental way. So were some of his advisers when they welcomed the start of a contest between Russia and Austria in the Balkans on the grounds that 'we shall not now be bothered by Russia in Asia'.[59] Hardinge said at the turn of 1907 that, in the Near East, Russia 'will constantly find herself in conflict with Germany and not in opposition to us'.[60] The latter point – that Russia should not be in opposition to Britain – was the main one. A reorientation of Russian policy towards the Balkans, and the possibility of her colliding with Germany through the pressure she would put on Austria, were welcomed at the Foreign Office less because Germany was considered a menace to Europe or to Britain than because Russia was considered a menace to the British position in the world.

As it was more to the future than to the present that the makers of the Anglo-Russian Conventions were looking, the passage of time only increased the importance to them of maintaining their achievement. Hardinge revealed in 1910, to Paul Cambon, the French ambassador in London, of all people, that he regarded the Russian railway systems in Central Asia as 'a sword of Damocles hanging over Britain's head'.[61] So far as he was concerned, 'our whole future in Asia is bound up with the necessity of maintaining the best and most friendly relations with Russia'.[62] Nicolson shared this outlook. He wrote in April 1912:

> it would be far more disadvantageous to have an unfriendly France and Russia than an unfriendly Germany. The latter . . . can give us plenty of annoyance, but it cannot really threaten any of our more important interests, while Russia especially could cause us extreme embarrassment, and, indeed, danger, in the Mid-East and on our Indian frontier, and it would be most unfortunate were we to revert to the state of things which existed before 1904 and 1907.[63]

As, with time, it became clear that Russia's recovery was indeed taking place, the consequences for Britain of not being on friendly terms with her were increasingly stressed. Nicolson wrote in April 1913 that Russia 'can, were she unfriendly, cause us very great annoyance and embarrassment in Central Asia, and we shall be unable to meet her on anything like equal terms'.[64] In May he received a letter from Hardinge, then Viceroy, expressing the devout hope 'that Russia may be pre-occupied for some years to come in the Near East with the interests of the Slav races, so that those who favour a forward policy in Asia may receive no encouragement'.[65] Rightly convinced that Grey was 'thoroughly in accordance' with his own and Hardinge's view that relations with Russia must remain on the best possible footing, Nicolson wrote again in April 1914:

The maintenance of our understanding with Russia is of the very greatest importance to us both in Europe and as regards India and our position generally in the Mid and Far East. Hardinge is continually impressing on me the urgent necessity of doing nothing which could in any way tend to alienate Russia from us . . . She could hit us where we were powerless.[66]

A few days later Buchanan wrote to him from St Petersburg: 'Russia is rapidly becoming so powerful that we must retain her friendship at almost any cost.'[67]

It was the fear of such consequences, I suggest, that accounts for Grey's categoric assertion to the German ambassador in May 1910: 'we cannot sacrifice the friendship of Russia or of France.'[68] It was this that explains his constant anxiety to avoid any 'new departures' in foreign policy. As he told Churchill on one occasion, the risks involved were greater than the advantages.[69] Hence his concern to avoid making with Germany any agreements into which France and Russia could not also be admitted.[70] As he told the Cabinet in July 1910, the difficulty of making any political arrangement with Germany was that

France and Russia would regard any such agreement with suspicion and all the blessings of the entente with France and Russia would go, and we might be again on the verge of war with one or other of these Powers.

He was supported in this instance by Morley, who urged from the Indian point of view that nothing be done to worsen 'our present happy relations with Russia'.[71] No more than his ambassador to Berlin did the Foreign Secretary, who continued to believe as others had done before him that Russia was both inaccessible and invulnerable to Britain, wish to see 'all the work of the last decade brought to nought, and all our old anxieties, which we set at rest by our Ententes, brought to life again'.[72]

It was these 'old anxieties', and not the more prominently advertised fears for the balance of power *per se*, that were throughout his tenure of the Foreign Office uppermost in Grey's mind. At the height of the Agadir crisis, when the prospect of British involvement in a Franco-German war was in sight again as it had been in 1906, Grey stressed that the break up of the triple entente would mean that 'we should be faced again with all the old troubles about the frontier of India'.[73] Early in 1912 he assured Hardinge that he was staking everything on pulling the Russian Agreement through all difficulties, for 'if it were to go everything would be worse'.[74] When on 3 August 1914 he told the House of Commons that the country would suffer but little more if it went into the war than if it stayed out it was of these consequences, basically, that he was thinking. Indeed in the fortnight before the declaration of war, he had been forcibly reminded of, and even blackmailed with, precisely these consequences by his staff at the Foreign Office, by certain of his Ambassadors, and by the French in the person of Paul Cambon. Crowe, who on 31 July was to appeal to 'the theory of the balance of power', minuted on 25 July: 'Should the war come, and England stand aside, one of two things must happen: (a) Either Germany and Austria win, crush France, and humiliate Russia . . . What will be the position of a friendless England? (b) Or France and Russia win. What would then be their attitude towards England? What about India and the Mediterranean?'[75] Buchanan telegraphed from St Petersburg on 2 August 1914:

> I venture to submit that if we do not respond to the Tsar's appeal for our support, we shall at the end of the war, whatever be its issue, find ourselves without a friend in Europe, while our Indian Empire will no longer be secure from attack by Russia. If we defer intervention till France is in danger of being crushed, the sacrifices we shall then be called on to make will be much greater.[76]

As recorded by Grey on 1 August the French Ambassador, helping the sword of Damocles on its downward path, 'urged very strongly the obligation of British interests. If we did not help France, the entente would disappear; and, whether victory came to Germany or to France and Russia, our situation at the end of the war would be very uncomfortable.'[77]

From 1904, associating with France and then Russia looked like supporting the weaker of the two major European groupings. It resembled, in this respect, classical balance-of-power politics. When the Foreign Secretary and his officials spoke and wrote of 'the work of the last decade', however, they did not have Europe primarily in mind. Nicolson might write in July 1911 of 'our policy since 1904 of preserving the equilibrium and consequently the peace in Europe'.[78] Mallet might write in 1912 that 'by the policy so happily inaugurated by Balfour's Government the outbreak of war has been twice averted in the last eight years'.[79] Essentially, this was a screen erected to conceal Britain's imperial vulnerability. Not only did those most concerned with, and most responsible for, British foreign policy know that she could make hardly any material contribution towards a balance of power in Europe; they knew that their alignment with France and Russia rather than with the Triple Alliance was for the purpose of enabling Britain more easily than otherwise to retain command of the sea and, above all, to secure the position of the British Empire in Central and East-Central Asia.

2. Publicity and Diplomacy: The Impact of the First World War upon Foreign Office Attitudes towards the Press

PHILIP TAYLOR

GOVERNMENT information services and official press departments were unknown in nineteenth-century Britain. Before 1914 it was not seriously considered to be a responsibility of government to explain, still less to justify, its policies to the public at large, whether at home or abroad. Apart from infrequent official announcements and ministerial speeches, the publication of Hansard, command papers and parliamentary bluebooks (which became less revealing in the years after 1880),[1] there was little public access to information concerning the workings of government. Moreover, attempts to secure public support for policies formulated by the ruling élite were considered unnecessary. The prevailing official attitude remained that 'opinion, like trade and industry, should under the old liberal conception be allowed to flow in its own natural channels without any artificial regulation'.[2] Despite a discernible trend away from this assumption in the years following the conflict with the Boers, a fundamental reappraisal did not take place until the outbreak of the First World War.

Between 1914 and 1918 it became necessary to mobilise elements in society which had hitherto remained uninvolved in the exigencies of national survival. It also became necessary for the British government to embark, essentially for the first time, upon a systematic campaign of national self-advertisement overseas in order to counter the effects of aggressive enemy propaganda directed against British interests and prestige. The ability to influence or even control public opinion, domestic and foreign, thus became a military asset, and propaganda emerged as the principal instrument of power over opinion. Moreover, with the gradual admission of propaganda into the national armoury as an additional weapon of wartime diplomacy, a process which culminated in the creation of a Ministry of Information in 1918, there developed simultaneously an appreciation of the potential value of the press as the chief medium then available through which public opinion could be most readily influenced. With broadcasting and the cinema still in their infancy, the press became a vital link between government and governed. By the end of the war, such was the degree of conviction concerning the success of the wartime propaganda experiment, and of the role played by the press in that experiment, that a reappraisal of government–press relations became inevitable.

Before the outbreak of war in 1914, the Foreign Office possessed no formal machinery for the regular supply of official information or for the issue of guidance to the press. There did not exist a British equivalent of the Press Bureau in the Wilhelmstrasse or the Maison de la Presse at the Quai d'Orsay. To the sheltered world of Whitehall, there appeared no need for such an organisation. Effective public opinion had, until relatively recently, been restricted by such factors as the limited electoral franchise, the absence of educational facilities and opportunities for those outside the privileged élite and, on the official side, a lack of means to disseminate information to an audience which lacked sophistication and which only occasionally expressed an active interest in foreign affairs.[3] Diplomacy remained 'the special business of kings, nobles and aristocratic persons';[4] any attempt to influence popular opinion would have stood out in sharp contrast to the traditional diplomatic etiquette of self-restraint and discretion. It was generally maintained that the conduct of foreign affairs required a high degree of freedom from public scrutiny, whether at home where it was believed that the majority of people were incapable of appreciating the subtle intricacies of diplomatic manoeuvres, or abroad where premature disclosures might prejudice Britain's interests. Diplomatic negotiations and transactions were therefore conducted beneath an umbrella of secrecy, while the Foreign Office 'abstained assiduously'[5] from creating any machinery that would encourage greater public participation in the exclusive realm of international politics. Indeed, such was the special position of diplomacy that even the House of Commons 'seldom or never presumed to press for an answer when the Foreign Secretary put a finger to his lips'.[6]

However, with the gradual trend towards universal suffrage and the improving standards of literacy and education – which served to subsidise and to reflect the new trends in journalism towards the close of the nineteenth century – there were developing new means and media of communication through the advance of technology. The implications for both publicity and diplomacy were dramatic. Increased speed of communication shortened the interval which elapsed between the transmission and receipt of diplomatic correspondence, allowed the Foreign Office more efficiently to control its representatives abroad, and reduced time available for making decisions. In the field of communications, wireless telegraphy and the cinematograph, like the heavier-than-air flying machine, were no longer figments in the imagination of men such as Jules Verne and H. G. Wells. The communications revolution had begun and its ramifications threatened to change fundamentally man's world picture. Britain was singularly well-placed to play a leading role in this development but despite the emergence of London as the major news capital of the world, at the hub of a vast global cable network, the government remained more concerned with the strategic defence of that network than with its use for the dissemination of British ideals and opinions.[7]

The Foreign Office, more often than not, proved to be a generally disappointing source of information for the nineteenth-century journalist. Indeed, one historian has claimed that 'the foreign secretary and his officials *prided* themselves on their detachment from the changing moods of public opinion',[8] and certainly there were numerous complaints concerning the secrecy with which diplomats conducted their business, and of their notorious treatment of the casual enquiry.[9] Kennedy Jones, a distinguished *Daily Mail* correspondent who later became editor of the *Evening News*, described how the permanent officials of the pre-war Foreign Office constituted a 'brick wall against which many a proprietor and editor has bruised his head' and who regarded the journalist 'who strayed into Downing Street as an unmannerly intruder to be mercilessly snubbed'.[10]

As public interest in foreign affairs inevitably increased during periods of international tension, so also did the demands of the press for more official information concerning British attitudes and actions. Bismarck had displayed his capacity to exploit his 'reptile press' in the service of diplomacy, and the French were not beyond such manipulation.[11] Whereas there was no exactly corresponding development in Britain, certain individual politicians, of whom Lord Palmerston is perhaps the most notable example, had fully appreciated the value of cultivating their relations with the press. However, attempts by governments to influence the press over questions of foreign policy were generally resisted by the non-party newspapers, as in 1852 on the occasion of the famous debate between Lord Derby and *The Times*. Journalists were forced to obtain information on foreign affairs from more consistent sources, but because the maintenance of foreign correspondents abroad was a luxury few papers could afford, the major European news agencies – Reuters, Havas and Wolff – enjoyed a period of rapid expansion. Unlike its continental counterparts, however, Reuters did not enjoy direct official subsidies and the overseas distribution of British news was left in the hands of private enterprise.

Nevertheless, as Oron J. Hale has argued with some force, between 1890 and 1914 British newspapers underwent many changes in spirit, content and physical appearance and millions of people who had not been subscribers to the older journals now became regular readers:

> The publicity given to politics and foreign affairs was increased a thousand times. More people were informed, or misinformed, about the Empire and England's relations to her neighbors than ever before. We cannot infer from this any extension of popular control over those relations, because the balance between parliament, cabinet and foreign office remained unchanged. A higher regard for the increasing power of publicity marked, however, the attitude of foreign office officials.[12]

Another American scholar has taken this argument one stage further by suggesting that, with the increasing appreciation of the value of publicity in domestic affairs, there developed an awareness of the value of applying similar methods in diplomacy. If public support could be aroused for internal political purposes, so it might also be enlisted to strengthen bargaining positions in foreign relations. Popular sentiment could furnish a convenient excuse for refusing concessions that negotiators, for various reasons, did not wish to grant. The press could be used to stir up public opinion in support of a particular policy, or it could be used to justify specific diplomatic aims, or merely to explain the official position of the government. However, the argument continues, 'although statesmen considered these uses of the press, those of even the late nineteenth century approached the potential of propaganda in diplomacy with extreme caution. To many, such activities seemed to stand in sharp conflict with their professional sense of responsibility and tantamount to opening Pandora's Box.'[13] It was this suspicion of the unknown, this uncertainty concerning the response of a largely ignorant and erratic mass audience, that prevented any real change in the organisation of the Foreign Office to meet these new trends in communications and publicity. Instead, the press was used more cautiously 'for the purpose of making announcements, or putting out feelers to foreign governments than as a means of influencing public opinion at large'.[14]

Just as the Foreign Office remained an alternative, albeit disappointing, source of information to diplomatic correspondents so also was the press considered a useful means of confirming, and sometimes supplementing, information gathered through the normal diplomatic channels. In this way a kind of symbiotic relationship developed between small groups of publicists and officials, each utilising the other's sources of information in pursuit of their respective duties. True, there did not exist any system of formal contact, but there did develop an unofficial and highly selective system of informal communication, often based upon personal friendship and mutual interests. This is a twilight area where hard evidence is not readily available, but it does seem that information was divulged in a private letter, at a social function or over a quiet table at White's or the Athenaeum, when an official would confide in a responsible correspondent or editor with whom he could feel safe, in the knowledge that any news divulged would not appear beneath sensational headlines on the following day. J. A. Spender has maintained that 'it was never the habit of the Foreign Office to inspire the newspapers',[15] but he nonetheless enjoyed a special privilege of confidentiality with the Asquith Government. Nor would his claim appear to stand up to closer examination of the numerous contacts known to have existed between permanent officials and such distinguished journalists as Valentine Chirol and Wickham Steed, both of *The Times*, E. J. Dillon of the *Daily Telegraph*, and Spencer Wilkinson of the *Morning Post*, to name but a few. It would be naive to conceive of these relations merely as personal friendships.[16] It appears likely that, by confiding in such men, permanent officials hoped to avoid serious misunderstandings concerning their policies in the press, thereby aiding the course of diplomacy. In this respect, the work of William Tyrrell, private secretary to Sir Edward Grey and the official chiefly responsible for maintaining contacts between the Foreign Secretary and trusted editors, should not go unnoticed.

Parallel to this growing appreciation of the value of official publicity, there developed an equal appreciation of the possible dangers. Writing in 1933, J. A. Spender observed that 'there has been much talk since the war of the evils of secret diplomacy, but the dangers of a rash and inexpert handling of publicity are written just as large in the records'.[17] Indeed, the poisoning of the international atmosphere through the arbitrary publication of information, as had happened during the so-called press 'war' of 1900–03, has been adjudged one of the underlying causes of tension which led to the outbreak of the First World War: 'The newspapers of two countries often took up some point of dispute, exaggerated it, and made attacks and counter-attacks, until a regular newspaper war was engendered, which thoroughly poisoned public opinion and so offered a fertile soil in which the seeds of war might easily generate.'[18] Such obvious excesses produce ample evidence that too much publicity was as dangerous as too little. It was because of this danger that in 1904 a standing sub-committee of the Committee of Imperial Defence was set up to examine the question of press censorship in the event of war. The problems deriving from an inexpert handling of publicity had become apparent during the Fashoda crisis which, as Kennedy Jones has pointed out, 'marked the breaking down of the barriers of Downing Street'.[19] The CID sub-committee debated the problem intermittently for a decade, pointing out in 1913:

> The danger to be met is that, in times of tension, the press has endangered the interests of the country by the publication of naval and military intelligence which it was of importance to withhold from the enemy.[20]

This might well have been so, but with the transformation of international allegiances between 1898 and 1907, the role of the press as a medium of explanation (tending as it did to lead rather than follow public opinion on questions of foreign policy) had become more important. And yet, as Sir William Tyrrell recalled, this development did not necessarily require the creation of a press department within the Foreign Office because, he wrote, once the issues had become clear, 'it was a comparatively easy task in pre-war days to deal with the press . . . The issues which presented themselves to the popular mind were . . . mainly confined to Anglo-German relations, and on this subject there was practical unanimity in our press so there was little to do on our part on the matter.'[21]

It was the First World War which provided the catalyst in the relationship between the Foreign Office and the press. Between 1914 and 1917, the News Department of the Foreign Office emerged as the proper channel through which official information was issued to British and foreign journalists. This is not to suggest that informal contacts did not continue to exist; merely that the distribution of news relating to foreign affairs was placed upon a more regular and systematic basis. The precarious armed neutrality that had characterised relations between the two professions now became an open and mutual co-operation 'in the national interest'.

The need to harness the potential of the press, both in a positive (publicity) and in a negative (censorship) sense, manifested itself in the creation of the Foreign Office News Department and of the Press Bureau in August 1914. The invaluable experience of journalists in the techniques of news selection, written communication and the propagation of opinion for a wide audience was eagerly sought after by officials who lacked similar experience and training. It was, for example, partly on the advice of editors and proprietors that Charles Masterman began to establish his War Propaganda Bureau at Wellington House.[22] George Mair resigned his position as assistant editor of the *Daily Chronicle* in order to take charge of the other important official propaganda body set up in 1914, the Neutral Press Committee.[23] Later in the war, Mair's former editor, Robert Donald, was mainly responsible for the recommendations which led first to the creation of the Department, and then of the Ministry, of Information.[24] The government began recruiting prominent journalists with Sir Edward Cook and Sir Frank Swettenham at the Press Bureau,[25] a development which reached its controversial apogee with the creation of Lord Beaverbrook's Ministry of Information and Lord Northcliffe's department of enemy propaganda at Crewe House in 1918. Thus, by absorbing whenever possible the power of the press into the service of government, by making some of its members an integral part of the war-time defence of the realm, by the provision of honours to proprietors thereby giving them a vested interest in the survival of the system, and by utilising the press as an instrument of national propaganda, the government made inevitable a reappraisal of its relations with the press.[26]

It was certainly ironical that the Foreign Office, traditionally the most difficult of government departments to penetrate and among the most zealously protective of its secrecy, proved to be the first in 1914 to open its doors to the press. On the outbreak of war, William Tyrrell continued his practice of seeing any journalist who called at the Foreign Office. The requests for news soon became too great a burden for one man to handle. Before long, when the propaganda value of the press, particularly in allied and neutral countries, took on added significance, a small News Department comprising three or four permanent officials was established to meet the increased demand for information about a war fought on foreign soil. Journalists were actually encouraged to call at the Foreign Office and F. D. Acland, the first head of the News Department, was held responsible for the officials 'unburdening themselves from time to time to correspondents'.[27] Under Acland's direction two traditions were established. The first was that the parliamentary under-secretary for foreign affairs, with his experience of meeting journalists in the lobby of the House of Commons, would act as nominal head of the News Department, an arrangement which prevailed until 1916. The second was that contacts between officials and newspapermen were placed on a regular basis. Meetings with correspondents for two-hour periods took place three times weekly, while the private secretary of the News Department's head, in Acland's case Guy Locock, made himself constantly available to answer enquiries.[28]

This rationalisation of contacts with the press was, from the outset, based upon a belief in the value of indirect techniques of persuasion: 'through showing one important editor the concrete evidence of this country's achievements, you can reach hundreds of thousands of readers'.[29] The chief targets of the News Department's propaganda were, therefore, the opinion-makers and influential members of society, the principle being that it was more effective to influence those in a position to influence others than to attempt a direct appeal to the mass of the population. The early emphasis on press propaganda did, however, give rise to two serious problems. In the first place, the News Department correctly sensed that newspapermen who cherished liberal traditions of freedom to report and criticise would continue to resent the incursions of the Press Bureau's censorship restrictions into those hallowed areas. The resulting tension was, however, to a great extent alleviated when, following enlightened appeals by the Foreign Office in October 1915, the political censorship of all material relating to foreign affairs – until that time the joint responsibility of the Press Bureau and the News Department – was discontinued.[30] Thereafter, considerable latitude was extended by the Foreign Office to journalists and a new period of frankness and mutual co-operation ensued, although this was not a trend initially welcomed by other government departments. Secondly, recognising the resentment caused by officials' attempts to influence opinion, the News Department tried to facilitate the efforts of journalists to report for themselves. Reports issued by the War Office's official 'eye-witnesses' at the front provided one such case, and it was only towards the end of 1915 that the Service departments relented, allowing allied and neutral correspondents to visit the front and the fleet for the first time.[31] Also on Foreign Office advice, General Maurice and Admiral Hall began to give weekly lectures on the military and naval situations to eager journalists, 'the success of which more than justified the experiment'.[32] With the same principle in mind, the News Department arranged visits to munitions factories, prisoner-of-war camps and even to the visitors' gallery at the House of Commons. Great emphasis was always placed upon personal contact between official and journalist in order to forge a relationship of trust and mutual confidence. This approach was entirely compatible with the training, experience and temperament of the 'foreign-policy-making élite' to which concepts of mass public opinion were either alien or incomprehensible. It was only in 1918, with the transfer of responsibility for propaganda from the permanent officials to such press lords as Beaverbrook and Northcliffe who, with some justice, claimed to understand public opinion better, that direct methods of propaganda involving film, leaflets and pamphlets were given greater emphasis.

For the first three years of the war, however, officials in the News Department preferred that any proposals for increased or improved propaganda through the press should originate with the journalists themselves. They conceived their own role merely as suppliers of information on demand. What happened to the information once it had left their lips was left to the discretion of the recipient. Those who lacked discretion and published sensitive material were damned in future. The fear that one of their most important sources of information may suddenly dry up at any time seems to have been an adequate deterrent. Emphasising the joint nature of the collaboration, one official wrote that 'the News Department and the correspondents are constantly racking their brains to think of subjects which it will be interesting to work up'.[33] Such co-operation was possible only with journalists who shared a common aim with the allies for the duration of the war, namely the defeat of the Central Powers and the achievement of victory. It was more difficult to apply in contacts with journalists from neutral countries. Nevertheless, the attitude of correspondents from that most important of neutral countries, the United States of America, was recorded as being 'everything that could be wished'.[34] The only exception was the pro-German Hearst press which, following repeated warnings not to publish misleading information, suffered an official news embargo in London between 1915 and 1917.[35] In general, however, it was considered that the American newspapermen in England were 'trustworthy people'[36] but had to be 'constantly nursed and humoured . . . There is a need therefore to get [them] in good temper', a task which was considered to be 'one of the most important bits of work that the News Department has to do'.[37]

It was this emphasis on press propaganda which was challenged by Robert Donald in this first investigation into Britain's propaganda organisation in January 1917. In recommending the creation of a separate Department of Information, Donald not only questioned the Foreign Office's priorities but also the capacity of permanent officials to undertake press work at all. He claimed that the main problem derived from the fact that Lord Newton, head of the News Department since early 1916, and his assistants had 'no experience in newspaper work until some time after the war began, and are hampered by the traditional atmosphere of the Foreign Office, its attitude towards the press, and its inability to appreciate the supreme importance of quick action'.[38]

This was not entirely fair. Whereas it is undoubtedly true that many of the more traditionally minded diplomats in the Foreign Office disliked the whole notion of releasing information to the press, those officials in the News Department had constantly fought for a more enlightened attitude on the part of other government departments. In defence of its methods, one official pointed out that 'the government departments have a tradition of silence and Parliament has not. It is this tradition of silence only very slowly breaking down that forms the chief difficulty with which the News Department has to contend.'[39] The same author concluded with a claim that reflected the dramatic transformation which had taken place since the beginning of the war concerning the attitude of some Foreign Office officials towards the press. He wrote:

> The correspondents, and especially the Americans, will come much more freely to the Foreign Office, *which is the natural place to seek information from*, than they will to an office known to be established for propaganda purposes.[40]

It was further claimed that 'it will be quite unpractical to supply the correspondents with the information they want (fully 75% of which concerns foreign affairs) except by having a staff for the purpose at the Foreign Office'.[41]

The establishment of the Department of Information under John Buchan in February 1917 did not threaten the position of the News Department as the major source of official information concerning the war to British and foreign journalists because Buchan chose to locate his headquarters at the Foreign Office. A year later, however, with the creation of the Ministry of Information, the Foreign Office was forced finally to hand over its responsibility for propaganda abroad, including its control over press relations. This development, which provided the signal for wholesale recruitment from Fleet Street into the service of the governmental propaganda machine, not unnaturally provoked an outcry in Parliament. Austen Chamberlain led the attack, claiming that the appointments of Beaverbrook and Northcliffe removed the line of demarcation which had previously existed between the functions of press and of government.[42] Moreover, it was not beyond the imagination of many politicians, particularly those in opposition to Lloyd George, that the new and dangerous weapon of propaganda could be used by an unscrupulous government as a means of sustaining political power. As Chamberlain wrote to Lord Milner and Lord Curzon privately:

> Some people think that Lord Northcliffe controls the Government. Others say the Government have 'nobbled' Lord Northcliffe. But no-one for a moment supposes that these appointments – whatever can be said for each on its merits – had any other object in the mind of the Prime Minister than to secure for himself the support of powerful groups of newspapers . . . This is a method of propaganda repugnant to the traditions of our public life and to the habits of our nation. But I venture to add that it is as short-sighted as it is dangerous. The support of such a journal as 'The Times' [owned by Northcliffe] would be invaluable to you if 'The Times' were thought to be independent. Its support under present circumstances has merely the negative value that it does not oppose you: in other words, from the moment that it is supposed that Government have bought the support of a paper their bargain becomes valueless to themselves. On the other hand, as long as the proprietors of these great papers and groups of papers are members of the Government, the

Government will be suspected of inspiring, and will be denounced for conniving at, anything which appears in their columns. This is a position equally injurious to the Government and the Press and there is no escape from it except by severing the connection so unfortunately made.[43]

The proposed severance did not take place; Lloyd George rode out the storm, and Beaverbrook and Northcliffe went on, at least in their eyes, to win the war with the aid of propaganda.

The closing stages of the war introduced a further consideration into the question of government–press relations: that of their future character. Lord Beaverbrook advocated the maintenance of the Ministry of Information during the coming Peace Conference and recognised a golden opportunity to secure public support for the British point of view. He wrote:

> The Ministry can only justify its existence during the period in which the terms of the Peace Treaty are being settled by maintaining the closest possible touch with the British representatives at Conference. Wherever it may be held, there will all the journalists of the world gather together. On the information obtained from the Peace delegates and their associates will depend the impression produced in every country as to the course of the negotiations – an impression which will react on the negotiations themselves.[44]

Given the developments which had taken place in government–press relations during the previous four years, it might be assumed that publicity would occupy a key position in the minds of British delegates attending the Paris Peace Conference in 1919, the more so with the return of Lloyd George to power at the 'coupon' election. Set in the context of President Wilson's appeal for 'open covenants openly arrived at' and for the creation of the League of Nations as an expression of the 'organised opinion of mankind', newspapermen from all parts of the globe flocked to Paris expecting no less. They could only have been disappointed. As one historian has shown, the scores of journalists soon discovered that 'open covenants openly arrived at' did not mean complete freedom to cover the proceedings but rather 'the receipt of prepared short news releases and the coverage of the rare and usually arid formal plenary sessions'.[45] Another observer noted that

The negotiators . . . seemed unaware of changed conditions in the realm of opinion; at any rate, they sought to close their ears to most of these voices. Negotiation to them was the concern only of the ruling class of political leaders and professional foreign office public servants. Narrow nationalistic views were hugged tight by these old-style diplomats in a new-style world.[46]

If publicity and public relations were examples of the 'new-style world' ushered in by the First World War, then the British delegation in Paris wanted no part of it. Lloyd George, more conscious than most of his contemporaries of the value of publicity in political life, had nonetheless done nothing to prevent the closure of the Ministry of Information after the armistice was signed. Moreover, he decided not to appoint an official spokesman for his delegation in Paris, writing instead of the 'very strong feeling inside the Conference room' that if the daily discussions were published before any decision had been reached:

> it would interfere materially with our efforts to reconcile differences and to arrive at a common understanding. It was pointed out that if it were known that the delegates of some particular country were putting up a fight on some special question on which opinion in that country took a somewhat different view from that which obtained in other Allied countries, it would be difficult for either side to give in or to compromise without an appearance of surrender.[47]

Here was the embodiment of those pre-war arguments in favour of secrecy at international conferences; 'open diplomacy' was in Paris a meaningless cliché.

However, the delegates were clearly out of touch with popular sentiment which, rightly or not, conceived of secret diplomacy as one of the underlying causes of the war. Almost immediately the absence of an official British spokesman began to cause problems for the British delegates. The demands of the press for more information could simply not be ignored. As a result, Lloyd George, William Tyrrell and Lord Riddell, Chairman of the Newspaper Proprietors' Association and the appointed representative of the British press at the Paris Conference, discussed the possibility of issuing communiqués to journalists on the lines already adopted by the American delegation.[48] Riddell, who was an intimate friend of Lloyd George, strongly urged the necessity for greater publicity and offered his services as liaison officer between the

British delegation and the press.[49] He appealed to the Prime Minister to release more news, although 'not necessarily for publication', in an attempt to clarify many existing misunderstandings, but warned him:

> Propaganda is not one of the functions for which I have been appointed by the newspapers. Nothing will satisfy the press but more information. Furthermore, you are dealing with questions which raise the most violent international antagonisms, and every nation implicated is endeavouring to make use of the press as a propaganda agent.[50]

Riddell continued to harass the Prime Minister on this issue and he was not entirely without success, but, as he noted in his diary in May 1919, Lloyd George and his colleagues had not favoured the use of publicity: 'We have had to fight inch by inch. Like all autocrats, they like to work in secret and to tell the public just as much as suits their purpose.'[51] Nevertheless, despite his disappointment, Riddell's position as intermediary between official and journalist was an indication of the changing demands of diplomacy and of the British response to them; the presence of such an official at a pre-war international gathering would have been unthinkable.

Between 1914 and 1918, the establishment of formal relations between Whitehall and the press had become a necessary expedient. Government departments were forced, often reluctantly, to abandon their traditional aloofness towards journalists and substitute for it a greater willingness to take them into their confidence. The British and foreign press had responded by providing, perhaps unwittingly in some cases, the chief medium by which government could speak to its people and the people of allied and neutral countries. A tentative alliance had been forged 'in the public interest', and the truce existed for the duration of the war although, as Northcliffe demonstrated during the shell-shortage crisis of 1915, the press retained its traditional freedom to criticise government if it chose to do so.[52] In general, however, Fleet Street had accepted the wartime restrictions with patriotic good grace.

Nevertheless, the co-operation of such bodies as the Newspaper Proprietors' Association, the recruitment of many journalists into the services of the Ministry of Information and Crewe House, combined with the widespread distaste for propaganda, had produced an atmosphere of public scepticism towards the press. Austen Chamberlain's warnings now seemed pertinent with the return of peace. Fleet Street accordingly resumed its sensitivity to any criticism of governmental influence. Co-operation may have been a necessary and even an acceptable expedient of war, but essentially the traditional line of demarcation between publicist and official had been preserved. It was largely because Lloyd George had attempted to cross that line that Robert Donald resigned as editor of the *Daily Chronicle* when the Prime Minister bought the paper in 1918.[53] Following Beaverbrook's example, Northcliffe had resigned his wartime office partly in order to pursue his normal newspaper duties in light of the coming general election. When, therefore, the wartime propaganda machinery was set in the process of liquidation after the armistice was signed and the question arose as to the desirability of maintaining those channels of communication between Whitehall and Fleet Street which had been built up during the war, the press became highly sensitive to any suggestion of malpractice in its relationship with the government. It became clear that any attempts at continued official control or influence in peacetime would be vigorously resisted. Hence the removal of two of the most symbolic wartime shackles was greeted with much relief: the Press Bureau was closed down on 30 April 1919 and the censorship was abolished shortly afterwards.[54]

However, many officials and journalists alike had welcomed the wartime regularisation of contacts between their respective professions. In many cases, an atmosphere of mutual trust and co-operation had developed. Officials were convinced that, by confiding in journalists, they had managed to prevent serious misunderstandings over many issues. An informed critic was considered more desirable than a misinformed sycophant. Government press departments had provided a valuable and much needed service, a sort of no man's land where the two professions could meet regularly to exchange information and discuss key issues. Moreover, the wartime contacts with foreign journalists had also proved invaluable not only in securing publicity for the British case abroad but also in enabling officials to keep a finger on the pulse of foreign opinion.

Thus when the Foreign Office began during 1919 to examine the possible peacetime role of publicity in diplomacy, the press received particular consideration. The British press after all provided an important source of information concerning Britain's domestic and foreign affairs for the overseas observer, and it was therefore necessary to consider this medium of national self-advertisement. Moreover, several enlightened officials argued that, as a direct consequence of the war, the

Foreign Office now had a moral responsibility to inform and explain its policies to an audience, both at home and abroad, whose opinions and actions were becoming increasingly important with the broadening base of political power. It was further argued that just as propaganda had been utilised as an effective instrument of warfare so also could it now be converted to serve the interests of international peace and understanding. For example, George Beak, former Consul-General in Zurich and largely responsible for the distribution of British propaganda material into Germany through neutral Switzerland, argued:

> The chief means by which the different peoples can arrive at a mutual knowledge and understanding of each other is the press . . . In the past, Great Britain was perhaps the only nation in the world which took practically no steps to inspire her own press or to influence the press of other countries and consequently, when the war came upon her, she was unable to make her own case known or understood.

The argument was developed further on the assumption that public opinion had now become a determinant factor in the making of policy:

> Without entering upon the advantages or disadvantages of either secret or public diplomacy, it may be taken for granted that the masses will now demand to know much more than previously of what is going on, and what is being done in the diplomatic field, and it would probably not only be futile but dangerous to attempt to keep knowledge from them. The great thing is to protect them from half-truths by letting them know as much as possible. Before the war owing largely to its being regarded as outside party politics, not only the people but even the House of Commons had become ignorant and apathetic on the subject of foreign policy. A general interest in that policy has now been revived by the war, and it is submitted that every step should be taken to maintain that interest, and to render it more intelligent.[55]

No doubt, not every member of the diplomatic service would have agreed with this view. But the theme was taken up and developed by another official who had been closely involved in wartime propaganda, S. A. Guest. He added that it was equally important for the Foreign Office to retain some form of machinery for the observation of foreign press opinion, particularly as he believed that labour questions and popular movements were assuming an increasingly important role in the government of foreign societies. He wrote:

> Whatever we may know about the legal or formal constitution of a foreign country, we seldom, if ever, know who 'runs' the country, or who 'runs' it in reference to any particular matter. We therefore do not know who is to be approached in order to deal at once and effectively with any particular difficulty or misunderstanding. In some cases and in some matters the ultimate power is split up in the hands of a very large number of persons and, therefore, the only means of influencing them is through the press or some other instrument of publicity.[56]

Such views were not uncommon at the end of the First World War; they belong in the context of a much wider body of opinion outside the Foreign Office which had been profoundly affected by such factors as the introduction of conscription and the mass destruction in the trenches, the revolutions in Russia and central Europe, and the widespread social and industrial unrest which had accompanied the return of peace, and which now called for the democratic control of foreign policy.[57]

The Foreign Office was not the only government department which gave serious consideration to the vexed question of press relations. In April 1919, the Cabinet considered a proposal for the establishment of what was called a 'Central Agency for the Issue of Official Communiqués from Government Departments' which was intended to fill the gap left by the Press Bureau.[58] The proposal encountered severe opposition, led by the Home Secretary, but also from the press, which had somehow been informed of the idea.[59] When one remembers the hostility of Parliament in February 1918 towards the appointments of Beaverbrook and Northcliffe, reinforced during the only major wartime debate in the Commons on the subject of propaganda in August of the same year,[60] this is hardly surprising. The Cabinet therefore decided that such a function would more properly be performed by the individual departments themselves, which were instructed to make their own separate arrangements for issuing statements to the press if they so desired.[61] Most departments chose not to consider the question until they could no longer resist the demand. By 1923, seven departments employed officials who specialised in the release of information to the press,[62] and by 1938 the number had increased to twelve.[63] But in 1919, only the News Department of the Foreign Office had existed solely to conduct press work.

Originally, the reconstituted News Department was amalgamated with the Political Intelligence Department under the direction of William Tyrrell. He was charged with the task of keeping the parliamentary under-secretary 'fully cognisant of all that was passing and would arrange for interviews between him and important journalists when this was found necessary'.[64] Nevertheless, the News Department remained conscious of the sensitivity of the British press and initially designed its arrangements to cater mainly for the release of official news to representatives of foreign newspapers.[65] The appointment of several press attachés at the more important embassies was a further facility provided to meet this demand.[66] Nevertheless, whereas the decision to retain a department for the supervision of British overseas propaganda marked a major departure from established peacetime tradition, the Foreign Office decided that for the moment it would revert to an improved version of the pre-war system whereby the responsibility for dealing with visitors from Fleet Street was placed in the hands of the private secretary to the secretary of state.[67]

J. W. Headlam-Morley, a member of the Paris Peace Delegation who was to become Historical Adviser to the Foreign Office, expressed his frustration at this retrogressive step, and at the post-war policy of retrenchment which threatened to close down the Political Intelligence Department. He expressed the view that 'it would perhaps be more agreeable if the whole work were stopped and we went back to the original system by which the government divested itself of any responsibility for the immediate control of foreign opinion', but, he continued,

This is now impossible. In a condition of things when the foreign policy of each nation is no longer determined by a small group of men at the head of affairs often in close connection with a court, but is becoming more and more the immediate concern of peoples and parliaments, we cannot ignore the importance of using legitimate means for influencing this opinion . . . It is also clearly necessary that there should be someone whose duty it is to keep in touch with the correspondents of foreign papers in London and the person who does this should obviously be the same as the one who communicates material to our agent in the foreign country. The object to be attained is that both in England and abroad there should be arrangements by which representatives of the press get to understand that they will receive ready assistance and information. This, it may be noted, is quite different from anything in the nature of bribing the press, or attempting to get an illicit control over it.[68]

Headlam-Morley did manage to secure the influential support of Hardinge, the Permanent Under-Secretary, and of Curzon, by then Foreign Secretary,[69] but despite negotiations on the subject throughout the first half of 1920, the Foreign Office was instructed to re-examine the entire position of the News Department with a view to effecting economies, a decision which was shortly to result in the closure of the Political Intelligence Department.[70]

As a consequence of the reorganisation which took place in 1920, representatives of the British press were, at least in theory, directed to the private secretary's office for their occasional ration of news and comment. During Lord Curzon's term of office this work was at first undertaken by Robert Vansittart who admitted that he more often tried to avoid journalists than meet them.[71] Relations between Whitehall and the press were in fact severely strained after the war, as was illustrated by the boycott imposed upon the Northcliffe papers by Lloyd George. Kennedy Jones commented upon the 'semi-contemptuous attitude' which prevailed and wrote cynically that officials chosen to supply information were appointed for their ability 'to gauge correctly the exact suppression of the truth in each statement, for these statements, though in the main true, are rarely the whole truth and nothing but the truth, and their nature varies according to the friendliness or hostility of the medium through which they are to reach the public'.[72] The Foreign Office soon appreciated that its reversion to pre-war methods had been a serious error; not only were journalists dissatisfied with the treatment handed out to them by officials, but the officials were unhappy with the printed results.

It was for this reason that Tyrrell wished to place peacetime contacts with Fleet Street on the same basis as those which had been laid down for foreign correspondents. 'I am not sure', he wrote with some justification, 'that we sufficiently realise the great change which has taken place in our relations with the press since the outbreak of war.' Commenting upon the apparent increase of public interest in foreign affairs which had prompted a corresponding increase in the news-papers' interest, he argued that there has been a simultaneous decline in the independence of the British press due to the growing influence of four proprietors on the editorial policies of the majority of newspapers. Because the British press was regarded abroad as a mirror of British opinion, the effect of strained relations between Whitehall and Fleet Street was distorting the image. While deprecating the dominance of Northcliffe, Rothermere, Beaverbrook and Dalziel in the formulation of newspaper opinion in Britain, Tyrrell observed:

> If their outlook happens to coincide with the national view, so much the better for the nation, but if these mighty men settle on a personal policy, so much the worse for the nation. In the latter case they will only accept information from here which suits their book and are quite willing to reject or distort what runs counter to their policy as distinguished from ours.[73]

In making this observation, Tyrrell touched upon perhaps the most fundamental problem confronting governmental publicity in a democratic system which cherished notions of a free press and freedom of speech. Ideally, both would speak with one voice in order to project an image of domestic harmony. In reality, however, this was rarely the case. Despite the recognition in 1922 of the need to remain in constant touch with the British press – which has remained a prime task of the Foreign Office since then – the most that the News Department could hope to achieve was the provision of a regular stream of accurate news and intelligent comment in an attempt to disarm any adverse press criticism of government policies based upon ill-informed or misguided speculation.

The Foreign Office decided that this task would be best performed by an official with journalistic experience, a man who could understand the needs of the press in its dealings with government. Accordingly, in 1921, Arthur Willert, former Washington correspondent of *The Times*, was recruited to serve in the News Department and he began his duties in London once he had completed his task at the Washington Conference where he had taken over from Lord Riddell as the British delegation's official spokesman.[74] Thereafter, not only was there a News Department official at every major international conference for the purpose of handing out information concerning the policies of the British government to the press, but there was also at least one official on constant call in London to meet enquiries. Under Willert's direction from 1923 to 1935, the press department of the Foreign Office became an established and legitimate point of contact between the world of

diplomacy and the world of publicity. As one of its officials,
J. D. Gregory, recognised in 1925:

> The era when it was possible either to lead opinion in foreign politics
> by mere authority or tradition, or to ignore it from Olympian heights,
> has long since vanished, and once modern contact, however vulgar,
> has been established, it is not possible to confine it to an intermittent
> dispensation of tit-bits of news at the will of one or two minor
> officials . . . It has become, and must be, practically a never-ceasing
> intercourse with the publicity world.[75]

Gregory was by no means alone in such views. Many contemporaries,
both within official circles and beyond, were quick to recognise the need
for the British government to meet the new requirements of a changing
world, a world that was becoming more familiar through technological
developments in the field of communications. The wartime contacts
between Whitehall and the press could not simply be terminated as if
nothing had happened to public opinion. The propaganda experiment,
combined with such factors as the wartime introduction of conscription,
the explosion of social and industrial unrest in the wake of the Bolshevik
revolution in Russia, and the anticipated increase of popular participation in the determination of governmental policy after the 1918
Representation of the People Act, had all served to heighten the
awareness of the British ruling élite concerning the power of publicity.
   The Foreign Office News Department may well be regarded as
having functioned 'on the edge of diplomacy'. Increased official
communication with the press was, however, merely one facet of a
much wider development. The advent of more sophisticated instruments of communication which were not dependent upon the written
word provided alternative means of reaching a much wider audience.
Indeed, the inter-war period witnessed the arrival of the genuinely
'mass' media. These new media could not be ignored as instruments of
political persuasion, either at home or abroad. In 1925, for example, the
Conservative Party began experimenting with travelling cinema vans
to disseminate its political ideals through the use of film. The following
year saw the creation of the Empire Marketing Board which was
instrumental in pioneering techniques of publicity based upon theories
of public relations imported mainly from the United States. In 1932, the
BBC launched its Empire Service and five years later it began
broadcasting in foreign languages. Meanwhile, in 1934, the Foreign

Office was responsible for the foundation of the British Council, which was designed to publicise British cultural achievements overseas along lines advocated by Sir Stephen Tallents in his influential 1932 pamphlet, *The Projection of England*.[76] At home, the National Publicity Bureau was set up to secure publicity for the policies of the National Government, while government departments such as the Post Office and the Ministry of Labour devoted more and more attention to new methods of securing publicity through the various media. By 1939 the House of Commons was in general agreement with the view of one of its members that 'the possession of efficient methods of publicity' had become 'an essential part of the equipment of the modern state'.[77] The Foreign Office News Department was perhaps the major pioneer in this development through its dealings with the press.

Much research remains to be done in this field which has rarely received the attention its significance deserves in, say, the major general histories of the twentieth century. But at least one thing is clear. During the inter-war years, publicity became an established fact of British political and diplomatic life.

3. The Foreign Office, the Dominions and the Diplomatic Unity of the Empire, 1925–29

NORMAN HILLMER

EXPEDIENCY governed the outlook of the Foreign Office and the Foreign Secretary on dominions questions in the 1920s. If the dominions – or some of them – insisted on laying claim to independent diplomatic action, then so must a great department of state, charged with the far-flung responsibilities of a major world and imperial power. In 1925 the movement away from an imperial foreign policy was ostentatiously confirmed: Foreign Secretary Austen Chamberlain negotiated and signed the Locarno Treaty on behalf of the United Kingdom alone, stipulating that no dominion need be bound unless its government formally approved. Thus, it seemed, the Foreign Office had declared against the diplomatic unity of the empire. It could no longer be taken for granted that the empire spoke with one voice on foreign affairs, except by the express consent and with the active collaboration of the governments of Canada, Australia, New Zealand, South Africa and the Irish Free State.[1]

The Foreign Office, however, did not readily admit that a choice had to be made between freedom of action and imperial unity. The Locarno policy was pursued in the name and interests of an empire that had to look to the Rhine, in Chamberlain's words, as one of its 'strategic frontiers'.[2] And so it must continue. 'It is vital', Permanent Under-Secretary Sir William Tyrrell wrote in November 1926, 'that *we* should conduct *all* political negotiations as affecting the Empire as a whole.'[3] Earlier in the year, in a memorandum which led to the formation of a

64

Dominions Information Department under his direction, Percy Koppell elaborated on the argument. Diplomatic unity, he asserted, remained an important tie of empire, cementing the links of common sovereignty and a common defence. The Foreign Secretary was still 'the director of Empire foreign policy'. Putting to one side the claims of dominion nationalism and the Foreign Office's own insistence on the need for efficiency and expedition in the conduct of foreign affairs, Koppell urged that 'it was impossible to have different members of a "Commonwealth of Nations" each expressing a foreign policy of its own and each negotiating on the basis of absolute sovereignty'. By impossible Koppell surely meant intolerable. If the diplomatic unity of the empire was broken, 'disaster and ultimate disruption' would follow; and without diplomatic unity 'the British Empire would lose weight and prestige in the councils of the Great Powers'.[4]

One means of asserting the continuing diplomatic unity of the empire and of preserving the empire's integrity as a legal and political entity in international law was the 'central panel', a system by which plenipotentiaries acting for the government in London were given unrestricted powers to sign League of Nations treaties on behalf of the 'British Empire'. Even though established constitutional procedures ensured that the dominions could only be truly bound by the signature of their own plenipotentiary, the Foreign Office insisted that the central panel was more than subterfuge, that 'the essential unity of the Empire' was thereby maintained.[5] The international community was reminded that different parts of the empire were not, *inter se*, separate contracting parties to international agreements and treaties. The more dominion representatives emphasised the need for separate signatures, the more foreign countries would insist on treating different parts of the empire as distinct units. The League of Nations and the International Court of Justice could assert jurisdiction to intervene in and adjudicate upon disputes within the empire. It would be difficult to resist claims that a commercial treaty granting most-favoured-nation treatment to a foreign country did not also entitle that state to the benefit of preferences given by one part of the empire to another. Ultimately, the empire's unique and recognised international position in matters of peace and war would be open to question.

The Dominions Office, newly-constituted under Leo Amery, doubted that the Foreign Office's arguments would hold up under the onslaught of the nationalist dominions – particularly South Africa and the Irish Free State – at the Imperial Conference of 1926. Amery preferred to concede the principle of full equality and trust the dominions to do the right thing. A prolonged debate took place, causing Assistant Under-Secretary Sir Hubert Montgomery to comment to the Foreign Secretary that the Dominions Office was 'much too inclined to take the extreme *Dominion*, as opposed to the *Imperial*, point of view'.[6] The Foreign Office finally expressed a willingness, if the dominions did not wish the central panel to continue, to accept the Dominions Office suggestion that treaties be made in the name of the king as contracting party, each dominion being given full powers equal to the British government and all adhering by geographically limited signatures. These signatures, though, would continue to be grouped under the heading 'British Empire' and to carry the covering sanction of a common head of state. In return, the Foreign Office wished open acceptance and written support of the *inter se* doctrine.

The Foreign Office's Legal Adviser, Sir Cecil Hurst, represented the British government at the Imperial Conference's committee on treaty procedure. 'You are in the happy position that you are represented twice over',[7] he told dominion delegates, the majority of whom were anything but happy at the prospect. In the face of the combined pressure of the Irish, South African and Canadian delegations, Hurst was driven quickly to a defence of the Dominions Office proposals that the department had earlier opposed. In the end, even the grouping of signatures under the term 'British Empire' was found to err on the side of unity to the detriment of the dominions' international standing. The committee decided that every treaty, whether negotiated under the auspices of the League or not, should be made in the name of heads of states; 'plenipotentiaries for the various British units should have full powers . . . indicating and corresponding to the part of the Empire for which they are to sign'; a treaty concluded on behalf of any or all of the empire governments should henceforth be signed in the name of the king as the symbol of the special relationship between the different parts of the empire. The latter provision rendered superfluous, it was stated at Hurst's insistence, the inclusion of a specific provision declaring the sanctity of *inter se*.[8] 'Sir Cecil Hurst . . . has been driven from pillar to post gallantly defending each position as he retired from it', an apparently straight-faced New Zealand delegate told the last committee meeting, 'and has met us all in a spirit that is not common with the Foreign Office.'[9]

When the Imperial Conference convened, the Foreign Secretary still hoped to achieve imperial unity on the Locarno issue: 'unanimous adherence', Chamberlain told dominion representatives, 'would produce a great effect, if it was felt that the whole weight of the British Empire was to be used to prevent aggression'. But this, too, was not to be. The dominions voiced their approval, even congratulation, but showed no enthusiasm for taking up obligations to defend Europe against itself. Nor could Chamberlain think of 'any serious consequence [that] would follow from the Dominions not adhering': 'people at large would think it almost certain that in a great crisis the Empire would act together'. And so it seemed, even to the reluctant South African and Irish delegates. The Canadian Prime Minister, indeed, went much further, echoing the sentiments of Australia and New Zealand: 'if the situation arose Canada would do her part'.[10]

From the signature of the Locarno Treaty, the editor of this volume has written elsewhere, there briefly developed 'a mood of helpfulness and co-operation in European politics' which lasted until 1929, and was never recaptured:

> Enmity between France and Germany, the cause of great wars in 1870 and in 1914, had been assuaged. Germany was to enter the League of Nations on equal terms. By her own free will, rather than by dictation, she had accepted that the Rhineland zone must be free of troops and military installations; and France and Belgium had in effect undertaken that there should be no repetition of the occupation of the Ruhr.[11]

For some, the successful foreign policy of the British government doubtless made the movement towards a decentralised commonwealth structure – symbolised by the declaration of the 1926 Imperial Conference that the dominions were 'equal in status' with the mother country – seem less painful, the questions involved less urgent. War, after all, and consequently the need for the closest imperial collaboration, seemed a long way off.

The Foreign Office had contributed mightily to the devolutionary trend in Anglo-dominion relations, but the Foreign Secretary, the Dominions Information Department and high-ranking officials in the department were now determined to establish an intra-imperial system of consultation on questions of foreign policy. Because it was clear that the dominions would not be willing to give their representatives in London sufficient scope and confidence, Foreign Office officials were to be sent to the dominions – as a method, minuted Chamberlain, 'of keeping the different Gov'ts of the Empire in step'.[12] But again the Foreign Office met disappointment. The main result of this initiative was the sending in 1928 of a *Dominions Office* appointment as the first British High Commissioner to Canada. There is reason to be sceptical about the willingness of the majority in the Foreign Office to enter into a real exchange with the dominions on questions of high policy. The dominions, at best, were only one factor in a complex international equation. Nevertheless, Foreign Office officials could not help noting the impact of dominion nationalism on the department's conduct of a foreign policy which they continued to call imperial. 'Experiments' such as Canada's election to a seat on the League of Nations Council in 1927, wrote Koppell, were likely 'to lead to some incident liable to shake the unity of the Empire' unless they were 'properly guided and controlled'.[13]

Another of Koppell's 'experiments', and the greatest threat to the concept of the diplomatic unity of the empire, came with the sending of dominion representatives abroad. The case for permanent representation at Washington had been conceded to the Canadians in 1920, and acted upon by the Irish in 1924 and Canada in 1927. It was believed, however, that imperial unity and efficient diplomacy would be safeguarded as long as the British ambassador in a foreign capital remained the sole spokesman on all matters that concerned common imperial concerns. When Irish and Canadian diplomatic appointments were made at Washington, the dominion ministers were accompanied by a formal note addressed by the British ambassador to the government of the United States which drew a distinction between imperial and dominion interests. 'Matters which are of Imperial concern or which affect other Dominions' would be handled by the British ambassador; the questions which remained, those relating only to the dominion concerned, were placed in the charge of the dominion representative. Within the British empire, the foreigner was told, all difficulties were solved by the closest contact and consultation, and so it would be among imperial representatives in a foreign country. The arrangements, in short, did not 'denote any departure from the principle of the diplomatic unity of the Empire'.[14]

The outsider might easily misunderstand. Foreign governments – Washington was a notorious example – were unversed in the metaphysics of a changing empire and unreceptive to a device which seemed to multiply the number of British voices in their capital, while rendering the practice of diplomacy all the more complicated. It was more convenient to continue to bring all matters of substance to the British ambassador. The Irish Free State and Canadian governments grasped the obvious: the co-operation and goodwill of the British government and the British ambassador in a foreign country were essential if a distinctive dominion diplomatic presence was to be established. Only at the request of the British would an appointment be made in the first place; only on their insistence would foreign governments approach the proper empire representative at the proper time. It was to gain that British co-operation and goodwill, and probably for this reason alone, that the Irish and Canadians accepted a form of wording which severely limited the competence of their ministers in Washington.

The Foreign Secretary hoped that Canada would for the time being be content with a single representative abroad, but the King Cabinet decided in late 1927 to seek an immediate exchange of representatives with Japan and France. The Canadians, indeed, wanted changes made in the Washington formula in time for the opening of the Canadian Legation in Paris. The Liberal Government of Mackenzie King was anxious to act quickly in order that the more important Japanese appointment could be expedited and so that the Prime Minister himself could open the French Legation during his autumn visit to Europe. No action had been taken by the time King arrived in Paris, however, and almost entirely with a view to saving time, he reluctantly allowed a note identical to the one used at the time of the Washington appointment to go forward to the French government. He was then subjected to considerable further delay, which he attributed partially to European inefficiency, but most of all to the malice of Britain's 'tory' ruling classes. 'I shall never feel the same again towards Great Britain,' King confided prematurely to his diary during the affair; 'this class of men are the natural enemies of freedom – the inciters of revolutions. – What I meant to say of goodwill and co-operation between Can. and Br. Govt. . . . will be said hereafter, if said at all, with more reserve and caution.'[15] King's embitterment made him all the more determined to see the note changed. At the same time, the Irish and South Africans, who were also contemplating appointments abroad, raised objections to the formula. As the summer of 1928 drew to a close, prolonged and complex discussions began which were not brought to a satisfactory conclusion until just before the defeat of the Baldwin government in June of 1929. This was an issue of real substance. One is continually impressed, as Professor Beloff has said, by the effort and ingenuity 'that went into the finding of verbal formulas to bridge the gaps between the independent nationhood of the members of the Commonwealth and the survival of the system'.[16]

Even if imperial affairs could be kept as the sole province of the British ambassador in a foreign country, the day-to-day business of the Foreign Office provided much evidence that dominion representation and diplomatic unity were not easily compatible. In February and March of 1928, the Foreign Office considered the hypothetical case of a rupture of diplomatic relations between Canada and Japan. In this instance, the British ambassador and the (as yet unappointed) Canadian Minister to Japan would in theory be the representatives of a single king. The Foreign Office realised, however, that if Canada withdrew her minister from Tokyo, it would leave relations between Japan and the rest of the empire unaffected only if His Majesty was recognised to be not one king, but the king of seven states whose relationships with a foreign country could conceivably all be different. It would then be obvious that 'the British Empire has ceased to exist as an international entity . . .. [We would] have destroyed, by dividing it into seven pieces, the only link which held the Empire together as an international unit.'

The Legal Advisers at the Foreign Office could only think of one way of convincing the foreigner that the British Empire remained united under these circumstances. Agreement must be reached beforehand that no part of the empire would recall its representative from a foreign country until the whole empire was prepared to take a similar step. The Foreign Secretary wished to approach the dominions formally, impressing on them the need for close consultation in such an event, but his Cabinet colleagues did not agree. It was apparent that Chamberlain and his colleagues were slowly coming to the view that Leo Amery and the Dominions Office had held since before the Imperial Conference of 1926: the breaking up of the empire as an international unit might be delayed, or even discouraged, but if so, it was on the co-operation and common sense of the dominions that the British government must rely.[17]

In the autumn of 1928, the Foreign Secretary visited North America. Upon his return, Austen Chamberlain explained to the Cabinet that he had discussed the note addressed to foreign governments with Ambassador Sir Esmé Howard in the United States before raising the subject with Mackenzie King in Ottawa. Howard had reported that the presence of Canadian and Irish representatives, far from doing any harm, had strengthened 'the general position' in Washington. The Americans had discovered that the British ambassador had often taken up a difficult attitude in the past, not on behalf of his own masters, but at the request of Ottawa or Dublin. With the appointment of dominion representatives, Howard escaped the embarrassment of constantly troubling the State Department and of being unable to obtain satisfactory replies for the Canadians and Irish on important issues. Certainly there was no reason for anyone in Washington to believe that there was disunity within the empire. Howard's relations with the Irish and Canadian missions were exemplary.

Chamberlain's interview with King substantiated the impression that the Foreign Secretary had gained in Washington. Chamberlain told his Cabinet colleagues that it was impossible and unwise to resist the consequences of the last Imperial Conference. He had suggested to the Canadian Prime Minister that ministers abroad should henceforth be placed in a position of absolute equality with the British ambassador, having authority over all matters concerning the dominion. To balance that concession, Chamberlain asked King to preserve the phrase 'diplomatic unity of the empire'. To this compromise King, and in its turn, the British Cabinet agreed.[18] The matter, even so, was far from settled. The formula that was circulated for the approval of the dominions at the end of 1928 was much as Chamberlain had arranged it with Mackenzie King. The amended note did not casually mention imperial diplomatic unity, however. Rather, it undertook to define the phrase as 'the principle that all His Majesty's Governments act in unison in matters which are of common concern'.[19] Precise terminology, obviously, still took pride of place beside the cultivation of goodwill and common sense in the conduct of Anglo-dominion relations.

Despite the advice of his closest adviser, O. D. Skelton, who railed against this dangerous and ambiguous assertion of diplomatic unity, King's reply to London's overture was moderate and carefully worded. He made several amendments in the formula, tactfully suggesting that if it was considered necessary to persist in making specific references to the bearing of dominion diplomatic appointments on empire solidarity, it might be best to omit any definitions. The Irish and South Africans, however, took a much stronger line, opposing even the mention of imperial unity. Diplomatic unity, stated the Irish response to the latest British suggestion, meant nothing more than consultative co-operation, a co-operation in matters of general concern which was so obviously based on the common and individual interests of all the parties that there was no need to make provision for it.[20] It was an ingenious, almost irresistible, argument and at least one member of the Foreign Office was prepared to acknowledge its cleverness. The British government, however, had no intention of giving in to the Irish and South African demands, especially when the Canadian suggestions for change were so much more palatable. The Cabinet decided to accept the new Canadian formula and thus to drop the words defining diplomatic unity from the note to foreign governments. Here they would take their stand. Any further concessions would be resisted.[21]

The tactics were Amery's. The Dominions Office had developed a sure touch in its search for a consensus on commonwealth issues. Mackenzie King usually represented a position somewhere in the centre – anxious to avoid any association with the consequences of British policy and yet having strong political and personal reasons for being sensitive about criticism that he would allow the British connection or a commonwealth of nations founded in an essential unity of purpose to be endangered in any way. Canadian attitudes on a given issue, although always progressive, could often be isolated from the more immoderate proposals of South Africa and the Irish Free State and used to convince the radicals of the error of their ways. Australia and New Zealand could then be brought into line and persuaded to accept a change in which the appearance of imperial unity was preserved. The result was always a British concession, but one which was thus rendered less painful – and less substantial.[22]

The Irish and South Africans refused to go along, however, and Mackenzie King himself soon returned with another, less palatable proposal, including a statement that the appointment of a dominion minister abroad should not detract from 'the principle of diplomatic unity of the *British Commonwealth of Nations*'. Not only that, King supplied a definition for his new concept. The expression, it seemed, meant that the representatives of the empire–commonwealth abroad would maintain the closest touch with one another and would consult where necessary, but nothing more.[23] It was true that a statement about the free and full co-operation of representatives abroad had always been part of the note addressed to foreign governments, but the British doubtless saw that Canada's notion of a limited 'commonwealth' unity would, if accepted, be quoted by the adversary in each subsequent war of words with the advanced dominions. Definitions, they had always insisted, were best avoided. But had not the idea of defining diplomatic unity come from London in the first place? That fact must now have haunted the British government. How much better it was to leave diplomatic unity undefined, allowing each country – including the dominions – to put their own construction on the phrase. Foreign governments could usually be counted upon to emphasise the bonds of empire rather than the 'independent' nationality of the dominions.[24] In maintaining the vocabulary of imperial unity abroad, the British government would to some extent be maintaining the reality of that unity.

The Dominions Secretary therefore moved to moderate the stand taken by the Canadian government. An appeal was made to King's better nature, to the conservatism in constitutional questions that had manifested itself since 1926. Amery told King that the government was pleased by Canada's acceptance of the *principle* of diplomatic unity. The Canadians were asked, however, not to press their wish to define that principle in such a limiting way, for surely diplomatic unity comprised 'consultation and co-operation in matters of foreign policy not only between diplomatic representatives of His Majesty's Governments at a foreign capital but also between the Governments themselves'. Canada was asked, in fact, not to attempt to define the concept at all and to accept that 'diplomatic unity of the empire' must be preserved intact. And in case this polite request might not prove sufficient, Amery implied that to prolong the controversy might seriously delay the Canadian diplomatic appointment at Tokyo. The Dominions Secretary offered one concession. The phrase 'British Commonwealth of Nations' (which had also been mentioned by the South Africans) found its way into Amery's new version of the note to foreign governments. It was, however, tucked into an unobtrusive corner, where it might easily escape the notice of the uninformed observer.[25]

The British, meanwhile, heard from their representative in South Africa, Bede Clifford. In a series of skirmishes with General Hertzog, Clifford had apparently outlasted and partially won the South African Prime Minister over to the British point of view. Hertzog now seemed ready, if reluctantly, to accept a formal and undefined assertion of imperial diplomatic unity. Hertzog's telegram, however, was hardly conciliatory. His strong words conveyed the impression that the British government had not heard the last from Pretoria and must have reinforced Amery's conviction, which was now shared by the Foreign Office, that the agreement of the Canadians must be secured if

Whitehall was to fashion a viewpoint acceptable to all shades of opinion within the commonwealth.[26]

A Canadian reply to Amery's proposals did not come until late April 1929, almost a month after the Dominions Secretary's telegram. Mackenzie King agreed that no difference of principle now separated the two sides. Canada was fully prepared to retain the phraseology of imperial diplomatic unity, but King again pointed out the advisability of clarifying and interpreting this difficult concept. Perhaps the governments of the empire could agree, he argued, that diplomatic unity meant 'the practice which prevails amongst His Majesty's Representatives in Foreign Capitals, as amongst H. M. Governments themselves, of consultation on all matters of common concern'.[27] The Dominions Office warmed to the Canadian reply, and although the Foreign Office remained unhappy about a definition of any kind, the newly-installed Legal Adviser, William Malkin, was willing to bend if it was made 'plain that it was not intended to be a complete and universally applicable definition of the phrase, but merely a statement of what it involved in the particular connection with which alone the draft note deals'. The decision was left to Amery. The Dominions Secretary recognised the obvious advantages of including Malkin's proviso in the note, but the Legal Adviser reported that Amery was 'anxious for political reasons to keep as close to Mr. Mackenzie King's wording as possible'.[28]

The 'political reasons' were imperial, not domestic. Amery was saving all his credit with the Canadian government in order to gain one last concession. King was told that the British would accept a definition of imperial diplomatic unity, but Amery asked in return Canada's permission to employ the term 'consultative co-operation' – words recently used by both Mackenzie King and the Irish – as part of the formula. The Canadians readily agreed to this change of wording, but the Irish Free State continued to oppose any intimation that an imperial unity still existed which restricted their freedom of action. The British negotiators, however, could now bear down on a single adversary. The Dominions Office could emphasise that the Irish Free State was alone, that the Canadian government in particular no longer supported Irish views. The Irish insisted upon, and won, a number of small additional changes in the formula, but they were forced in their turn to accept a reference to imperial diplomatic unity.[29]

Final agreement was reached in early June of 1929. Soon thereafter, it was used as the basis for the appointment of Irish ministers to Berlin, the Holy See and Paris and the sending of a Canadian minister to Tokyo. The note that now went forward from the British ambassador in these capitals[30] was couched in terms which made diplomatic appointments derive unmistakably from the will and initiative of the dominion government. The dominion minister was empowered to deal with any matter upon which his government might choose to instruct him. The role of the British ambassador was the restricted (but significant) one of being the medium through which this information passed, a role which served to highlight the statement that none of these arrangements detracted from the principle of imperial diplomatic unity.

'Diplomatic unity of the empire' had a curious ring, in the light of what the rest of the note said and meant. And yet who could deny that diplomatic unity remained a key element in the formula? Or that dominion rights remained a murky concept in foreign capitals? The principle of imperial unity was defined, it was true, spelled out as meaning nothing more or less than consultative co-operation between the component parts of the self-governing empire on matters of common concern. The Foreign Office's Dominions Information Department, however, could consider even this a victory: the principle of consultative co-operation had now been 'formally enshrined' in imperial practice.[31] Outsiders might easily conclude that nothing much had changed.

Things had changed, of course, and were changing. That is why the Foreign Office had taken the episode so seriously. The negotiations that led to the compromise formula had often seemed concerned with the most tiresome details, but vital issues were involved. Concessions had been made which placed Foreign Office prerogatives in the area of 'imperial' foreign policy in serious question. There had been, in addition, some evidence during the recent talks 'that Canada, the Union of South Africa and the Irish Free State were working towards a joint policy, and were inclined to dissent from the theory that each of the members of the Commonwealth must necessarily be consulted beforehand and agreement reached on any proposal in which some members were not immediately concerned'. This was a situation which the United Kingdom could not tolerate. The Foreign Office insisted upon full consultation with Australia and New Zealand before final agreement was reached.[32]

The Foreign Office had never been a great believer in the consultative process when it was not in its interest. In the protracted discussion of constitutional matters, however, when the 'radical' dominions threatened to destroy the forms and traditions of empire, consultation with the Australians and New Zealanders had its uses. Their desire to retain the reference to imperial diplomatic unity provided an important arguing point during the negotiations on the formula for sending dominion ministers abroad. There was a certain irony in this. At the 1926 Imperial Conference, the conservative stance of Australia and New Zealand had also been used to advantage, but it was Hertzog, the Irish and Mackenzie King, not Bruce and Coates of Australia and New Zealand, who were cajoled and catered for and whose views had been seen to prevail. As seemed self-evident in even the best family, the more obtrusive the child, the more attention he had to receive.

Taken collectively, of course, the dominions of Australia and New Zealand (and Newfoundland) were of measurably less consequence in the imperial scheme of things than Canada, South Africa and the Irish Free State. But there remained more than a suspicion in Whitehall that men like Bruce and Coats were representatives of a silent majority of loyalist opinion throughout the empire. 'We must be careful not to alienate the people who really matter in the Empire', Amery had written to Lord Balfour during the Imperial Conference of 1926, 'for the sake of the representatives of the extreme section in South Africa or of the Irish.'[33]

What, then, of diplomatic unity of the empire? The Foreign Office, oddly enough, admitted to no certain knowledge of the phrase's precise origin or meaning. Did it imply some central authority for the conduct of foreign affairs? Did it mean that the empire spoke with one voice *vis-à-vis* foreign powers, but not necessarily as a result of central direction? Or did it signify, as Malkin thought, that 'as regards certain fundamental matters (such as peace and war or the maintenance or rupture of diplomatic relations) the constitution of the British Empire necessitates the position of all its component parts being the same'?[34] There had been a time, not a decade before, when such questions were unnecessary. Now empire unity – however defined – was in jeopardy. Malkin was reluctant, even so, to concede that the international status and autonomy of the dominions was incompatible with the existence of the British Empire as a constitutional unit. With the 1929 Conference on the Operation of Dominion Legislation about to open, and another, potentially more damaging, attack on the imperial fortress soon to begin, he admonished the Dominions Office: 'our motto ought to be (in a Pickwickian sense of course) Napoleon's maxim "Engage the enemy everywhere, and then see" '.[35]

Despite the developments that led to the Statute of Westminster in 1931, establishing the theoretical right of the former colonies to legal independence, there remained aspects of the imperial in all the dominions. For that very reason, the Irish and South Africans soon took steps to emphasise and extend their new freedoms; Australians and New Zealanders, on the other hand, never uniformly uncritical of imperial policies but valuing the British connection for reasons of self-interest as well as sentiment, would have nothing to do with the Statute of Westminster until the 1940s. Canadian governments, for their part, tenaciously held to the middle ground. They sought autonomy but never independence. They made no further diplomatic appointments between 1929 and the beginning of 1939, being content to rely on the services of the Foreign Office everywhere except Washington, Paris and Tokyo. As a European war loomed in 1939, and as all the dominions (except Eire, as it was now known) moved closer to eventual involvement, the Mackenzie King government pointed to the use of British diplomatic and consular services around the world as one of the reasons why Canada *had* to go to war at Britain's side. This was only one of the many ways, the Minister of Justice explained, in which dominion sovereignty had never been disentangled from that of the mother country. Neutrality was simply not possible.[36] For some, it seemed, the unity of the empire remained a very real thing.

4. Britain and Germany: the Search for Agreement, 1930-37

NORTON MEDLICOTT

I

WE may count among our blessings under the thirty-year rule the opportunity to take a closer look at the diplomacy of the 1930s, and to supplement the great series of published Foreign Office documents with fresh evidence from the unpublished minutes, correspondence, and private papers. The theme of this paper is accordingly the formulation of British foreign policy and in particular the attitude of the Foreign Office towards Hitler's rise to power in Germany and in Europe.[1]

It has been rather widely asserted that if British foreign policy took an unfortunate turn – or several unfortunate turns – at this period it was because of the failure of the Foreign Office to make its voice heard, and in turn to listen to the warnings of its own ambassadors. Lord Londonderry told the House of Lords on 29 March 1944 that the Foreign Office had not existed since the days of Sir Edward Grey.[2] In after years the officials themselves, to judge from the memoirs, tended to see their role as that of keen-eyed opponents of concessions to Nazi Germany whose advice was ignored. Lord Vansittart, the Permanent Under-Secretary at this time, talks in his own memoirs of his failure, and he repeats the curious legend of the Cabinet's unwillingness to read Hitler's turgid masterpiece, *Mein Kampf*. There is a lot to read: politicians rightly rely on their advisers for succinct summaries. These were supplied in abundance.[3] Again, the poignant story of the despair of another official, Ralph Wigram, after the German occupation of the Rhineland in March 1936, is well-known from Churchill's memoirs.

Wigram is recorded as·saying, 'I have failed to make the people here realise what is at stake . . . Winston has always, always, understood, and he is strong and will go on to the end.'[4] But in fact the Foreign Office documents show that Wigram was quite willing to agree to the German reoccupation of the zone in the changed conditions of early 1936, providing that Great Britain 'could get some little benefit in return for its disappearance'.

It is far from being the case that the expert advice was ignored, either by the foreign secretaries of the day or by the cabinets. Great Britain alone, of all Germany's neighbours, sought consistently to assuage her sense of grievance in a general settlement, and the Cabinet accepted, by and large, the proposals of the permanent officials to this end. In December 1936, looking back over the preceding three years, Vansittart defined the resulting negotiations as falling into two main phases. Their aim was, he said, to meet and divert the coming crisis

first by a comprehensive European settlement and, when that failed, by a Five-Power Agreement that should lead to a European settlement, less comprehensive, but none the less effective, by being confined to settlements first in Western and Central Europe, without the complication of any further agreement in Eastern Europe.[5]

Vansittart's memoirs have little to say about these negotiations; writing in the 1950s, he was at pains to vindicate his reputation as an opponent of all compromise with Germany.[6] There was nevertheless a steady search for agreement with Germany initiated by officials who undoubtedly trusted the new Germany very little.

In their interpretation of German attitudes they appear to have had no serious disagreements among themselves, although there were the inevitable differences over matters of tactics. The Central Department of the Foreign Office, responsible for German affairs, still seems, in the Eyre Crowe tradition, to have accepted German militarism as the all-sufficient cause of war in 1914, and to have been little impressed by the academic revisionism which was at its height in the late twenties. Reports from Germany were closely scrutinised from 1930 onwards for signs of a revival of the 'Old Adam' of German militarism. Sir Horace Rumbold, British ambassador at Berlin, discussed the prospects in his private correspondence with the Foreign Office: in January 1931 he thought that the evacuation of the Rhineland by allied forces had merely whetted the German appetite, so that 'the German Old Adam came on the scene again without apparently much loss of vigour'. But he also believed that the Hitler movement was largely economic.[7] On the other hand, Orme Sargent, the head of the department from 1928 to 1933, and his successor, Ralph Wigram, Vansittart's closest ally, who was head of the department until his untimely death in December 1936, both readily agreed in condemning various parts of the 1919 peace settlement as 'untenable and indefensible'.[8]

Vansittart, a formidable and able man and a good German scholar, who became Permanent Under-Secretary on 1 January 1930 at the relatively early age of 48, shows the same curious contrast: he believed fiercely in the need to retain the war-guilt clause but less dogmatically it would seem in the validity of the rest of the Versailles treaty.[9] Far-reaching proposals which he made to a new Secretary of State, Sir John Simon, in December 1931 included the abrogation of the military clauses of the Versailles treaty and Germany's right to introduce conscription and to build up to the French naval strength.[10]

It has been suggested, notably by Mr Valentine Lawford in a sympathetic essay on Wigram, that a show of interest in negotiations with Germany by Vansittart and others was merely a desperate device on their part to keep some hold on the attention of the Cabinet.[11] Undoubtedly the officials wished not only to solve the German problem but also to regain the initiative in policy-making: their sensitivity on this point (the one which Lord Londonderry had in mind in 1944) is not surprising when we remember the extent to which problems of economics and defence made up the substance of Anglo-German discussions after 1931. The first and often the last word on these matters was spoken by the Treasury or the Bank of England or the service departments rather than by the Foreign Office. Sir Victor Wellesley, Deputy Under-Secretary to the Foreign Office, refers briefly and discreetly in his book, *Diplomacy in Fetters* (pp. 89–92) to the Foreign Office exasperation on this point, but other officials, such as Mr Ashton-Gwatkin[12] and Sir Walford Selby,[13] openly accuse Sir Warren Fisher, who combined the offices of Head of the Civil Service and Secretary of the Treasury, of stifling Wellesley's efforts to strengthen the Foreign Office on the economic side. There is in fact little evidence in the Central Department files of such interference by Fisher: Sir F. Leith-Ross, economic adviser to the government, is much more in evidence in Anglo-German negotiations in the thirties.

The Foreign Office wished, not to control economic policy, but to use it to reinforce diplomacy. It was a problem of timing: how to identify, encourage, and ensure the dominance at the right moment of the relatively peaceable elements that were believed to exist in Germany, and to restrain the rest. Was it better to keep Germany lean – a course which Vansittart and Wigram generally favoured after 1933 – or to offer her economic aid as an antidote to political extremism? There was general agreement as to the wisdom of economic help to bolster the Weimar regime between 1929 and 1932, but also much annoyance at the failure of the Treasury and Bank of England, in this and other cases, to work closely with the Foreign Office in order to use economic concessions as a political weapon. The importance of bringing the government's new role in tariff manipulation and monetary policy into line with the country's diplomatic policy in Europe was being urged from November 1931 onward by a group in the Foreign Office who were to man the new Economic Relations Section in 1934.[14] But the notion was novel, and the argument appears to have made little impression outside the Foreign Office itself. Germany secured the virtual abolition of reparations in July 1932 but the negotiations were conducted by the Chancellor of the Exchequer, Neville Chamberlain, and the result came too late to save the Brüning Government.

II

The fact that Hitler's accession to office on 30 January 1933 did not kill Foreign Office hopes of a reasonable solution of the German problem does not mean that the more alarming features of the new situation were ignored. The alliance between the old professional military caste and the new radical élite was ominous and obvious: German rearmament, illegal but poorly concealed, proceeded apace. Referring to its aggressive possibilities in August 1934, Vansittart could fairly write,

I have said it *ad nauseam* since Hitler reached power. Other countries also have an inkling of the truth. I am still none too sure about this vacillating and indifferent country of ours, though I feel that *some* impression has been made during the past year. Not enough though. Any shortcoming will not be, and has not been, the fault of the Foreign Office.[15]

If there remained hopes of a more peaceful turn they were not due to the organised foreign sympathy for the German cause which was one of

Hitler's most valuable inheritances from the Weimar regime, but rather to the fact that a reasoned assessment of Hitler's difficulties gave some plausibility to his angry asseverations of goodwill. There was no doubt about the parlous state of the German economy (so that rearmament could for a time be plausibly equated with unemployment relief), and he desperately needed a political success. He insisted that German honour would be satisfied with a limited measure of permitted rearmament, and he appeared to yearn for agreement with England. There is no truth in the view that the Foreign Office ignored the ambassadors' reports, or that *Mein Kampf* remained unread. A copy of the unexpurgated edition was placed in the Foreign Office Library in 1933. But the ambassadors' reports, closely scrutinised, were often equivocal, and advice when given (as in the case of Sir Walford Selby from Vienna) often impracticable. And how far should *Mein Kampf* be believed (or disbelieved)? It had after all made Anglo-German friendship one of Hitler's chief objectives.

The retiring ambassador at Berlin, Sir Horace Rumbold, after many warnings as to the grim possibilities of Nazi power, ended his final despatch, No. 642 of 30 June 1933, on a question mark: he felt it impossible to forecast the development of Germany during the next few years, but denied that there was 'any hostility to Great Britain on the German side, particularly in official circles'. He also said that Hitler was concentrating his attention on reducing unemployment and hoped that he might 'succeed in getting rid of the undesirable leaders and elements in his party who have given it a bad name'.[16] His successor, the lively Sir Eric Phipps, Lady Vansittart's brother-in-law, in a similar survey of 25 October, stressed the dangerous possibilities but thought that 'with skilful handling Herr Hitler and his movement may be brought to contribute some new impulse to European development', and that 'a sound disarmament convention with present day Germany is, perhaps, not entirely a Utopian idea'. This was written ten days after Hitler had flounced out of the Disarmament Conference and the League.

If the clue to Hitler's aims and personality eluded the ambassadors (as it continues to elude historians at many points) this was partly because they saw so little of him. Phipps did not have more than three or four serious conversations with him during 1933 and 1934. Austere, vegetarian, celibate, socially remote and boringly declamatory even in private conversation, Hitler gave few hints as to the real working of his mind. Phipps on occasion rather jocosely describes the public figure: he remarked after his interview with Hitler on 27 November 1934, 'whilst I spoke he eyed me hungrily like a tiger'.[17] He noted that this was the first occasion on which he had seen Hitler for any length of time since the 'blood bath' of 30 June, and that the delay 'has not increased his charm or attractiveness'.[18] But he evidently found other Nazi leaders easier to size up: he refers to General Goering's almost pathetic naïvity, showing his bison and other toys like a big, spoilt child;[19] von Ribbentrop, 'that ambulant and compromising windbag'; von Neurath, the foreign minister, 'rather a poor creature, who roars rudely only in the Tiger's presence and out of it bleats like a lamb'.[20] Baldwin reflected later that Phipps' despatches from Berlin had too much wit and not enough warning: they did not alarm the Cabinet enough.[21]

But it can be asked whether Phipps wished to be alarmist at this stage. He, more than anyone else, kept alive the theory that Hitler might be more reasonable than his chief henchmen, although he also spoke of Hitler as an 'unbalanced being' who might see red and shoot wildly and run amok someday.[22] He did believe that Hitler's offer early in 1934 to accept only a limited measure of rearmament in return for its legalisation was probably genuine. So too did the Central Department. Anthony Eden, the Parliamentary Under-Secretary, told Mussolini on 26 February 1934 that Hitler seemed sincere in desiring a disarmament convention, as he wished to push on with a long programme of internal reconstruction. He added that 'speaking frankly, he was less sure' of 'those who surround Herr Hitler'.[23] As late as June 1935 Phipps reaffirmed his conviction that Hitler would have kept this bargain, if the French had not rejected it on 17 April 1934.[24]

Certainly Phipps, and the officials in London, were not entirely pessimistic about Hitler's intentions during the summer and autumn of 1934. The 'blood-bath' of 30 June 1934 might, it was thought, have shaken his position and made circumspection necessary. Commenting on Germany's economic plight Vansittart remarked on 5 July: 'a scapegoat for the hardships *may* be necessary. Hitler *might* be the goat, now that he has destroyed so many of his own original supporters.'[25] And Phipps, in a private letter to Sargent on 7 November, reported that General von Blomberg, the Reichswehr minister, had won Hitler's confidence with very satisfactory results.

> The whole regime has been modified; Goebbels has been practically silenced; the wild men have been shot; the balance between Right and Left is being maintained very skilfully. One might almost say that the country is now being ruled by the permanent officials while

Hitler looks on benevolently. No doubt the murder gang . . . would slay him but this is a chance that Hitler must take.

The idea that expediency, as Hitler saw it, called for Anglo-German agreement was strengthened when he bitterly reproached Phipps on 27 November 1934 over Britain's action in turning a deaf ear to his proposals from time to time for a bilateral agreement on armaments, and among the torrent of words Phipps thought he detected the mention of a thirty-five per cent naval ratio.[26]

The view which was emerging in the Foreign Office and which Vansittart put strongly to Simon at the end of December 1933 was accordingly that a satisfactory agreement with Germany was possible if direct negotiations were substituted for the machinery of Geneva, but that France could be brought to accept some measure of German rearmament as its indispensable basis only if Britain herself rearmed and gave France additional promises of support.[27] The Secretary to the Cabinet, Sir Maurice Hankey, warmly supported the plan for direct Anglo-German negotiations, but was silent about additional commitments. The departmental argument was elaborated in a Cabinet paper of 21 March 1934, drafted by Orme Sargent. 'Part V of the Treaty of Versailles . . . is, for practical purposes, dead, and it would become a putrefying corpse which, if left unburied, would soon poison the political atmosphere of Europe. Moreover, if there is to be a funeral, it is clearly better to arrange it while Hitler is still in a mood to pay the undertakers for their services.' The wording betrays the growing sense of an opportunity slipping away as each successful Nazi defiance of the western powers increased Nazi self-confidence. On Hitler's position, the memorandum was, from the British point of view, strangely optimistic.

The false position in which the illegal rearmament of Germany places her is in general a source of diplomatic weakness. Germany is still isolated abroad; Herr Hitler wishes to make her 'alliance worthy' . . . He also needs to be free of foreign complications until he has effected the constitutional and administrative reorganization of the German Reich . . . In these circumstances, ought we not to consider whether we are not in a position to make Germany pay for the legalization of her rearmament? Her desire for such legalization is an asset in our hands.[28]

However, the disarmament euphoria was at its height and the

Cabinet, and particularly the Prime Minister, Ramsay MacDonald, found it impossible to contemplate a bargain (on the basis of some measure of German rearmament) until the end of the year. The reasons were complex and did not include any disagreement, as far as one can see, with the Foreign Office's estimate of Hitler. But the Cabinet preferred to go along with the French, who, after rebuffing the Germans in April, appealed to the British to stand firm on the letter of the Versailles treaty, and set to work to bolster their position with an eastern security pact.

There are many signs of the mounting alarm of the officials at this situation during the summer and autumn of 1934. There was no prospect of early British rearmament, although the Cabinet had accepted it in principle, with Germany visualised as the country's chief potential enemy.[29] Baldwin allowed himself to be persuaded by the Air Ministry in the early summer of 1934 that the Foreign Office figures for Germany's growing air strength were too alarmist; the Air Ministry was probably right in this, but Vansittart was indignant: 'for those who attach importance to an independent foreign policy,' he wrote later, 'this tale of rejected advice is a chapter not easily forgotten'.[30] Simon, who had every qualification of a great foreign secretary except the power of initiative, was in a very negative mood during most of 1934; fortified by MacDonald's opposition to fresh commitments he rejected suggestions from Vansittart during the summer for additional guarantees to Belgium and even for a message of encouragement to Mussolini after the assassination of Dollfuss in July.[31] There was again much uneasiness in the autumn at the forbearance displayed by the Treasury and the Bank of England over Dr Schacht's exchange manipulations and the refusal of payment for goods supplied by British commercial firms. Wigram remarked that it was based on the assumption, which had proved wrong on countless occasions during the past fifteen years, 'that the Germans are a people with whom one can avoid a definite conclusion'. The Foreign Office was further alarmed by the discovery that the signature of the Anglo-German payments agreement of 1 November 1934 (Cmd 4726), negotiated by Sir F. Leith-Ross of the Treasury, was facilitated by opportune loans from the Bank of England, with no political strings. The Foreign Office was not consulted. Vansittart, however, in a private letter to Leith-Ross on 17 December, said that he was 'so impressed by the unpleasant potentialities' of the Bank of England's gestures that he felt he must put his misgivings on record.[32] But by this stage the Cabinet had arrived at much the same

position as that of Wigram: late in November it accepted the proposals
of the Foreign Office for the negotiation of a comprehensive agreement
with Germany, whereby she would make concessions in return for the
legalisation of her armaments. Baldwin's speech of 28 November broke
the disarmament deadlock by publicly admitting, while condemning,
the fact of German rearmament and suggesting renewed discussions. He
foreshadowed British rearmament.[33]

The long and exasperating negotiations that followed involved all the
European powers for the next nine months; they await their historian
and I wish to comment here only on the effect on the Foreign Office
outlook. The Foreign Office had certainly regained the initiative, but
the change had come too late to give the officials much joy: there was a
note of apprehension as well as of urgency in Vansittart's comment to
the French ambassador on 14 December. He thought that after the
forthcoming Saar plebiscite there would be a short period when 'certain
and valuable concessions might still be wrung from Germany', but that
the last of Hitler's Sibylline books would have been burned by the
spring.[34] The plebiscite gave Hitler an enormous and most gratifying
majority on 15 January 1935; the resulting jubilation in Berlin was
gloomily interpreted by Vansittart as evidence that 'the true German,
and the true Germany, has always become arrogant and impossible
with success'.[35]

And yet there seemed no doubt that Hitler, in his moody, incalcul-
able way, was still ready to do business of some sort with England. He
continued to deplore her failure to respond to his earlier approaches. He
assured trusting and distinguished visitors, such as Lord Lothian and
Lord Allen of Hurtwood, of his desire for a long period of peace. Lothian
told Phipps that he was 'impressed by the sincerity of Herr Hitler,
whom he regards as a prophet'.[36] Talking to Phipps on 23 January
Hitler displayed an almost touching solicitude for the welfare of the
British empire and fervently hoped that India would never be lost to it:
that would, he declared, be a catastrophe for the whole civilised
world.[37] Although these blandishments, believed to be inspired by
Ribbentrop,[38] were received sceptically in the Foreign Office, the
officials seem to have been reasonably sure that a good professional
negotiator (Phipps in fact) feeling his way and tying the German
government down point by point might achieve results as opportunity
and Hitler's moods and domestic needs allowed.

But Phipps' ride with the Tiger suffered many interruptions. The
French were demanding and apprehensive, and Laval, the French

foreign minister, insisted on a stiff *quid pro quo* in return for his formal acquiescence in German rearmament. He could do this because it was considered axiomatic in London that Britain and France, and indeed Italy, must keep in step. The British were unable to agree to Anglo-French staff talks[39] or an Anglo-French air agreement, suggested on 1 February during Anglo-French talks in London, and rejected by the Cabinet on the 2nd, despite Sir John Simon's recommendation of acceptance.[40] They were then asked to secure instead German agreement to a system of full political security for France, including the eastern pact, a Danubian pact, an air pact applying to all the Locarno powers, a reasonable limitation of Germany's armed strength, and Germany's return to the League.[41] Hitler on 14 February received this programme politely, but with reservations on every point except the air pact.[42] The Italians were interested in the air pact and the Danubian pact, but not in the eastern pact;[43] the Soviet government wanted the eastern pact, but showed no enthusiasm at all for the rest of the programme.[44] The French insisted sternly that although negotiations for the various pacts might proceed simultaneously, all must be finalised before a comprehensive agreement was signed.

This was the ambitious programme which the Foreign Office sought to push through, although much beset by worries as to the way ahead. The departmental discussions reveal a fundamental cleavage over the future of the eastern pact, the basic, and at the same time the most impracticable, French requirement. Hitler had already rejected it in its earlier, mutual assistance, form. Sargent strongly objected to support for a Franco-Russian alliance, the only practicable alternative, which he thought would be rejected by British opinion as the encirclement of Germany; he certainly disliked it himself as a confession of failure in the shape of a return to the pre-war system of alliances. Laurence Collier, the head of the Northern Department, retorted that he honestly didn't believe that any large body of opinion in England cared two hoots about the encirclement of Germany: in his view anything would be better than a Soviet–German pact, which Vansittart considered a not impossible alternative. The debate veered off into dark speculation as to whether the Soviet government were less concerned about the eastern pact in itself than about its use as a means of preventing a general improvement of relations between the other European powers.[45] Failing departmental agreement, Vansittart himself put to the Cabinet on 21 February a plan for a network of non-aggression agreements in eastern Europe as the basis of the pact.[46] But Phipps thought little of the proposal and remarked on the following day that he could not 'conceive of a plan which would have enough "teeth" to please the French and Russians, and at the same time be sufficiently toothless to be acceptable to the Germans'.[47]

Nor could the Foreign Office view without secret alarm Simon's public-spirited decision to conduct the vital discussions with Hitler in person. The Germans were agreeable to this; they had earlier hinted at a visit by Baldwin, and on 23 February Hitler actually invited Vansittart too for an exchange of views, 'precisely because', wrote Phipps, 'he is convinced you are opposed to him'.[48] Wigram believed that Hitler intended to use his wizardry on Simon to divide Britain and France.[49] Vansittart declined Hitler's invitation on 5 March, but insisted that he was 'not anti-German in the least'; if Germany's recent 'warlike preparations of body and spirit and steel were to change,' he wrote, 'I should revert instantly to my old and very friendly feeling'.[50] Whether this message ever reached Hitler is doubtful. It was certainly not the cause of Hitler's abrupt announcement on 16 March 1935 of the reintroduction of conscription and an army of thirty-six divisions (500,000 men, roughly equal to the paper strengh of the French army). This action was maddening because it upset the whole British bargaining position: it was not really a shock otherwise, for the inevitability and indeed the fact of German rearmament were already accepted. The announcement was almost pointless and certainly stupid, whether it was the German aim merely to gain time for rearmament or genuinely to secure an Anglo-French-German agreement. The German ambassador in London, Hoesch, implied as much in a courageous message on 19 March in which he warned his government that only British goodwill stood between Germany and almost universal hostility.[51]

It was again the Cabinet's tactical sense that was in question when the British ministers, in a remarkable spirit of self-abnegation, denied themselves the pleasure of a searing retort. After hasty ministerial discussion on the next day (Sunday 17 March) the Cabinet agreed on 18 March that a visit by Simon and Eden to Berlin should still take place, although they were instructed to be 'crisp but firm' in asking Hitler what he was up to. A British protest note was delivered on the same day, but it ended by asking somewhat lamely whether the German government still desired the visit to take place.[52] In a minute on the following day Vansittart said that he thought the Cabinet had gone too fast and too far. Phipps on the other hand welcomed the decision.[53]

And in fact the negotiations of the next three months seemed to confirm Phipps' view that the storm aroused in France, Italy, and Russia, although not in London, by the announcement of 16 March had had a sobering effect in Berlin. Hitler assured Simon and Eden during their conversations on 25 and 26 March of his peaceful intentions, his acceptance of the territorial clauses of the Versailles treaty, his readiness for an eastern pact (on a non-aggression basis only), and for naval and air agreements with England. He was also ready for parity with France in land armaments. He said that he wanted colonies and would not return to the League without them, and he had a great deal to say about the communist menace, but Germany would never declare war on Russia.[54] In mid-April, worried apparently by the Stresa front of Britain, France, and Italy and the League's condemnation of the unilateral action of 16 March, Neurath reiterated Germany's willingness to enter a modified eastern pact. The British proposal for Anglo-German naval talks was accepted. When a Franco-Soviet pact was concluded on 2 May, Germany did not react violently; on 29 May Hoesch gave Simon the draft of an air pact, which his government desired to discuss in the first instance with Britain alone.[55] The naval agreement was signed on 18 June. It is true however that the uninhibited General Goering announced a greatly raised air target in May, and the Foreign Office was not inclined to wave this aside as 'mere boyish naughtiness' on his part.[56]

Certainly the great general settlement visualised in February was no nearer completion. In London Hankey at any rate still took the German approaches seriously, and was alarmed lest Britain, by loyalty to the rigid French requirements, should miss 'this possibly last chance for years of obtaining a settlement'. In the Foreign Office the mood was apparently one of increasing exasperation, combined however with a dogged belief that something could still be achieved. Vansittart's comments on 8 June on the prospects of an air limitation agreement are typical. 'In the existing spirit in Germany we shall almost certainly be swindled anyhow,' he wrote, 'but that matters less if, besides limiting at a high figure, we [maintain] close relations with the powers that are not dangerous.'[57] These were, above all, France and Italy: a new Foreign Secretary, Sir Samuel Hoare, coached by Vansittart, told Laval on 10 September that the overriding problem in the Abyssinian dispute was not Italy's quarrel with a backward country but the effect of the crisis on Germany's growing ambitions.[58]

There is no doubt that the comprehensive agreement with Germany was Hoare's chief preoccupation throughout the summer and autumn of 1935, and he emphasised the importance of the eastern pact in his House of Commons speech of 1 August. Without it, he said, progress with the air pact would present great difficulty. This attempt to bargain, which had caused Hankey's uneasiness, was due to the belief that while the Germans disliked the first they still really wanted the second. But at the end of July the German ambassador told Hoare that owing to the Franco-Russian pact Neurath's offer of 13 April with regard to the eastern pact had lapsed. The German Foreign Office was content that the negotiations should come to a standstill after this, with bland references to the holiday season, for Neurath was now convinced that the Abyssinian crisis was rapidly changing the international situation in Germany's favour.[59]

III

The collapse of this nine-months' quest for agreement might well have been followed by a period of disillusioned, and preferably ominous, silence on Britain's part. But as Winston Churchill remarked somewhat cryptically in December 1937, 'we can lay down the proposition that the Angel of Peace is unsnubbable'.[60] The Cabinet view, shared and urged by the Foreign Office, was that a new and more thoroughgoing effort must be made to secure a settlement. This was not due merely to a nervous itch to be doing *something*, however pointless. It was certainly not due to lessening apprehension about Germany: the British decision to rearm, endorsed by the government's electoral victory in November 1935, was primarily directed against her. A new note, an insistence on negotiation as a means of gaining time for rearmament, now appears in departmental minutes. But as hopes of a successful agreement lingered we must also assume continued belief in some ultimate sense of expediency and moderation, separating him from his wilder colleagues, on Hitler's part. 'No one thinks that Hitler himself is a monster', wrote Sargent in November 1935, 'but it is more than probable that he is a Frankenstein, and has created a monster which is fast growing up.'[61] A year later, following an Italian comment on Hitler's ultimate reasonableness, Vansittart did not disagree, but remarked that it left out of account 'Goering and the lunatics'.[62]

The urgency of the case for fresh negotiations was expounded on 21 November 1935 in a remarkable joint memorandum of thirty-eight pages by Germany's two stern critics, Sargent and Wigram. They rejected policies of drift (or inaction) and also of encirclement. 'We might become the centre force in a great anti-revisionist block dressed in the cloak of collective security . . . In reality this block would differ little from the old pre-war defensive alliances.' After an elaborate analysis of all the possible German objectives, including expansionist aims in the centre and east of Europe, they concluded that 'a policy of coming to terms with Germany in Western Europe might enable Britain and France to moderate the development of German aims in the Centre and East', although they recognised that there were 'tremendous objections to the further increase of German power and influence' in these areas.

> The fundamental idea is of course that the ex-Allied Powers should come to terms with Germany in order to remove grievances by friendly arrangement and by the process of give and take, before Germany once again takes the law into her own hands. This is the only constructive policy open to Europe – the alternatives of drift and encirclement are avowedly policies of negation and despair. There will in this memorandum be no suggestion that this policy should be abandoned.

The memorandum also remarked that this had been British policy since the early 1920s, and had 'brought about the London Declaration of last February'.[63]

This was a bold, but also somewhat equivocal, proposal, which engendered much uneasy debate, not all of it unfavourable, among the officials. The Economic Relations Section argued as usual in favour of economic aid to Germany, on the ground that a 'weak, hysterical individual, heavily armed, is a danger to himself and others'.[64] On the other hand Collier, the Russian specialist, stoutly opposed the Sargent–Wigram programme, which he thought was not a continuance but a reversal of the previous policy. It would be impossible for example to discuss with Germany the Rosenberg plan of detaching the Ukraine without ruining British relations with Soviet Russia. If Britain could not prevent the realisation of German ambitions she should not condone them: she would then at least be able to come before the public with clean hands.[65] Vansittart too distrusted the idea of 'moderating' German expansion. 'Does it mean, for example,' he wrote, 'that she might have Austria and Memel, but not Russia and Czechoslovakia?' He had been speaking of a colonial settlement since the previous

summer, and he now took the position that if Germany's desire for
expansion could be satisfied by the return of her colonies, he would
favour this as the lesser evil.[66]

Sir Samuel Hoare took these papers with him to Switzerland for the
ill-fated holiday which included the signature of the Hoare–Laval pact
on 8 December; he resigned on the 19th. Eden succeeded and
Vansittart stayed in office, although, as he rightly said later, the Hoare–
Laval pact should really have been called the Laval–Vansittart pact.

The new Foreign Secretary put to the Cabinet on 17 January 1936
the proposal that, while pursuing rearmament, Britain should seek a
modus vivendi with Germany, 'which would be both honourable and safe
for this country'.[67] The wording suggests that a permanent agreement
was visualised, although his hopes were not high. A Foreign Office
memorandum of 31 January on German expansion suggested that the
return of economic prosperity to Germany would end Naziism.[68]
Summing up the varied proposals in a massive paper on 3 February,
Vansittart now firmly advocated colonial concessions. He wrote:

> No lasting bargain can be made with present day Germany without
> the payment of a high price – that is, provision for territorial
> expansion . . . We cannot immorally seek that price, or connive at its
> being sought, at the expense of others, that is, in Europe . . . such
> expansion can therefore only be pursued at our expense, that is, in
> Africa, by the restitution of the former colonies of Germany.

In return, however, Germany must limit her armaments, abandon expansion in Europe, and rejoin the League.[69] Meanwhile the Cabinet,
which had many other preoccupations in January, had discussed
Eden's proposal, and a new Cabinet committee began on 17 February
the examination of more detailed plans.

In preparation for this the Foreign Office put forward its own
programme, now quite elaborate. On 14 February Eden recommended
acceptance of the German remilitarisation of the Rhineland as part of
the comprehensive agreement[70] and the essential elements in this
agreement, as Eden and his advisers visualised it, were set out in a
memorandum of the following day.[71] It proposed, in western Europe,
the substitution of the 'air pact', extended to cover land attack, for the
treaty of Locarno, with the following features: disappearance of the
demilitarised zone; French and German guarantees of Britain; bilateral
arrangements for mutual inspection of armaments; and the inclusion of

Holland in the arrangements. Secondly, the limitation of air and land armaments. Thirdly:

> In Central and Eastern Europe, recognition by Great Britain and France of the special interests of Germany owing to her geographical position; no request to her (which would be foolish) not further to exploit those interests, but the requirement of a promise not to do so in a manner which will conflict with the principles which we ourselves profess under the Covenant of the League of Nations; as a corollary to this, a readiness, so far as we are concerned, not in these regions to stand, in the commercial and economic sphere, on the letter of rights which we cannot in practice exercise.

Fourthly, an 'assurance to Germany of our readiness to bear in mind her need of maintaining and developing her export trade, in the matter of our tariff policy, financial assistance and our colonial policy'. Fifthly, with regard to the League of Nations, it was felt that it would raise all sorts of difficulties to propose Germany's return to the League during the preliminary soundings. Finally, the colonial question was one for Germany and not Britain to raise, and it was for her to offer something equally concrete in order to obtain the return of her colonies.

So the Cabinet committee was well supplied with proposals when it began to discuss British concessions and German counter-concessions without, it would seem, much enthusiasm. Economic aid, which Eden on balance favoured, was opposed by Runciman, the President of the Board of Trade. In the end it was agreed, on Ramsay MacDonald's suggestion, that the air pact would be a good starting-point.[72] Germany had been told through Wigram and Lord Cranborne in mid-February that the Cabinet was drafting a working agreement between Germany, France, and Britain.[73] But it was not until 6 March that Eden invited Hitler to open serious negotiations for an air pact as a preliminary to a real improvement in British–French–German relations (the delay, which certainly reduced the chance that Germany would take the *modus vivendi* hints seriously, was due among other things to the oil-sanction crisis in the Abyssinian negotiations).[74]

There was really very little in all this to attract Hitler.[75] If his aim was to divide and confuse the western powers, then Mussolini was doing this for him in Abyssinia. As the Cabinet had not responded to the Foreign Office hints of a bargain over eastern Europe there was no certain prospect of help or acquiescence in his expansionist plans in that region.

The British no longer insisted on linking the air pact with the eastern pact, but the eastern pact had lost its significance with the ratification of the Soviet–French agreement by the French chamber on 27 February. However, he still had hopes of some success for his divisive tactics, and both governments needed time for rearmament.

His mood, accordingly, did not seem unpromising and some members of the British embassy staff at Berlin – although apparently not the ambassador – were rather hopeful.[76] Germany agreed to open negotiations for a further naval agreement on qualitative questions.[77] Hitler used remarkably conciliatory language late in February to a French journalist and an English professor. 'Let us be friends', he told the Frenchman, Bertrand de Jouvenel, on 21 February. He said that *Mein Kampf* was outdated, and that 'the correction of certain pages in his book . . . would be made upon the page of history'.[78] Speaking non-stop for one and three-quarter hours he told the Englishman, Professor Toynbee, on 28 February, 'I want England's friendship, and, if you English will make friends with us, you may name your conditions – including, if you like, conditions about Eastern Europe.' Toynbee was evidently impressed. Through his friend, Mr Thomas Jones, he forwarded an account of the interview to the Foreign Office; Hitler, he thought, was seeking British friendship as an alternative to his anti-Russian role, and he concluded that 'any response from the British side to his overtures for our friendship would produce an enormous counter-response to us from Hitler'.[79] But then on 7 March, German troops without preliminary warning occupied the demilitarised Rhineland.

British officials and the Cabinet had long been expecting this event, since at least the time of the Anglo-French talks in February 1935; they thought of it, not as the last opportunity to overthrow the Nazi regime, but as possibly the last opportunity to make a profitable deal with it. This is quite clear from the Cabinet discussion on 5 March, which shows that early German action over the demilitarised zone was anticipated; it was decided that Eden should make haste to open discussions about the air pact as this would be almost certain to lead to an early discussion about the zone and to the solution of the problem by negotiation.[80] Hitler had repeated the trick of March 1935, seizing what he knew was about to be offered as part of a bargain. The Foreign Office reaction was on much the same lines, as becomes clear from Eden's exasperated comments to the Cabinet two days later. 'By reoccupying the Rhineland', he said, 'Hitler has deprived us of the possibility of making to him a concession which might otherwise have been a useful bargaining counter in our hands in the general negotiations with Germany which we had it in contemplation to initiate. Such negotiations are now inevitable, but we shall enter them at a disadvantage, for we have lost the bargaining counter to which I have just referred.' He believed nevertheless that Hitler was still in the mood to negotiate a far-reaching and enduring settlement. He was quite untrustworthy: but there were some safe and advantageous agreements which might last because Hitler would be making no inconvenient concessions (he thought of the air pact, the non-aggression pacts, Germany's return to the League).[81]

The negotiations of the following twelve months show both sides determined to avoid a breach, to give nothing away, and to probe for weaknesses. Hitler had seized the initiative on 7 March by offering what was certainly an attractive programme if he meant it seriously. With later elaborations it included twenty-five-year non-aggression pacts between Germany and France and Belgium, guaranteed by Britain and Italy, and supplemented by an air pact – in short, a re-furbished Locarno. He was also willing to sign military assistance pacts in this western security system, non-aggression pacts in eastern Europe, and to return to the League.[82] It was agreed on 10 April by the three remaining Locarno powers that as Great Britain was not prepared to apply sanctions she might at least make herself useful by putting to the German government some rather searching questions in order to clear up ambiguities in the German programme – in other words, to test German sincerity.[83] Hitler had himself suggested that the British government should, as before, conduct negotiations for the western pact. The moment for French intervention, if it ever existed, had by this point passed. The French blamed the British, who for their part were convinced that neither the French government nor British opinion regarded the matter as an occasion for the use of force.

It certainly seems today that Hitler, having won this round, soon lost interest in his own peace plan and was content once again to leave the German Foreign Office to talk the matter out. To the British however the proposals seemed as good a basis as any for a settlement, or at least for negotiation. Eden urged the Cabinet on 29 April to consider the possibility of a *détente* with Germany, and several members argued that Britain's principal aim at this stage was to play for time and for peace. There was every advantage in coming to terms with Hitler and fastening him down to help keep the peace in the west. 'Did it matter if the French said they could not rely on us? How far could we rely on the

French? . . . In the long run French interests were bound up with our own.'[84]

The *questionnaire*, which asked among other things whether Germany now regarded herself as being in a position to conclude 'genuine treaties', and whether she intended (subject to free negotiation) 'to respect the existing territorial and political status of Europe', does not sound today a particularly tactful document, even after the Cabinet had toned down the Foreign Office draft, much to the indignation of Wigram and Vansittart.[85] Hitler gave instructions that the answers should be postponed, on one pretext or another. Yet the atmosphere was friendly enough when on 14 May Phipps had an interview with Hitler, who, after an outburst against the 'unholy Russian alliance' which would drag Spain and France 'into the Bolshevik pit', and other German grievances, went on to outline the forceful measures, preliminary to a bargain, by which the British should have dealt with Mussolini over Abyssinia. When Phipps objected that 'it was a religion in England that there should be no more aggression', Hitler replied, smiling pityingly, 'with dictators nothing succeeds like success'.[86]

The negotiations languished during the summer of 1936, while Eden awaited a reply to his questions, and Hitler awaited the result of the French elections (as good a reason for delay as any). M Blum, the socialist leader, came to office in a most conciliatory mood towards Germany, but it was then explained that Hitler was absorbed, during July and August, with the Olympic games in Berlin (Germany won thirty-three gold medals). Vansittart visited Berlin, had a chilly lunch with Ribbentrop, an affable meeting with Hitler (when high politics were avoided), and an important talk with Herr Dieckhoff, Under-Secretary to the German Foreign Office. No one wanted to talk seriously about a western pact.[87] It looks as if there had still been some hope in the Foreign Office until this point of a real agreement with Germany, and that after this the tactical aim became more and more that of buying time until British rearmament had reached the stage of defensive impregnability in 1939. The Thirty-Niners, as Vansittart called those who accepted this estimate (misreading his American history apparently in the process) included himself but with the reservation that there was no certainty that Hitler would wait so long.

IV

Time had seemed important in 1935 while Hitler might still be in the mood for agreement: now the position was reversed. This was Vansittart's view, and it was shared, although with differing degrees of pessimism, by others. The Cabinet was more hopeful. Eden's assumption was that negotiations must continue, but with no one-sided concessions.

This rather stiffer attitude is best illustrated perhaps in the colonial sphere, the only one, it must be remembered, in which Britain could make direct territorial concessions. A subcommittee of the CID, set up on 9 March 1936 under the chairmanship of the Earl of Plymouth, reported three months later that while a blank refusal to discuss the colonial question with Germany was impracticable unless a general settlement was to be entirely ruled out, there were objections to the transfer of any mandated territory to Germany either in full sovereignty or under mandate. The least objectionable course would be to join with France in the surrender of the whole or part of Togoland or the Cameroons. But they condemned any settlement which involved irrevocable concessions *to* Germany and no such irrevocable concessions *by* her.

None of the Foreign Office officials who commented on the report could now see any justification for the surrender of territory; Vansittart, after referring to his advocacy in February of a colonial transfer as part of a durable European settlement, now concluded that there was no sign that such a settlement could be obtained. Nevertheless he had consistently exaggerated Hitler's interest in colonies, and he was still worried about the consequences of refusal. Ultimately, he said, 'we shall have to fight to keep Germany out of the colonial sphere. Will the nation think the game worth the dizzy taper? I wonder – when we get to the point. And unless we are both careful and clever we shall get these hostilities before we are ready.'[88]

However, the conclusion was clearly against any colonial concessions to Germany, and Eden favoured a plain statement to this effect before Hitler committed himself on the point too deeply. The Cabinet a month later preferred a form of words suggested by Lord Halifax in a statement which Eden made to the House of Commons on 27 July: '. . . as far as His Majesty's Government are concerned, the question of any transfer of mandated territories would inevitably raise grave difficulties – moral, political and legal – of which His Majesty's Government must frankly say that they have been unable to find any solution'. This left the door slightly ajar.[89] When Blum, at the end of August, after private talks with Dr Schacht, President of the Reichsbank, also suggested a

colonial settlement, Eden was unyielding: he said that his statement in
July had made it impossible for him to open conversations at this stage.
Blum said he was reluctant to let an opportunity slip by, and that
Schacht had assured him that Germany would be willing to give
guarantees for a European settlement and for the reduction and
limitation of armaments in return. He had stressed the official character
of his approach. Why then, asked Eden, did Germany not use the
diplomatic negotiations for a western pact that were already in
progress?[90]

Why indeed? The available German evidence, which is scrappy,
proves only that at this point Hitler was launching the last stage of
rearmament in the form of the four-year plan. The plan, made
economically possible by the Rhineland occupation, visualised readiness for war in four years and Russia as the enemy.[91] In October he
signed the German–Italian agreement, and received from Ciano, the
Italian foreign minister, a purloined copy of Eden's proposal for a *modus
vivendi* of 17 January 1936, with its accompanying anti-German
documentation. But we do not know how deep an impression this made,
and whether it really told Hitler anything about the British that he did
not know already; he did not reveal his ultimate plans to Ciano, and
they are not stated elsewhere.[92] Certainly there was no breach with
England: the approaches and reproaches continued: Ribbentrop was
sent to London as ambassador to exercise his charms. Did the British
themselves, as the Germans claimed, throw away the chance of an
agreement?

The answer is that they had always been open to agreement on
certain terms, and at this stage were seeking it on the basis of Hitler's
own proposals of the previous spring. Over these they did their best. A
meeting of British, Belgian, and French representatives on 23 July 1936
invited Germany and Italy to a five-power conference over the western
pact, which if successful would naturally lead, it was suggested, to
discussion of other matters affecting European peace.[93] After first
urging preliminary Anglo-German discussions, Germany accepted the
invitation on 11 September, but on condition that there must be
adequate diplomatic preparation.[94] A British memorandum of 17
September then put forward certain points for discussion, including a
guarantee of the United Kingdom as an extension of the Locarno
system.[95] Four weeks later the Germans rejected this proposal as
impracticable, and also declined to commit themselves to a discussion of
wider issues, as suggested on 23 July. A further difficulty now emerged.

Britain and France felt that they must have a form of words which reserved their position under the League Covenant and under any mutual-assistance pacts that they had signed. Germany strongly objected to such 'exceptions'.[96] Ribbentrop's comment in December was that the British attitude had been a grievous disappointment to Hitler.[97]

If we can assume the continuity of Hitler's anti-Soviet policy, first sketched in *Mein Kampf*, then his disappointment over the 'exceptions' is not surprising. By accepting the western pact on his terms France would have abandoned her liberty to go to the assistance of the Soviet Union and of Poland and Czechoslovakia, according to her treaty obligations, and Great Britain would have been without any assurance of French assistance in the event of a German attack on the United Kingdom alone. Hitler did not admit that the essential anti-Soviet formulation of *Mein Kampf* still applied. Goering and others were more frank, although not necessarily good guides to his intentions.[98]

The position, however, as Eden and his advisers viewed it in the winter of 1936–7, was one of obvious disillusionment, and it is this, rather than any difference of policy, that explains their growing uneasiness with Neville Chamberlain's initiative in foreign affairs after becoming Prime Minister in May 1937. Sargent, in a long minute of 29 December 1936, thought that Hitler had definitely failed in his original aim, which had been to pose as the saviour of European civilisation and rally Europe round him against communism. But he had also failed to solve the internal economic crisis, to secure victory for Franco in Spain, and to achieve the prestige of a colony. Would he, like Lenin when faced with analogous reverses, be strong enough to abandon his earlier policy? If not, he would seek the success that he must have by the old policy of expansion, and this could mean only Czechoslovakia or Spain. He suggested that, of the two, Czechoslovakia was the more likely objective, and Eden agreed that the Czech problem should be studied by the Central Department. As to the former solution, Sargent commented:

If he is, then we may look forward to a new Locarno treaty; Germany's collaboration in clearing up the present economic and currency chaos in Europe; the limitation of armaments; the return of Germany to the League; the establishment of a real policy of non-intervention in Spain; and a *détente* with Russia and Czechoslovakia. Enumerated in this fashion such a *volte face* sounds, alas, too good to be true or even possible.[99]

Vansittart, writing on 31 December, also thought that the second main attempt at a European settlement had failed:

> Time is the very material commodity which the Foreign Office is expected to provide in the same way as other departments provide *other* war material . . . To the Foreign Office falls therefore the task of holding the situation until at least 1939, and . . . there is no certainty of our being able to do so, though we are doing our utmost by negotiating with Germany, and endeavouring to regain lost ground with Italy, and reducing the demands on our still exiguous strength by a treaty with Egypt.[100]

The Foreign Office hoped to 'hold the situation' until at least 1939 by maintaining a relationship with the Führer just sufficiently amicable to avoid stampeding him into violence, while keeping in his mind the possibility, clearly implied in the 'exceptions' controversy, that as Great Britain had not disinterested herself in Central Europe she might, in a European war, not stand aside. The point was clearly formulated in these terms by Mr William Strang in an attempt to define his position after succeeding Wigram as head of the Central Department in January 1937. In a note of 1 February 1937 he wrote:

> The best we can do is probably to follow and develop our present line of policy: i.e.
> (1) Arm.
> (2) Maintain close relations with France.
> (3) Make it clear beyond doubt what we will fight for.
> (4) For the rest, neither say that we will fight nor that we won't.
> (5) Profit, so far as we can, by the strength of Russia, without engaging ourselves to her.
> (6) Use our power of manoeuvre, our still undoubted prestige, and all the imponderables, to the uttermost: these are still useful in relation to Italy . . . .

The fourth point covered the problem of a Central European policy, or lack of it. Six months later, Strang again commented on the deliberate ambiguities of British policy: 'The means by which we are seeking to restrain Germany', he wrote on 2 July, 'are our rearmament, plus speeches . . . about our interest in Central Europe. I think that we should all admit that even these statements, moderate as they are, have in them a fair admixture of bluff.' Sargent agreed. 'We are all playing a game of poker. I wish we were not, and like Mr. Strang I can see no alternative.'[101]

My conclusion is that the tactical programme implied in these comments, and the story in general of the two major attempts in 1935 and 1936 at a settlement with Germany, demonstrate the essential continuity of British policy towards Germany throughout the 1930s. In the process of enquiry the lines of distinction between the popular stereotypes, appeasers (or peacemakers) and warmongers (or resisters), between the doves and the hawks of the 1930s, tend to disappear. Neville Chamberlain, like Vansittart, was a Thirty-Niner. He was a little more hopeful than the Foreign Office people that Hitler might still mend his ways. He showed a strange predilection for Treasury advisers. He thought that Eden had missed chances of a settlement. But as to the time schedule of resistance, the need for armaments, the sinister alternatives to agreement, even the basic lines of a settlement – on all these matters they agreed. This is not to say that his policy in action was any more successful than theirs.

5. British Military Preparations for the Second World War

MICHAEL HOWARD

In tracing the sad, confusing, and nearly disastrous history of British attempts to come to terms with the realities of power politics in the 1930s, it is useful to bear in mind the three major factors which determined British defence policy between the wars.

British Defence Policy was, in the first place, concerned with the protection of an empire; of what we would today call 'a global system'. British defence planners had to provide not simply for the security of the United Kingdom, but for that of such countries as Egypt, India, the Federated Malay States, Australia, New Zealand and a host of minor colonial possessions. The foundation of this Imperial system was, in the 1930s, as it had been in the 1890s, the Royal Navy's capacity to maintain 'command of the sea', in order to safeguard Imperial communications. In 1896 the Admiralty had laid it down in words which were to be repeatedly quoted in official documents:

> The maintenance of sea supremacy has been assumed as the basis of the system of Imperial defence against attack from over the sea. This is the determining factor in shaping the whole defensive policy of the Empire, and is fully recognised by the Admiralty who have accepted the responsibility of protecting all British territory against organised invasion from the sea.[1]

All British territory: this was a heavy responsibility, and one which grew heavier as the 1930s pursued their increasingly depressing course. In 1932 when it was clear that the Japanese were pursuing a 'forward policy' on the mainland of China which it was feared might lead to an equally forward policy elsewhere in the Pacific, the Australian government made anxious enquiries in London as to whether the Royal Navy still felt itself capable of fulfilling those responsibilities. They received from the British Chiefs of Staff the following answer:

> Provided that the British fleet arrives in time and finds a properly equipped base at Singapore, Australia has nothing to fear beyond a sporadic attack.[2]

But if the Fleet did *not* arrive in time, and if it did not find a properly equipped base at Singapore, then, it was clearly implied, Australian interests and even territory become exposed to attack on a considerable scale. And not only Australia would be at risk: New Zealand, Malaya, Burma, India, the Persian Gulf, the British possessions on the east coast of Africa, in short the whole of the Indian Ocean would be vulnerable to Japanese naval attack. So throughout the 1930s the eyes of the Admiralty were fixed on what appeared to them to be the greatest threat to the British imperial system: the navy of Japan, second in size only to that of the British and the United States. We have to bear this in mind if we are to understand the reluctance of successive First Sea Lords and First Lords of the Admiralty to see the Navy saddled with additional responsibilities in Europe and in the Mediterranean, especially at the time of the Italo-Abyssinian war.

The Chiefs of Staff in the 1930s were not a particularly memorable group, but by far the most impressive among them was the First Sea Lord between 1932 and 1938, Admiral Sir Ernle Chatfield, Chairman of the Chiefs of Staff Committee. Chatfield was one of those primarily responsible for the conclusion of the Anglo-German naval agreement of 1935, whereby the Germans agreed not to build more than thirty-five per cent of the British strength in all classes of vessel, with the remarkable exception of submarines; a self-denying ordinance which in the existing state of the German economy and rearmament imposed no sacrifices on Nazi Germany but which left the Royal Navy (or so it was hoped) free to fulfil its commitments in the Far East. Chatfield, moreover, was particularly insistent at the time of the Italo-Abyssinian crisis in 1935 that Britain should not become involved in a conflict in the Mediterranean; not because the Royal Navy doubted its ability to defeat the Italian navy, but because in the process of doing so it might incur losses which would make it all the more difficult to get an effective fleet to Singapore if a crisis developed in the Far East.[3] In the eyes of the Royal Navy, the Far East enjoyed overriding priority almost until the end of the decade.

The Army also saw its duties primarily in terms of Imperial defence. The garrisoning and the protection of India, Burma, the Middle Eastern countries and the colonies in Africa had been the main and continuing concern of the British Army ever since those regions had come under British suzerainty. It was an *actual* commitment to which the Army had to give a standing priority in terms of training and equipment, over a *hypothetical* involvement in a Continental war which there was a profound reluctance on the part of the entire country, including the Army itself, to contemplate at all. A skeleton 'Expeditionary Force' existed on paper, but when in 1925 the British government assumed certain specific obligations to continental intervention under the terms of the Treaty of Locarno, the Chiefs of Staff warned the Cabinet that although

> the Expeditionary Force, together with a limited number of Air Force squadrons, constitute the only military instrument for immediate use in Europe or elsewhere outside Imperial territory in support of foreign policy, they are so available only when the requirements of Imperial defence so permit. It follows that so far as commitments on the Continent are concerned, the services can only take note of them.[4]

It is hard to conceive of a more alarming disjunction between foreign and defence policy than that expressed in this statement.

Imperial Defence thus enjoyed absolute priority in the plans both of the Royal Navy and of the Army, and European obligations received only such crumbs as could be spared from that table. This situation was gradually to be modified in the course of the 1930s, but it was not wholly transformed until the very eve of the Second World War.

The second factor was the vulnerability of the United Kingdom to air attack. It was to deal with this problem that an independent Royal Air Force had been reconstituted after the First World War. If the Admiralty accepted as its responsibility the defence of imperial territory and communications, the Royal Air Force existed in order to prevent an air attack on the United Kingdom from a European adversary. But it was assumed until about 1937, for good technical reasons, that effective defence against aerial attack was not feasible. There could be no physical defence; there could only be deterrence. So it was the function of the Royal Air Force to provide a *deterrent* against any conceivable attack on the United Kingdom, by possessing the capacity to inflict unacceptable and unavoidable punishment against the homeland of any aggressor. The concept of 'deterrence' with which we have become only too familiar since the Second World War was in fact developed by the British Air Staff in the 1920s in a very sophisticated form.[5] The vulnerability to air bombardment of Britain in general, and of London in particular, increasingly haunted the British government and British public opinion between the wars. A sub-committee of the Committee of Imperial Defence in 1921 drew a gruesome picture of what could happen in the event of air attack. 'Railway traffic would be disorganised, food supplies interrupted, and it is probable that after being subjected for several weeks to the strain of such an attack, the population would be so demoralised that they would insist on an armistice.'[6]

This forecast was based on an assumed attack from France by an Air Force capable of dropping only seventy-five tons of bombs a day. But by 1939 planners were expecting raids on a scale of 700 tons a day; coming not from France, against whom retaliation was comparatively simple, but from a Germany whose own civilian targets were too dispersed and too distant for an effective return strike to be at that time feasible. Not only did they foresee a daily strike of 700 tons; they also warned of the possibility of an immediate 'knock-out blow' against London of 3500 tons, inflicting some fifty casualties per ton of bombs.[7] In fact the heaviest load dropped on the United Kingdom during the war was to be 1000 tons dropped in a raid on London in April 1941; the next heaviest, the 500 tons dropped on Coventry in November of 1940. Otherwise the general average of raids fluctuated between about 40 tons and 300 tons.[8]

Clearly the prime responsibility of the Government was to protect the people of the United Kingdom, which obviously involved a high priority for expenditure on the Royal Air Force. But it also involved an additional responsibility for the Army. In any case the Army was responsible for anti-aircraft defences; but in addition it would have the task of maintaining order in a civil community whose reaction under this kind of bombardment was unpredictable, and might well be one of

uncontrollable panic. So in 1938 the air defence of Great Britain was
accepted as the Army's main responsibility, one even more urgent than
that of imperial defence.

The third factor in planning was, simply, money.[9] Much has been
made by hostile critics of the unwillingness of British governments in the
1930s to spend enough on rearmament, or to interfere with the normal
course of trade. It is easy and perhaps legitimate to condemn the
Treasury officials who advised them for a certain narrow-minded
conservatism, for ignoring the words of wisdom, laced plentifully with
acid, which dropped from the lips of Maynard Keynes, for the caution
imposed on them by the disastrous experiences of 1929 to 1931, in short
for their conviction that the convalescent economy of the United
Kingdom was simply not in a state to support the heavy additional
charges required by rearmament on the scale which the Chiefs of Staff
demanded. When it was suggested in 1934 that a defence loan might be
raised to meet some of the costs of rearmament, Neville Chamberlain,
Chancellor of the Exchequer, described this as 'the broad road that
leads to destruction'.[10] The idea of raising the standard rate of income
tax to something above five shillings (25p) in the pound was regarded as
almost inconceivable in the financial climate of the 1930s. Yet the
problem which faced the government was not simply that of redistribut-
ing resources from the civilian into the military sector, of reallocating
priorities. It was the more basic one of enabling the country to go on
earning its living during this period. The Permanent Under-Secretary
to the Treasury, Sir Warren Fisher, defined the problem in 1934 as
follows:

> Raw materials, not to mention food, are only produced within this
> country in relatively negligible quantities, and therefore have to be
> secured from other countries who will not of course give us them. And
> when our international purchasing power is exhausted they will not
> continue indefinite credit to us.[11]

So even if the British government committed all its resources to
rearmament and defence, it would still have to trade abroad in order to
purchase the necessary raw materials and food for its civilian popu-

lation and its armies. It had considerable overseas assets but not enough to make possible an unfavourable balance of payments for the indefinite future.

This was the nightmare which stalked the corridors of the Treasury in the 1930s, and when war finally came, the nightmare came true. Early in 1940, the Treasury reported that by the end of that year the United Kingdom's overseas liabilities would total some £400 million. The assets in gold reserves and marketable securities were only £700 million; Britain would be bankrupt by the end of 1941 even if the rate of spending did not increase; which in fact it did.[12] It is easy now to forget that in the 1930s there was no reason to assume that the United States would bail the United Kingdom out of any war in which she became involved. In fact Congress, by a succession of Neutrality Acts, was making it clear that she would do nothing of the kind. The British empire was alone, with such Continental allies as it might be able to recruit. There was no exaggeration in the statement which Sir Thomas Inskip, the Minister for the Co-ordination of Defence, made to the Cabinet in February 1938:

> the plain fact which cannot be obscured is that it is beyond the resources of this country to make proper provision in peace for the defence of the British Empire against three major powers in three different theatres of war.[13]

These, then, were the three factors which governed all military planning in the 1930s: Imperial Defence, vulnerability to air attack, and financial stringency. When the Minister for Co-ordination of Defence made the statement quoted above, there were three probable adversaries – Germany, Italy and Japan. In 1933 when the British government for the first time began seriously to contemplate the possibility of rearmament, there was only one: Japan. Even so, the situation was serious enough. The deterioration of the situation in the Far East after 1931 led first to the abrogation of the 'Ten Year Rule', and secondly to the resumption of work on the long delayed fortifications of Singapore. But by the autumn of 1933 the course of events on the Continent, and particularly inside Germany, suggested that a threat might soon develop very much nearer home.

In October 1933 the Chiefs of Staff submitted a report to the Cabinet, in which they stated that from a naval point of view, 'the defence of our possessions and interests in the Far East remains the greatest and most immediate of our commitments'. But they also gave a remarkably prescient warning about the future course of German policy, which emanated partly from the Foreign Office, then under the guidance of Sir Robert Vansittart, and partly from the General Staff of the Army. As a result of the course of German policy, they warned,

> at any time within the next three to five years, we may be faced with the demands for military intervention on the Continent, either as a result of repercussions arising out of attempts to prevent German rearmament by means of threats or sanctions, or in order to implement our obligations to provide assistance in case of aggression by Germany under the Covenant of the League or the Locarno Treaties.

It was a remarkably accurate prognosis. The Chiefs of Staff went on to quote a statement by the Foreign Office to the effect that 'the more the nations of Europe become convinced of our readiness to fulfil our guarantee [Locarno], the less likelihood there will be that we should be called upon to do so'. But they commented on this: 'this may be true, but we feel it our duty to call attention to the slender means which we would have at our disposal for carrying out these guarantees, and the dangers to the defence of the Empire which such action on our part might entail'.[14] And in 1936 the same theme was to recur: 'the greater our commitments in Europe, the less will be our ability to secure our Empire and its communications'.[15]

This was a straightforward presentation of disagreeable alternatives, of a dilemma which could only be resolved by the making available of vastly greater resources than, in the view of the Treasury, the country could afford. But in consequence of this warning the Cabinet set up, in the autumn of 1933, the famous Defence Requirements Committee, which was to lay the foundation for all subsequent measures of rearmament. It consisted of the ubiquitous Sir Maurice Hankey as Chairman, of the three Chiefs of Staff, of the Permanent Under-Secretary of the Foreign Office, Sir Robert Vansittart, and of Sir Warren Fisher, the Permanent Under-Secretary of the Treasury. Their report in February 1934 was a clear recommendation of priorities. They agreed, in the first place, that it was necessary to press to completion the defences of Singapore, but an attempt should be made to restore good relations with Japan. Germany was the greater adversary; Japan could be and must be 'pacified'. (The word 'appeased,' in any pejorative sense, has not yet appeared.) There must be an ultimate policy of accommodation and friendship with Japan. Germany, ran the Report, was the 'ultimate potential enemy against whom our "long range" defence policy must be directed'.[16]

The views of the Admiralty were thus overlaid by those of the Foreign Office, the Army and the Royal Air Force. In order to deal with the threat from Germany the report proposed increases in the size of all three Services, including the creation of an effective British Expeditionary Force to fight if necessary on the Continent. This would be only a small force of five or six divisions as in 1914, but it was hoped that it might act as a deterrent to an aggressor and exercise an influence for peace out of all proportion to its size. It would be an indication of British resolution if necessary once more to fight in the defence of France and Belgium. The defence of the Low Countries, the Report pointed out, was now more vital to British security than ever before, since their possession by Germany would greatly increase the damage which a German Air Force could inflict on the industrial areas in the Midlands and the North.

The total cost of the measures proposed by this Report, which were designed only to remedy the worst deficiencies in the Armed Forces, was some £70 million on top of current defence expenditure. The Cabinet decided that even this minimal increase was unacceptable, both to public opinion (which some ministers believed had just made its voice heard at the Fulham by-election)[17] and, in the existing state of the economy, to the Treasury. What could be done?

It was now that the Chancellor of the Exchequer, Neville Chamberlain, took the lead in the formulation of defence policy – a lead which he did not relinquish until May 1940. With an enviable clarity of mind he defined the central issue. The problem, he maintained, was not so much to *fight* a war as to *deter* one. This could best be done by the establishment of an air force based in Britain of a size and efficiency calculated to inspire respect in the minds of any possible enemy. This could only be done by cutting down on all other commitments, including Imperial Defence. Chamberlain did not lack courage. He even proposed to his incredulous colleagues that the Singapore base should be abandoned, and with it the whole commitment to send a fleet to the Far East. This was even more than the former pacifist Ramsay MacDonald was prepared to accept.

Mr Chamberlain allowed himself to be overborne on this issue by the unanimous voice of his colleagues. But they supported his proposal that another commitment should be delayed, if not entirely abandoned – the British Expeditionary Force. The Cabinet believed that in its hostility to any military involvement on the Continent it faithfully reflected public opinion. This was the time when the popular emotional reaction against the First World War was reaching its height. Captain Liddell Hart, the military correspondent of *The Times*, was preaching persuasively that the whole involvement in land war between 1914 and 1918 had been a great mistake, and ran counter to 'The British Way in Warfare'.[18] The Peace Pledge Union was becoming active. The works of Siegfried Sassoon, Edmund Blunden and Robert Graves were receiving public acclaim. The creation of a BEF to repeat the horrors of the Somme and Passchendaele was felt to be politically out of the question. Chamberlain summed up the situation when he said in May 1934 that it seemed to him and the Cabinet 'that our experience of the last war indicated that we ought to put our major resources into our Navy and our Air Force; the Army must be maintained so that it could be used in other parts of the world'.[19]

This view was accepted. The Army was given the lowest priority of all three Services. Its request for new appropriations was cut from £40 million to £19 million. The RAF's requests for appropriations were, on the other hand, overfulfilled. Instead of the fifty-two squadrons it asked for, it was given eighty. And this pattern – emphasis on the RAF, downplaying of the Army – remained more or less constant until 1939. In the first Statement on Defence in March 1935, the first of the White Papers on defence which have been issued annually ever since, the Army was barely mentioned. The Paper dealt with the role of the Navy in Imperial Defence and defined the Royal Air Force's 'principal role' as being 'to provide for the protection of the United Kingdom and particularly London against air attack'. It is interesting to observe that it made no claim to be able to *defend* the United Kingdom. The role was to be fulfilled by a bomber force: a *deterrent*.

All depended on the deterrent's working. It did not. In March 1935 Hitler claimed that Germany already had parity with England in the air. This was not yet true, but it was to become so within the next couple of years. It did not require any information from Hitler to see that the pace of German rearmament was alarming. A few months later the Abyssinian crisis broke, and in July 1935 the Defence Requirements Committee was reactivated to give renewed advice on what ought to be done. In an immediate interim report the Committee made two points. First, Britain should be ready for war by 1 January 1939: the Committee's appreciation of the rate of German rearmament led them to suppose that there would be no safety beyond that date. Secondly, adequate preparation could be made only if the government were to widen its financial horizon and finance defence expenditure by loan as well as out of income. The full report in November 1935[20] stated that in view of the enormously increased output of German aircraft

> there is the possibility of attack so continuous and concentrated and on such a scale, that a few weeks of such an experience might so undermine the morale of our civilian population as to make it difficult for the Government to continue the war.

To make matters worse, a totally unforeseen crisis had now arisen in the Mediterranean. In 1932 Italy together with the United States and France had been written off as a possible menace. Now it was clearly hostile, lying across the most vulnerable point of imperial communications. And the Labour Opposition in the House of Commons, having strongly opposed the modest increase in defence appropriations of 1934, now joined in the demand, which commanded a great deal of public support, that sanctions, if necessary military sanctions, should be imposed on Mussolini.

The Committee therefore recommended in the first place considerable increases in first-line air strength, involving building up to 8000 front line air craft by 1939 instead of the figure of 3000 visualised hitherto. Secondly they urged that the Navy should be increased to an explicit Two-Power, Two-Ocean standard, so that it could handle both a European and a Far Eastern adversary. Finally they insisted that the Army must be strong enough to provide not simply for Imperial and Home defence but for an Expeditionary Force as well, to be available on the Continent within two weeks. This was necessary, they pointed out, first to make Britain a convincing ally and so encourage France in her resistance both to Germany and to Italy; and secondly, to protect the Low Countries against German attack. But they insisted, in language which was to run continuously through all strategic reports for the next five years, that:

it is a cardinal requirement of our National and Imperial security that our foreign policy should be so conducted as to avoid the possible development of a situation in which we might be confronted simultaneously with the hostility of Japan in the Far East, Germany in the West, and any power on the main line of communication between the two.

In other words, it must be the task of British foreign policy to ensure that the United Kingdom should not become involved in a three-front war which she would never have the resources to fight. One of those three possible adversaries had to be at least neutralised and if possible made a friend; and the power that appeared easiest to conciliate was Italy.

The proposals of the report were in general accepted by the Government. They involved an increase in defence expenditure amounting to £394 million over five years, to be financed partly by a defence loan. The Labour Opposition opposed this increase with a declaration that

> the safety of this country and the peace of the world cannot be secured by reliance on armaments but only by the resolute pursuit of a policy of international understanding, adherence to the Covenant of the League of Nations, general disarmament, the progressive improvement of international labour standards, and economic cooperation so as to remove the causes of war.[21]

Nevertheless, in 1936, over the strong protests of both the Labour and the Liberal Parties, serious rearmament began.

Heavy weight was still placed on the air deterrent, and Chamberlain and his colleagues continued to resist the creation of a British Expeditionary Force. In the summer of 1937 Chamberlain became Prime Minister, and shelved the proposal by setting up a new enquiry under the new Minister for Co-ordination of Defence, Sir Thomas Inskip, whose task was to advise how British defence commitments could be brought in line with her financial capacity.

The abolition of the BEF was not entirely the result of Chamberlain's insistence. Outside events played into his hands. In the Mediterranean the explosion of Italian power put Egypt under direct threat for the first time. Simultaneously, there was the outbreak of civil disturbance in Palestine which began in 1936, and continued at an intensity which ultimately absorbed eighteen battalions of the British Army; disorders on the scale of those in Northern Ireland today, and only less serious in that they were rather further away. Further, the disturbance in Palestine affected all the Muslim countries in the Middle East, where Britain was with increasing difficulty trying to preserve her precarious suzerainty; which involved further 'peacekeeping' obligations for the Army in Egypt and Iraq. Finally the growing anticipated weight of the German air attack on the United Kingdom made it appear necessary to divert increasing military resources to the Air Defence of Great Britain. This did not leave much for an Expeditionary Force for the Continent. By February 1938 it had shrunk to two infantry divisions and one mobile division, lightly equipped 'for an eastern theatre'. It was to be available for Continental commitments, in the words of the Secretary of State for War, Mr Leslie Hore-Belisha,

> only if the situation in the rest of the world permits, and it would be necessary for the General Staff to review the whole field of possible action open to the enemy before this could be determined.[22]

Once more we see how the primacy of Imperial defence, combined with the constraints imposed by limited resources, eliminated the option of making a military contribution in Europe. This was the position in March 1938 when the *Anschluss* between Germany and Austria pointed to the possibility, in the very near future, of a German attack on Czechoslovakia. Immediately after the *Anschluss* the Chiefs of Staff were asked to report on the military situation which would result from such an attack. In the course of their review they gave the following warning:

> No pressure that we and our possible allies can bring to bear, either by sea, on land, or in the air, could prevent Germany from invading and over-running Bohemia and from inflicting a decisive defeat on the Czechoslovakian army. We should then be faced with the necessity of undertaking a war against Germany for the purpose of restoring Czechoslovakia's lost integrity and this object would only be achieved by the defeat of Germany and as the outcome of a prolonged struggle. In the world situation today it seems to us that if

such a struggle were to take place, it is more than probable that both
Italy and Japan would seize the opportunity to further their own
ends, and that in consequence the problem we have to envisage is not
that of a limited European war only, but of a world war.[23]

This would be the war against the three adversaries which at all costs
had to be avoided. As for the balance of terror in the air, it was
estimated in autumn 1938 that Germany had some 5000 first line
aircraft against the British 1500, while the French did not have any
aircraft capable of bombing Germany at all. So if Germany were to
concentrate on a 'knock-out blow' against England – a possibility which
could not be discounted – she would be able to deliver the tonnage of
high explosive described above: 500 – 600 tons a day for two months.
Since the Royal Air Force could only retaliate with 100 tons a day for a
far shorter time, measurable at most in weeks and possibly in days, and
since Germany presented no comparable targets, the Air Staff advised
that it would be unwise to initiate air attack upon industrial targets in
Germany; it would be 'inadequate to produce decisive results and must
inevitably provoke immediate reprisal action on the part of Germany,
at a time when our defence measures at home, both active and passive,
are very far from complete'.[24]

Such was the advice given by the Chiefs of Staff to the British
government of the day. It was advice that Chamberlain could not
ignore, even if it was not the primary factor in his decision, in September
1938, to conclude the Munich agreement with Hitler at the expense of
the Czechs. Certainly that agreement was greeted by the Chiefs of Staff
with profound relief. It gave them time to press on with their defences,
above all with the Air Defence of Great Britain which was now giving
them some hope of being able to counter the threat of German air
bombardment.[25]

The Chiefs of Staff had always reckoned that by 1939 they might just
be in a position to undertake a serious war against Germany. And since
1937, developments had been taking place in the field of aerial
technology and radar, which was for the first time making defence
against air attack a feasible proposition. But it was going to take another
two years before fighter aircraft of adequate performance, Hurricanes
and Spitfires, and radio-location stations in sufficient quantity could be
installed and in working order. But the surrender at Munich had one
unforeseen result. It had to be accepted that as a result of the cession of
the Sudeten areas, Czechoslovakia would be virtually defenceless.

What had not been foreseen was the effect which this would have on French morale. In December 1938, reports began to reach the Cabinet from the British embassy and the British Military Attaché in Paris, about the fundamental reappraisal which was taking place in Paris about the whole direction of French policy. France no longer had the ally in the East on whom she had been relying to tie down a substantial proportion of the German Army. She looked with increasing alarm at the growing imbalance, not simply of military strength, but of male population between Germany and France. And there seemed to the British officials to be a distinct danger that France in the near future might reorientate her policy completely and line up with Germany if the British did not do something drastic and dramatic to prevent it. What the French wanted from Britain was, in the gruesome words of the British Military Attaché, *un éffort du sang*: an effort of blood. They wanted, in short, British troops. It would not be enough for Frenchmen to be told that the Royal Navy was commanding the seas from the Mediterranean to Singapore, or that the Royal Air Force was knocking all hell out of Düsseldorf while the German army was trampling through the fields of Picardy and massacring Frenchmen by hundreds of thousands as they had done between 1914 and 1917. As the Chiefs of Staff admitted in a report to the Cabinet in February 1939,

> it is difficult to say how the security of the United Kingdom could be maintained if France were forced to capitulate and therefore defence of the former may have to include a share in the land defence of French territory.[26]

So in February 1939 the Cabinet agreed to throw financial caution to the winds and create not simply an expeditionary force of six divisions, but a full-scale Continental army of thirty-two divisions. But it was a little late in the day to do this. There were no training facilities and above all no armament. If sometimes one wonders why the British Army did not perform better in the first three years of the war, the short answer is that it only came into existence as a force organised for Continental warfare in the early spring of 1939.

The decision to create a Continental army, and to enter into staff conversations with the French, was taken even before Hitler overran the rest of Czechoslovakia on 14 March 1939. This event, however, set on foot a very belated search for allies in Eastern Europe, including the Soviet Union, in order to re-constitute an eastern front, to deny the economic resources of south-east Europe to Germany, and to create a protective glacis to the north of Britain's position in the East Mediterranean.

And what of the Mediterranean? The Chiefs of Staff assumed that Italy would enter the war on the side of the Germans. They therefore favoured the creation of an alliance in the Balkans consisting of Greece, Yugoslavia, and Turkey, to hold her in check. But those powers could only provide, and be provided with, help if the Royal Navy commanded the Mediterranean; and that, also, would be the necessary condition if the restive Muslim world in the Middle East was to be kept under control. Yet the first priority of the Royal Navy was to hold a fleet in readiness to go to the relief of Singapore. What would happen in the Pacific if Japan took the offensive?

In the summer of 1939, in a series of anguished papers, the Admiralty wrestled with this problem. They simply did not have enough ships to go round. It had always been assumed, and the Australians in particular had always been assured, that the Far East would enjoy an absolute priority over the Mediterranean. Now the situation was transformed. The Admiralty could only report in June 1939 that

> there are so many variable factors which cannot at present be assessed, that it is not possible to state definitely how soon after Japanese intervention a fleet could be despatched to the Far East; neither is it possible to enumerate precisely the size of the fleet that we could afford to send.[27]

This was the situation when war broke out in September 1939. Of the three problems which I listed at the beginning of this paper as dominating British defence policy, not one had been solved. In the field of Imperial defence, Britain was no longer in a position to ensure the defence of her eastern empire. In economic terms she was within two years of total bankruptcy. Only in the defence of Britain against air attack had progress been made. Such defence was at last becoming feasible, in spite of the dogma on which all RAF strategic thinking had rested, that any such development was out of the question. What however was certainly not feasible was the kind of 'deterrent' air attacks against Germany which the Royal Air Force had believed to be the only way of defending the population of the United Kingdom.

Nevertheless in April 1939 the British Chiefs of Staff produced in discussion with their French colleagues a realistic plan for winning the forthcoming war, which was to become the basis of Anglo-French strategy, and later of Anglo-American strategy. This saw the war as consisting of three phases. In the first, nothing could be done except hold the line against a German attack which was bound to be ferocious but could only be short-lived. If that could be survived, then there was some hope. In the second phase, the Allies should contain Germany while dealing decisively with Germany's expected associate, Italy; and the elimination of Italy would be facilitated if Italian morale had been undermined by the capture of Italian possessions in North and East Africa. During this phase the allied bomber effort should be directed against economic and industrial objectives in Germany with the object of contributing to the ultimate breakdown of her resistance. Third, 'the final object of the Allies is to defeat Germany. In view of the magnitude of the reserves which would have to be employed no date and no possible line of action can be fixed for this phase. But meanwhile,' concluded the plan, 'in peace, as later in war, all the resources of diplomacy should be devoted to securing the benevolent neutrality or active assistance of other powers, particularly the United States of America.'[28]

This was what British military planners were intending to do in April 1939. It is consoling to observe that this was precisely what Britain and her allies ultimately did. It would be too much to claim for the planners of 1939 a substantial share of the credit for winning the war. But it was certainly due in some degree to their sensible and far-sighted provisions that the war was not quickly and irretrievably lost.

6. The Hoare–Laval Pact Reconsidered

NORTON MEDLICOTT

NEWS of the signature of the so-called Hoare–Laval pact reached the English newspapers on the morning of 10 December 1935; it was speedily accepted as a surrender to fascist aggression as inexplicable as it was shameful, and this impression was deepened by recollection of the comparatively brave words with which the League of Nations' sanctions programme against Italy had been launched in the preceding weeks. As the British negotiators of the agreement were evidently quite taken aback by this almost universal condemnation we may well ask, in the light of present day evidence,[1] how they had managed to put themselves at such cross purposes with the rest of the world.

By 9 December 1935 the Abyssinian (or Ethiopian) crisis was almost exactly a year old. It had begun with a small battle between Ethiopian tribesmen and Italian-led tribesmen on 5 December 1934 at a place called Walwal, well inside Ethiopian territory. Negotiations over what Signor Mussolini, the Italian dictator, insisted on treating as an act of blatant Ethiopian aggression had dragged on during the first nine months of 1935; and Italy had gone to war on 3 October. The 'Hoare–Laval' plan was an attempt at a compromise settlement which failed. Serious fighting began in January 1936, and Ethiopian resistance finally collapsed in the following May. We can start by being quite definite on one point: on Italy's part this was undoubtedly planned aggression of the most deliberate kind.

On Mussolini's instructions war against Ethiopia was being prepared by the Italian government from 1932 onward. The complete plans of the Italian War Office in connection with the war were published in 1970 in an important book by Professor Georgio Rochat on the military and political preparations of the Italo-Ethiopian campaign.[2] The decisive document, one might almost call it the Hossbach memorandum of Italian fascism, was dated 30 December 1934, and it gave Mussolini's detailed instructions to Marshal Badoglio, the Chief of the Italian General Staff, for war to be launched against Ethiopia in October 1935 (the rainy season normally ends in September). Forces were to be built up in the adjacent Italian colony of Eritrea on the Red Sea to a total of 200,000 men, with 300 aircraft, 200 tanks, artillery and gas.[3] The Italian generals wrangled a good deal about the plans. Among other things Mussolini's choice as leader of the expedition of a rather brutal old gentleman, General de Bono, Minister of the Colonies since 1929, was disliked by his fellow generals.[4]

If it was planned aggression it was nevertheless rather shrewd planning. Mussolini was still determined to keep the Germans out of Austria but he had persuaded himself that Hitler would not be ready for a major war for two years and that he had time in the meantime to conquer his Italian empire. The only two powers likely to make difficulties were France and England and he believed he could arrange matters with Pierre Laval, the French Foreign Minister, with whom he signed an agreement on 7 January 1935 giving Italy a free hand in economic matters in Ethiopia, subject to the maintenance of French interests in the Djibouti–Addis Ababa railway zone. This innocent-looking agreement was published. What was not published was a resulting secret military agreement providing for joint Franco-Italian military operations in Austria, should Hitler invade that country, and visualising therefore the virtual demilitarisation of the Franco-Italian frontier, where both powers had been maintaining large bodies of troops in the recent past. An understanding between Badoglio and General Gamelin on these lines was concluded in Rome on 28 June 1935. This if fully implemented would enable Laval to move ten French divisions into northern France to meet the possibility of a German attack and it would of course release Italian divisions for Mussolini's adventure in Africa. The British ambassador in Paris, Sir George Clerk, reported on 22 August 1935 that France had already been able 'to withdraw her garrison troops from the Franco-Italian frontier and concentrate them on the Franco-German frontier – a most valuable factor in the "Années creuses" '.[5]

Mussolini evidently planned a somewhat similar agreement with England. On 29 January 1935, three weeks after the conclusion of the Franco-Italian agreement, the Italian ambassador in London, Count Grandi, proposed to Sir John Simon, the British Foreign Secretary, an agreement providing for a definition of the respective economic spheres of the two countries in Abyssinia.[6] The implication was that England should give Italy a free hand there as France had done and that England could ask for some *quid pro quo* for herself. It is pretty evident that the *quid pro quo* which Mussolini may well have contemplated (to judge from his later proposals) was a naval agreement covering the Mediterranean, together with a firm Italian guarantee of the specific British economic and strategical interests in Ethiopia.

The Italian approach came at an extraordinarily awkward moment for the British Foreign Office. All the efforts of Sir John Simon were bent at this point on negotiations whereby Germany would be allowed to rearm up to a reasonable figure in return for participation in a general settlement. French ministers who visited London, 1–3 February, wished to impose more stringent conditions on the Germans and were more sceptical than the British as to whether a bargain was possible. Italy shared the French distrust of Germany's goodwill. The British hopes that Germany might be persuaded persisted despite the shock of Germany's unilateral declaration of rearmament on 16 March, although the British Cabinet's White Paper on defence of 4 March showed that their credulity was not inexhaustible. Everything pointed to the need for Britain, France, and Italy to stand together in handling the German problem.

So the Foreign Office evaded an immediate answer to the Italian approach of 29 January, though not through failure to grasp the dangerous possibilities of the Italian initiative or through belief that any net advantage could accrue for Great Britain from a bargain with Italian imperialism. Sir Robert Vansittart, the Permanent Under-Secretary of State for Foreign Affairs, commented on 10 February:

> I think it would be dangerous to encourage the Italians to develop their ideas until we know our own minds . . . For we know that otherwise they would open their mouths pretty wide. If left to themselves they would ask from us a self-denying ordinance, such as they have obtained from the French.[7]

After some inconclusive debate in the Foreign Office Vansittart proposed the appointment of an inter-departmental committee under Sir John Maffey of the Colonial Office to define British interests in Ethiopia, and this course was agreed to by the Cabinet. The committee's terms of reference took the form of a letter of 6 March from the Foreign Office to the Colonial Office which visualised the possibility of a violent absorption and political domination of Ethiopia by Italy, and asked for an examination both of the effect of this advance on British interest and authority in surrounding areas such as British Somaliland, Kenya, Tanganyika, Uganda, the Sudan, and Egypt, and of the effect 'on the general political relations between His Majesty's Government in the United Kingdom and the Italian Government'. But the committee, whose unhurried deliberations lasted until 18 June, decided that it was not qualified to discuss 'the general situation in Europe and the role which it is desired that Italy should play on the European stage', and its report accordingly did nothing to elucidate the wider issues of policy, although it concluded that no such vital interest was concerned 'in and round Ethiopia as would make it essential for His Majesty's Government to resist an Italian conquest of Ethiopia'. The practical result was unfortunate: four months had gone by without either a clever formula emerging from the committee or any indication to the Italians that the British were at least studying the problem. Vansittart, rather unfairly perhaps, blamed his subordinates for a failure in communication: 'The Italians have asked for an answer several times, and, as far as my knowledge goes, have not even had an interim one', he remarked on 22 June. 'This has provided them with a grievance and a suspicion, both unfounded . . . None the less it would have been both wise and courteous to let them know that no early answer could be expected, since it was necessary to consult so many colonial authorities.'[8]

The committee had done little more than emphasise the complexities of a problem which was evidently not going to solve itself. It was clear that there was not one Ethiopian problem but at least four. There was the problem of defining the area in the Ethiopian province of Ogaden in which tribes from British Somaliland had long established grazing rights: a joint Anglo-Ethiopian commission had nearly completed a survey of this area when its work was suspended in December 1934 by the Walwal episode. There was secondly the Walwal incident itself and the increasing Italo-Ethiopian tension which resulted from the refusal of the Emperor Haile Selassie to settle the affair by an admission of guilt and payment of compensation. Even if the Italian Government had no broader imperialist intentions this dispute might lead its prestige-conscious colonial leaders into reprisals. But there was thirdly the possibility, which was beginning to loom more and more ominously before the British Foreign Office after January, that Italy was indeed planning the conquest of the entire Ethiopian state. And there was a fourth complication, which arose from the close links which the Foreign Office had developed with the Emperor in recent years, and which, while strengthening his position in return for the removal of causes of Anglo-Ethiopian tension, was not likely to please the Italians.

From 1932 to 1934 there had been intermittent but prolonged Anglo-Ethiopian bargaining over a possible territorial exchange. Ethiopia was an entirely land-locked state and the Emperor had his eye on an outlet to the sea through either Assab in the Italian colony of Eritrea (as he suggested to the Italians in 1931) or the port of Zeila in British Somaliland. In either case he would expect a narrow corridor of territory to be ceded to give communication with Ethiopian territory. Naturally the Emperor would be expected to reciprocate. Counter-concessions suggested by the British Foreign Office on 27 March 1934, after much cogitation and argument with the Colonial Office about the alternatives, included the cession by Ethiopia of the area of the Ogaden province over which British-Somali tribes had their well-established rights of grazing their flocks, together with small frontier adjustments on the Kenyan and Sudanese borders. The Emperor had seemed interested in this plan, but became alarmed in September (1934) when he realised that the area proposed for cession to British Somaliland in the Ogaden actually included the oases of Wadair and Walwal, to which Italy already had claims. The Foreign Office was alarmed too, and promptly pigeonholed the Zeila proposals; it suspected that the Italians had speedily learned of the plan through a leak in Addis Ababa. The combative attitude that the Italians adopted over the Walwal battle was ascribed to a belief that the British were encouraging the Emperor's resistance. The important point is that the British Foreign and Colonial Offices had become familiar even before 1935 with the notion that rather large areas of the Ogaden province would constitute a fair exchange for the small but (to Haile Selassie) valuable Zeila corridor.[9]

It was in these circumstances that a British plan for a settlement emerged, and it cannot fairly be judged without a recognition of the impracticability in the British Government's eyes of any obvious alternative. Laval was determined to do nothing to jeopardise the precious military agreement with Italy. In the last resort he preferred the British, uncertain, coy, and hard to please though they were, to the

Italians as allies, but his whole purpose was to prevent the necessity for making a choice, to retain the friendship of both powers.[10] Facing a malevolent and resurgent Germany, Britain could not afford to alienate her two partners, France and Italy, in the front which found public expression at the Stresa conference in April. A League of Nations sanctions programme against Italy in the event of her invasion of Ethiopia might well have this effect, and yet at the same time be unlikely to succeed without the exercise of belligerent rights, which would almost certainly mean open war. Full-scale war with Italy was a horrifying alternative justified neither by Britain's own colonial interests nor by her League of Nations' obligations, and the naval balance which she needed to maintain against two potential enemies, Germany and Japan, might be upset even after a victorious struggle against Italy. Mussolini's approaches to both France and Britain pointed to a quite different solution, namely a bargain whereby Italy would receive a free hand in Ethiopia and consolidate her political and military co-operation with France against Germany. This would have completed the encirclement of Germany in the south and west and incidentally greatly simplified Britain's problem of finding the extra naval strength which she needed to deal with the future hostility of both Germany and Japan. But at this stage of world history it was impossible for a British (although not perhaps a French) government to strike this sort of bargain. The vague and muddled but highly respected concept called Collective Security effectively ruled out any action which was frankly in the national interest alone. Later, in May 1936, Hitler seemed genuinely surprised that the once bold British had not handled Mussolini more toughly. He told the British ambassador that with dictators 'nothing succeeds like success': Britain at the beginning of the Ethiopian crisis should have thrown troops into Ethiopia, staked out her vital sphere of interest there (around Lake Tana and the source of the Nile), and settled matters afterwards in a friendly way with Italy. But the ambassador was well aware that this Fashoda-style operation would have been distasteful to the British mood of 1936. He could only reply to Hitler that it was 'a religion in England that there should be no more aggression'.[11]

The Stresa conference had been concerned only with German problems, although in talks between the British and Italian officials present the possibility of an Italian attack on Ethiopia after September had been mentioned, and had elicited a warning that Italy could expect no co-operation from the United Kingdom in an attack on Ethiopia.

This was a repetition of similar warnings by the British ambassador, Sir Eric Drummond, and Vansittart in February, which had clearly not made much impression in Rome. Sir John Simon had been too engrossed with German rearmament to give close attention to Ethiopia, although he did surprise the Italians by calling rather sharply at Geneva on 15 April for early progress in the Walwal negotiations. But he was succeeded on 7 June by Sir Samuel Hoare, and the more positive phase of British activity in the crisis began.

Hoare undoubtedly had the makings of a very good Foreign Secretary, but he was tired after four years of successful struggle over the Government of India Bill, unfamiliar with the details of foreign policy, subject to fainting fits, and very much in need of a rest and of time to think out, and even read up, foreign policy.[12] Ethiopia was only one of several problems with which he had immediately to deal. He came into office right in the middle, for instance, of the Anglo-German naval negotiations and had to take vital decisions in those negotiations almost at a moment's notice. It was natural, therefore, that he should turn to and rely on the great civil servant at his elbow, Sir Robert Vansittart.

Vansittart, who had been head of the Foreign Office since January 1930, was at the height of his powers and self-confidence; a very formidable figure, ranked with Sir Maurice Hankey and Sir Warren Fisher as one of the three great civil servants of the day. As members of the Defence Requirements Committee in 1934 they had laid it down that, in her severely disarmed state, Britain was scarcely strong enough to cope with her two potential enemies, Germany and Japan, and could never contemplate war with Italy, France, or the United States in the forseeable future, a view which the Cabinet had accepted.

Hoare, with the utmost conscientiousness and perhaps a little naïvety, listened to all the advice including that of his colleague Anthony Eden, Minister for League of Nations Affairs, and tried to base his policy at every stage on League of Nations principles and procedure, as he understood them. Whether he shared the somewhat mystical faith of some of his contemporaries in that institution is doubtful, but he was shrewd enough to realise the publicity value of League approval. There is no sign of disagreement with Eden or Vansittart or his Cabinet colleagues over the main lines of the policy which he followed in the Ethiopian crisis, although they were quite willing afterwards to suggest that he was striking out on a line of his own. Most of the more detailed moves throughout the crisis were in fact initiated by Vansittart, although one would hardly gather this from Vansittart's own memoirs,

The Mist Procession, published in 1958. He did say later, however, that the 'Hoare–Laval' pact should really have been called the 'Laval–Vansittart' pact.

Hoare had scarcely entered the Foreign Office on 8 June when Vansittart presented him with a weighty memorandum, which looked very like a proposal for the gradual dismantlement of the British empire. It included this passage:

> I have long thought the distribution of this limited globe quite untenable, and quite unjustifiable. Like fools we made it far worse at Versailles. What *has* happened in regard to Japan; what is happening in regard to Italy, and what is about to happen in regard to Germany, should surely confirm this view to anyone with political antennae. We are grossly over-landed (and British Somaliland is a real debit).

His plan was to give away part of the British Somaliland in order to facilitate agreement between Italy and Ethiopia. He wrote:

> The position is as plain as a pikestaff. Italy will have to be bought off – let us use and face ugly words – in some form or other, or Abyssinia will eventually perish. That might in itself matter less, if it did not mean that the League would also perish (and that Italy would simultaneously perform *another* volte-face into the arms of Germany, a combination of haute politique and haute cocotterie that we can ill afford just now).
>
> I agree that we cannot trade Abyssinia. The price that would now satisfy Italy would be too high for Abyssinia even to contemplate.
>
> If we are all clear and in unison about that, it follows clearly that either there has got to be a disastrous explosion – that will wreck the League and very possibly His Majesty's Government too, if the League is destroyed on the eve of an election – or else we have got to pay the price . . . with British Somaliland.

Personally, he said, he opted unhesitatingly for the latter course.[13] In short, the British Government should not leave Ethiopia to its fate, but in order to produce an acceptable settlement should cede to Ethiopia the port of Zeila and a corridor in British Somaliland, and in return should require Ethiopia to cede territory to Italy in the Ogaden country.

It was a curious proposal, under which Britain would ask for nothing for herself. The Foreign Office perhaps had exaggerated hopes of the Emperor's willingness to make sacrifices to secure the corridor; but as the Ogaden area was largely stony desert he might be willing to abandon some of it, although for the same reason Italy might not find the bargain particularly attractive. Vansittart included Germany in the far-reaching plans that he was contemplating for diverting totalitarian energies into peaceful channels by cessions of colonial territory, and he clearly attached too much significance to the Zeila offer, which he was prepared to widen if necessary. He was perhaps influenced too by a tendency in the Foreign Office to view the Italian sense of grievance with a certain sophisticated tolerance, if not with sympathy, and to underrate the degree of long-term planning in Mussolini's Abyssinian programme. The Foreign Office was conscious of Italy's complaints about her own limited colonial possessions, and particularly her conviction of having failed after the Versailles treaty to get the just reward for her warlike efforts; it was also aware of the fact that numerous international agreements since the 1890s had undoubtedly conceded that Ethiopia was Italy's special sphere of interest. Moreover the Foreign Office, although respecting the Emperor, did regard his country as in many ways barbarous and in need of foreign aid and reform. These attitudes, and the urgent need to keep Italy on the right side of the European balance, help to explain this unorthodox proposal, although the vehemence of Vansittart's representations also reveal perhaps some undercurrent of uneasiness about the wisdom of his own plan. It was always difficult to visualise any peaceful exchange or settlement limited enough to give Haile Selassie satisfaction and security, and far reaching enough to give Mussolini the prestige of a major triumph.

Vansittart put his proposals to Hoare; Hoare and Eden discussed it; they were converted; it was put to the Cabinet and they, after showing surprise, agreed on 19 June. The plan was then taken to Rome by Eden and immediately rejected, angrily rejected, on 24 June by Mussolini. He simply said it wasn't enough, he wanted the whole of Abyssinia, and if she resisted him she would be blotted off the map of the world. In his memoirs Vansittart omits all reference to his own share in the proposal; he gives the impression that he rather disapproved of it all and that he disapproved in particular of the sending of Eden to Rome. But in fact it was he who proposed the sending of Eden, and he was ready to go himself if Eden didn't want to do so. The documents clearly establish his initiative throughout the affair.[14]

Moreover in spite of Mussolini's reaction Vansittart did not abandon the basic idea, which he could commend to his colleagues and the Cabinet as *faute de mieux* the only practicable means of peaceful change in East Africa. A revised version of the plan was put to the Italians again in mid-August with the exchange of territory as before, Zeila for Ogaden, and with some provision for a reform programme for Ethiopia, in which Italy would be allowed to take part, and from which she would presumably gain some advantage. Haile Selassie had indicated that he was now willing to cede the whole of Ogaden to Italy in return for the outlet to the sea, and he asked that the French should agree to add a small strip of territory (of French Somaliland) to the corridor. Eden found Laval more favourable to the plan than he had been at the end of June, and Alexis Léger, Vansittart's opposite number at the Quai d'Orsay, strongly supported the plan as 'a good opening move'. However it was again flatly rejected by Mussolini.[15] The same basic ideas were embodied in a programme by a committee of five set up by the League of Nations in September: a substantial reform programme in which Italy would participate, an exchange of territory and an international gendarmerie or foreign legion to keep the peace on the frontier, because the Italians were always complaining, quite rightly as a matter of fact, that their frontiers were being continually raided by Ethiopian tribes.[16] It is important to notice, for the subsequent history of the crisis, that the Emperor Haile Selassie accepted the three proposals of June, August, and September. He rightly said later that he had accepted them for tactical reasons and the situation changed when war began; but nevertheless he *had* accepted them and he was prepared to make some sort of peace on that basis. Mussolini rejected outright the plans of the committee of five and the war started on 3 October.

During July the British Cabinet had been slowly making up their minds that some action under the League's sanctions procedure would be necessary if Italy went to war against Ethiopia. The Prime Minister, Stanley Baldwin, agreed on 6 August that in the forthcoming tripartite talks it must be made clear to the Italian representative that his government must choose between a negotiated settlement with Haile Selassie and the 'carrying out by the League of Nations of the procedure laid down in the Covenant'. After the failure of the Paris meeting he agreed on 21 August to the removal of the Mediterranean fleet from its vulnerable station at Malta to the Eastern Mediterranean and to preparations for the Home Fleet to sail for Gibraltar; he is said to have remarked, 'I am afraid this means war with Italy'. However, the Chiefs of Staff, invited to comment, insisted that it would be unwise to risk a naval war with Italy, and after meeting for over four hours on 22 August the Cabinet agreed that it must keep in step with the French Government, particularly in the matter of sanctions, and avoid any commitment which France was not equally prepared to assume. They should follow the procedure laid down in the Covenant 'not in any quixotic spirit and with due regard to the many difficulties'. As it happened, Italian naval and air force experts were warning Mussolini just at this time through Badoglio that war with England would be disastrous for Italy (they were particularly impressed by the fact that Britain had six aircraft-carriers which would constitute a mobile base for attack). The apparent discrepancy between the expert views on both sides is, however, more apparent than real. Even a successful naval war against Italy would be won at a cost which Admiral Chatfield estimated as equivalent to the loss of four capital ships, and this could decisively tilt the naval balance against England as she faced the possibility of naval war against both Germany and Japan. In any case she would be fighting at a disadvantage against Japan in the Far East, partly because of the length of her communications. (It could also be argued, although no one appears to have done so, that it would be a net advantage to Britain to cripple Italy before she gravitated to the German side.) It must be said that the British fleet and its officers in the Mediterranean had far greater confidence than the Chiefs of Staff in the strength of their position.[17]

Thus the British Government had reached the decision that it could act only through the League, and that meant that British action would be as bold as that of France, but no more. So everything turned upon Laval's initiative and tactical sense. In fact, Laval had been talking quite toughly throughout most of July. A British official wrote from Paris on 18 July as follows: 'Laval lunched at the American Embassy this morning when he was in great spirits declaring that there would certainly be no war between Italy and Abyssinia as France would not tolerate it.'[18] But in August Laval made it clear that he was not prepared to support any but the mildest form of economic sanctions, little more in fact than moral or psychological pressure, on the Italians. If he had refused outright, the British Government might well have felt morally justified in doing nothing itself, but Laval was not likely to put himself openly in the wrong in that way. He had to deal with a strong radical political element in France who believed very warmly in the League of Nations although the right wing took the opposite point of view, and thought that anything approaching a war with Italy would be a disaster. This point of view was strongly supported by the Paris press, largely in Italian pay. So Laval told Hoare on 10 September that France would agree to some economic sanctions, but in no case to military sanctions. The British Cabinet decided on 2 October that owing to the French attitude they too would not go beyond economic sanctions.[19] The French attitude was decisive in this matter. If Britain had been prepared to impose military sanctions, France would not have followed her; if France had been prepared to impose military sanctions, probably the British Government *would* have done so. The war began and on 11 October fifty out of the fifty-four nations at Geneva condemned Italy as an aggressor under Article 16 of the League Covenant.

Every British politician and official in 1935 claimed belief in the League of Nations. What that belief meant in practical terms is harder to define. Hoare, new to diplomacy, certainly sought League endorsement for every step he took. Vansittart favoured demonstrative action by the League against Mussolini as a means of warning Hitler to behave himself, but his willingness to pacify the Germans as well as the Italians with colonial gifts meant, it would seem, that he regarded the League as little more than a means of moral or psychological pressure. Hoare made a celebrated speech, largely written by Vansittart, to the League Assembly on 11 September, when he affirmed Britain's support for collective resistance to any manifestation of aggression; but he stressed the word 'collective'. It was hoped that the speech would fulfil the original purpose of the League, by mobilising world opinion against a potential aggressor: but the bluff was called. Mussolini took no notice. Both Hoare and Vansittart claimed later that the speech was intended as a warning to Germany; but Hitler was equally unimpressed.[20] The most effective way to contain Hitler would have been to complement the Franco-Italian agreement with an Anglo-Italian guarantee of the naval position in the Mediterranean, which Mussolini's approach of 29 January had made possible and which he referred to on at least half a dozen occasions in October and November.

The British Foreign Office documents seem to make it clear that Mussolini was hinting at a naval agreement which would have added to the Franco-Italian military agreement and completed the encirclement of Germany. But, as already suggested, the British Government simply could not at this time conclude such an apparently self-seeking bargain. We are still very far away from the mood of six years later, when

Churchill could say that if Hitler invaded Hell, he would make at least a favourable reference to the Devil in the House of Commons.[21]

The other point that must be stressed is that Hoare, always striving to be ·the good League of Nations man, felt that he had a double task. Economic sanctions must be applied as long as Mussolini proved recalcitrant; at the same time there must be mediation and pressure to secure an agreed and if necessary compromise settlement between the two parties. Article 15, paragraph 3, of the League of Nations Covenant provided for the settlement of disputes by conciliation. This was quite clearly understood by the League Assembly, which appointed a Committee of Eighteen to draw up a sanctions programme and a Committee of Thirteen to seek conciliation between the two parties, and it was assumed that Britain and France would take the lead in both Committees. As far as the conciliation procedure went – the attempt to arrange a compromise settlement between Italy and Abyssinia – Britain and France were specifically asked to undertake the negotiations. Hoare called this his double policy and he defends it in his memoirs.[22] At the time there was not considered to be any rivalry between the two functions and as late as 2 November the Committee of Eighteen, that is the Committee that was drawing up the sanctions programme and on which Eden represented Great Britain, unanimously requested the two powers to continue their conciliatory efforts. It was a kind of 'carrot and stick' diplomacy. It was only after the Hoare – Laval fiasco in December that the idea spread that the two functions, sanctions and conciliation, were in some way incompatible. Eden seems to take this line in his memoirs but at the time he specifically affirmed the need for the double policy.[23]

There is little doubt that the willingness to seek a negotiated settlement was strengthened by doubts in the mind of the British Government as to the likelihood of success of the sanctions programme. If it failed, a compromise between Italian and Abyssinian interests might be the best solution for all concerned. One must say, however, that the permanent alienation of Mussolini, rather than the collapse of Haile Selassie, was the real preoccupation of the British Government. Economic sanctions, which came into force on 18 November, were as complete as circumstances allowed. In fact they formed quite an elaborate programme if we consider that the scheme was drafted and put into operation in just over six weeks. They included all the economic embargoes, except that on food, which it was in the power of the League members to apply on their own initiative, but they did not include such industrial commodities as oil, which came substantially from non-League sources. The idea was to get into operation as quickly as possible those sanctions which could be applied at once by the League powers themselves, and then to start negotiating with the other powers, particularly the United States, regarding the further proposals which came in category 4(b) of the programme. In reality there was little hope of persuading the other powers to take part. Venezuela, although a member of the League, was exporting largely to Italy and vital oil supplies went from America to the Italians. The United States Government had entire goodwill towards the League; they wanted to stop Mussolini, but professed their inability to help. American oil exports to Italy and its African colonies, right to the scene of the war in other words, increased by thirty-five times during the last five months of 1935, as compared with the figures for the same period of 1934.[24]

So the idea of bringing the war to an end by an early ceasefire and a settlement more or less fair to both sides had its attractions. If anything was to be done on these lines it was essential that Laval should take a sufficiently tough line with Mussolini to ensure a fairly reasonable settlement. But Laval was always desperately anxious not to quarrel with Mussolini and for a time seemed likely to back out of his earlier commitments altogether. There was a major crisis in Anglo-French relations, entirely unknown of course to the general public, in mid-October, when Laval refused to promise military support to England if Mussolini, in a mood of desperation, committed a 'mad-dog' act and attacked the British fleet in the Mediterranean. Laval's argument was that Britain had reinforced her fleet in August before sanctions had been agreed on and therefore the sanctions Article 16(3), which covered the provision of support, did not apply. This caused a Cabinet crisis in London on 16 October. A section of the Cabinet opposed to sanctions (described by Hoare as 'our enemies') proposed to abandon them altogether, but was defeated by Hoare with Baldwin's support; an ultimatum was then sent to Laval. In the meantime Eden was told to go slow in the discussion on sanctions pending the result of this ultimatum.[25] Vansittart was quite furious with the French and drafted an extremely violent message to Laval, which Hoare endorsed. Privately Vansittart called the French attitude 'disloyalty and treachery in its dirtiest and blackest form'. Laval did in fact give a profuse assurance on 18 October and Vansittart was mollified; but he remarked that they had had to get it out of the French with forceps and biceps.[26]

It thus became possible to embark on the negotiations which led

directly to the Hoare–Laval agreement. The Foreign Office felt that
there was a reasonable basis for agreement in the now well-defined
plans to which Haile Selassie had agreed in principle in August and
September. They were based on three points, namely the cession of
some territory to Italy in return for an Ethiopian outlet to the sea; the
delimitation of the Italo-Ethiopian frontiers in the Ogaden and Danakil
areas, where they had remained undefined and the cause of a great deal
of trouble since the 1890s; and the need for internal reform in Abyssinia,
a need which would not be shirked now that the League discussions had
focussed attention on Abyssinian slavery, backwardness, and the like.
In the discussions Laval easily slipped into the role of Italy's advocate
and was supposed to have a direct line to Mussolini. In some of the
discussions he would pick up a telephone and apparently have a little
chat with the Duce, although the British delegates suspected that he was
talking to a clerk in the next room. But on 17 October Mussolini himself,
pressed, it was said, by the Vatican, gave his own terms and these were
very different from the sweeping demands that he had made to Eden in
June (the annexation of the whole of Abyssinia). Now he wanted an
Italian mandate for the non-Amharic areas; Italian participation in a
League mandate for the central area; frontier rectification in the
Danakil and Ogaden districts; limitation of Ethiopian armaments; and
in return a commercial outlet for Ethiopia at Assab.[27]

The basic Abyssinian state consists of the Amharic-speaking area,
which goes in a semi-circle of rather mountainous country from Addis
Ababa to more or less the frontiers of Eritrea. Areas such as Danakil,
Ogaden, and the Galla country in the south had been conquered since
the 1890s, and there is no doubt that Abyssinian rule there had been
oppressive and unpopular. So Mussolini made a distinction: he was
really giving up his demand for the annexation of Ethiopia proper; he
was asking now – it was really a much more modest demand than
people realised – for parts of the Danakil and Ogaden and perhaps the
south Galla country. Much of this was desert, although the area south of
Addis Ababa in the province of Bale was much more suitable for white
settlement and that is really the area on which most of the controversy
turns.

His demands on 17 October therefore fell considerably short of what
he had been asking for in the summer and Vansittart called it a distinct
advance, although still not satisfactory. A British official, Mr (later Sir)
Maurice Peterson, was sent to Paris late in October for detailed
discussions. Laval proposed a smaller non-Amharic area, but with an

exclusively Italian administration. Mussolini had asked for the non-Amharic areas under a League mandate. Hoare preferred the British proposal of the previous June, that is, a corridor to the sea for Ethiopia and some area in the south for Italian settlement in an outright exchange. This was assumed to be a fair exchange in view of the importance which Haile Selassie was still believed to attach to the outlet to the sea. Thus by the end of October the British had turned down both the French and the Italian plans. There was then a break of about a fortnight while England had a general election, in which Mr Baldwin was re-elected on 14 November; and when that was over the talks started again. Peterson went back to Paris.

The discussions became very complicated as far as the details went, such as where the exact frontier line should run, but the main lines are clear. There were various slight Italian retreats and counter-demands, usually supported by Laval, and on the British side it seems fair to claim, a real effort to find terms which were fair to Ethiopia. It is interesting, in view of the later criticism, to notice how anxious Hoare was to keep the League in the picture. He even put forward a plan on 14 November for the League Council or the Committee of Five, if it still existed, to lay down in principle what the main lines of a settlement should be, after which the British and French delegates would merely have to work out the details. Laval rejected that as impracticable on the ground that talk about the League Council really meant England and France because they were the only two powers that mattered on the Council. If he referred it to the Council, it would merely mean that England and France through the same representatives would carry on the discussions in perhaps a different place.[28] So the negotiation went on in Paris and on 27 November Hoare and Eden, in spite of a quite anguished plea from Vansittart for delay, asked the British Cabinet to consider, as a matter of urgency, the imposition of an embargo on oil imports into Italy.[29]

At this point General Garibaldi turned up in London. He was the grandson of the famous Garibaldi, and a personal envoy of Mussolini – just how important was not clear. But he came to the Foreign Office on 25 November and had several discussions with Hoare and Vansittart. He gave Mussolini's latest terms, which however turned out to be identical to those of October. It looked as if Mussolini was becoming a bit dissatisfied with Laval as intermediary and was trying to establish a direct contact with London. At the same time, Hoare insisted that the area to the south, in which it had now been more or less accepted that

Italy would have the right to settlement, must remain under the ultimate control of the League of Nations. Laval having held out for a long time, saying that Mussolini would never accept it, at the end of November gave in on this point.[30]

This seemed to the Foreign Office to be the breakthrough in the negotiations for which they had been hoping, for it was assumed that Laval would not have agreed to this modification without Mussolini's consent. The Hoare–Laval meeting in Paris was the result. Having made his concession, Laval offered to come to London to complete the talks. Hoare, who was not feeling very well and didn't want to be bothered with the entertaining of Laval, said that he was himself about to take a holiday in Switzerland and would stop over in Paris and have a chat. This at least is the normal account of what happened; but it is a curious story and other theories and explanations circulate.[31] Vansittart actually makes the absurd statement in his memoirs that he was himself on leave in Paris all through the early days of December and was roped into the discussion at the last minute on 7 December and did not even know Hoare's instructions.[32] This is an extraordinary statement for a permanent head of the Foreign Office to make. Hoare himself, writing his own memoirs in the 1950s, copied this story and blamed himself for not calling a meeting of the Cabinet to discuss the plan.[33] Of course, things are not done in the British Foreign Office in quite so casual a manner as that. The King's permission was needed before both the Foreign Secretary and the Permanent Under-Secretary could be out of England at the same time and that permission was given by the King in writing on 1 December – the letter is in the Windsor archives. On 2 December there was a long Cabinet meeting, which had before it the Garibaldi and other proposals for the peace settlement, although the talk very quickly moved to the oil sanction which was the Cabinet's main concern.[34]

In the discussion Hoare supported the oil sanction and Baldwin postponed any decision on it till after the forthcoming Paris meeting. Vansittart was certainly in London all through this period; in fact he had a last round of intense talks with Grandi, the Italian ambassador, on 3, 4, and 5 December. The Cabinet on 2 December gave Hoare a free hand in the negotiations. He was to bring the Ethiopian question back to the Cabinet only if his peace discussions 'did not offer any reasonable prospect of settlement'.[35] That is the phrase used in the Cabinet conclusion. It is evident that the Cabinet regarded the matter by this stage as essentially one for the specialists.

Grandi's high demands had depressed everyone; he wanted much more territory than had been discussed before and he also wanted a railway from Eritrea right across Abyssinian territory to Italian Somaliland, with a 20-mile-wide corridor. One of the objections to this was that it would cut the French Djibouti–Addis Ababa railway, and the French were not likely to accept it. When this point was discussed in the Foreign Office Eden was rather in favour of the railway – he said it was worth trying – and he remarked that the French had been 'both greedy and grubby' throughout the discussions and it would be no bad thing for them to have to give up something. It was thought that a bridge over the French railway would meet the crossing problem. So the British team went to Paris in a rather depressed mood, with Grandi's steep terms in their heads; and when the actual negotiations in Paris on December 7 and 8 went very well everybody was correspondingly pleased. The British officials found Laval in an accommodating mood, although they had their usual distaste for his proximity. Vansittart wrote in his memoirs that Laval was 'troublesome and displeasing, as were the grubbiness of his white ties and a chain-smoking swarthiness suggestive of sun rather than soap' (a good example of Vansittart's literary style).[36]

Hoare started on 7 December by sharply raising what he called the main issue; this was French action in the event of a mad-dog Italian attack on the British fleet. Laval now gave absolutely definite assurances that France would honour her engagements and he also agreed to immediate staff discussions, which took place during the next few days between British and French military experts. The meeting then turned to the territorial proposals and the British succeeded, as Hoare himself put it, in greatly reducing the scope of the proposed cessions, as proposed recently by Grandi and Laval. They were reduced in fact, in the Danakil and Ogaden areas, to frontier rectification (but one may wonder whether Hoare quite realised how extensive were the territories that could be covered by that term); there was also to be the exchange of a port, either Assab or Zeila, for the territory occupied by Italy in the recent fighting in the eastern Tigre province. And in view of that rectification, wrote Hoare, 'it seemed possible to extend the area in the east and south-west, in which Italy, through a chartered company, would enjoy an economic monopoly and the right of settlement'. The obvious satisfaction of the British officials in Paris at these terms is the important thing to notice. Whether the terms were good or bad, the fact remains that the British officials were pleased with them and were convinced that they had scored a triumph, that they had defeated Laval's more extreme pro-Italian inclinations. An optimistic telegram which was sent to London early on 8 December, said that the first day's talks had shown a real attempt on the part of France to come into line.[37] After the second meeting Hoare was congratulated and told, apparently by Vansittart, that it had been a great day for him.[38] The meaning was evidently that he had secured vital concessions, which Peterson perhaps had been unable to secure in November.

Of course this view may have been too optimistic and they may well have been deceiving themselves; it had still to be seen whether Mussolini and Haile Selassie would accept. But it is quite clear that they were not themselves conscious of surrender. The terms were meant as recommendations, rather than as any kind of arbitral award; they were not intended to be published until they had been considered by the League and the two parties. But by a famous newspaper leak through the celebrated French journalist, Madame Tabouis, they appeared in the Paris press on Monday 9 December, and all over the world on the Tuesday morning.[39]

There is certainly a case to be made out for the proposals. Mussolini's main demand for the control of the basic Ethiopian state was ignored. The definition of frontiers in the Ogaden and Danakil areas was overdue; they had remained undelimited since the 1890s and caused endless disputes, such as that at Walwal. The Emperor would have secured his much-prized outlet to the sea in exchange for the cession of territory, limited in extent, to Italy. The large zone available to Italian development in the south was in an area which was not being made much use of by Abyssinia herself; it was very largely depopulated, it was to remain under the supervision of the League, Italy was pledged to introduce reform into the area, and it was an area undoubtedly crying out for good administration. It must be remembered too that Haile Selassie was a reformer in intention and had agreed on the need for the reform programme under League supervision. But the case, with whatever good points it had, was swept away in the universal cry that Hoare and Laval had rewarded the aggressor by giving him a third of all Abyssinian territory.

In the post mortem that followed the collapse of the plan it was sometimes complained that this was an example of the old diplomacy, and some critics thought that the old diplomatist, Sir Robert Vansittart, was really to blame. In fact the Paris plan was in no sense an example of the old diplomacy: it was rather a proof of the imperfections of the new diplomacy. The old diplomacy before 1914 would have handled the matter very differently. Still, somewhere along the line someone was to blame for a complete failure to anticipate the leakage of the plan and the rich possibilities of misrepresentation that it presented. Even if the terms were academically acceptable, as one can argue, many would say that it was the job of the Foreign Secretary, if not the Foreign Office officials, to understand and prepare public opinion.

The Cabinet agreed that Hoare must resign. His resignation speech of 19 December, largely written by the inevitable Vansittart, was by no means a matter of sackcloth and ashes, and behind the scenes the Cabinet blamed Vansittart. It is very unusual in the British Cabinet minutes to find any criticism of permanent officials but in the meeting of the Cabinet on 18 December there is some very frank criticism of Vansittart's role. Mr Neville Chamberlain, the Chancellor of the Exchequer, said that he thought the Foreign Secretary had been greatly misled by his staff. Mr Ormsby Gore, the First Commissioner of Works, said that Hoare's resignation was a tragic solution; his being caught by M Laval in Paris had involved the Cabinet in a humiliating crisis. In the circumstances he was unlikely to remain. If he did, said Ormsby Gore, he must put a 'British' official at the head of the Foreign Office. It was, he said, the same trouble that had brought down Sir Austen Chamberlain (apparently a reference to Chamberlain's naval negotiations of 1928).[40] Vansittart's career and equanimity were undoubtedly shaken by the crisis, and he had thoughts of resignation. But his basic notions, including that of providing safety valves for totalitarian exuberance, remained unchanged. On 3 February 1936 he presented a weighty memorandum to the Cabinet, advocating the return of some of her colonies to Germany as part of a general settlement, an idea which for a time attracted at least some of his colleagues, including Eden.[41]

But there were no further moves for a compromise settlement over Abyssinia. Eden succeeded Hoare. Laval won a vote of confidence on the Paris proposals in the Chamber of Deputies on 27 December, but was forced to resign on 22 January 1936, to be succeeded as Foreign Minister by M P-E. Flandin. Eden was quite unresponsive when on 10 January Grandi delivered a message from Mussolini enquiring whether he might expect any initiative on the part of Eden or Laval for conciliation in the Committee of Thirteen: Eden replied that he was confident that the British Government could undertake no individual initiative at that time, and he saw no prospect of it in the future. He thought the same was true of Laval. He gave Grandi the same answer to a similar enquiry a week later. The Cabinet did not ask for action. It had treated the details of the 'peace plan' in 1935 as a matter for the experts, and they now had no alternative scheme to offer, apart from the fact that they would receive no thanks for their pains if they did so. Flandin at first agreed with Eden that there could be no 'initiative in conciliation', but it soon became clear that he shared all Laval's yearning for the maintenance of the Stresa front, and he told the British ambassador in Paris on 7 February that Italy 'must be rescued from the Abyssinian muddle and brought back into the European fold'. When the British Cabinet, with an eye on public opinion, decided, at the end of February, to support the imposition of the oil sanction, Flandin was consternated, and Eden had sharp exchanges with him on 2 and 3 March. Flandin refused his agreement on the ground that the oil sanction would lead to Mussolini's repudiation of the Badoglio– Gamelin agreement (which he evidently regarded as being still in force). Then a few days later the momentum, such as it was, in the Abyssinian discussions was lost for ever in the greater excitement and controversy over the German occupation of the Rhineland.[42] Abyssinian resistance collapsed in April, and on 4 May the Emperor and his family left the French port of Djibouti in a British cruiser.

In summary we can perhaps say that if the crisis served any useful purpose in British policy-making it was in demonstrating the fundamental futility of the League of Nations Covenant in the circumstances of the mid-thirties. Economic sanctions were impossible to apply effectively in this type of situation when war was ruled out, when belligerent rights could not be exercised, and when at least three of the world's major industrial powers were neutral and quite willing to conduct profitable business with the belligerents on the side. In the circumstances it was fatuous for the supporters of the League to demand what amounted to Italy's total and unconditional surrender. But this attitude equally ruled out any comfortable compromise settlements which would enable potential critics to extricate themselves without losing too many feathers. The curious thing is that the British Foreign Office, in spite of its realistic professional approach in most matters, had shared some of the current optimism about the League, and the crisis resulted in a grave upsurge of disillusionment, significant for many transactions in the future.

7. Appeasement and 'Intelligence'

DAVID DILKS

The Permanent Under-Secretary of the Foreign Office from 1938 to 1946, Sir Alexander Cadogan, once remarked that there is a 'missing dimension' in most diplomatic histories: the information gathered by clandestine means, and the assessments based upon it, which statesmen weigh when they make their decisions. The importance of such material lies not in its uniqueness but in its value when measured against evidence, or even hints, derived from other sources. In diplomatic and military questions, the main founts of information are the missions abroad, the reports of military, naval and air attachés, scrutiny of the technical press, careful reading of the newspapers, and conversation with those who know other countries well. The heads of British missions in the 1930s were generally men of perception and industry. They did not always forecast correctly the actions of the governments to which they were accredited. Nor did anyone else. They are not to be blamed too harshly for it; Hitler and Mussolini, however fruitfully they might pretend to embody efficiency, resolution, planning, boldness, often made decisions at the last minute (as Hitler did over the invasion of Austria in March 1938) or changed their minds with bewildering effect. Moreover, information had to be gained and transmitted in extraordinary circumstances. For practical purposes, Stalin never had any dealings with British diplomats before the war. Hitler rarely saw Sir Nevile Henderson; in the whole summer of 1939, when Italy had signed the openly offensive Pact of Steel with Germany but was wobbling towards neutrality, Mussolini met the British ambassador twice only, and then for the most frigid of conversations. Because Germany was a more mighty and aggressive power, the difficulties in Berlin mattered more than those in Rome or Tokyo or Moscow. In all four capitals, the normal opportunities to gather good intelligence did not exist. The political and technical press was strictly controlled. The employment of locally-recruited staff made it extremely hard to maintain security inside the embassies. Horrible deaths awaited those suspected of spying.

Largely on the strength of its achievements during the First World War, the British Secret Service had become celebrated for its excellence. In particular, the ability to read the communications of other powers had played a substantial part in Britain's diplomatic and naval policy during the First World War, had helped to bring the United States into that war, and had persisted – despite severe economies in peacetime – into the 1920s. Churchill observed that he attached more importance to intercepted messages of foreign powers, as a means of forming a true judgment of public policy in foreign affairs, than to any other source of knowledge at the disposal of the state.[1] In the spring of 1939, after Italy had seized Albania at a moment when (as he characteristically expressed it) a good part of the Royal Navy was lolling about in Italian ports, Churchill observed in Parliament:

> Here let me say a word about the British Intelligence Service. After 25 years' experience in peace and war, . . . I have always believed, and foreign countries have always believed, that it was the finest in the world. Yet we have seen both in the case of the subjugation of Bohemia and in the case of the invasion of Albania that apparently Ministers of the Crown had no inkling or at any rate no conviction of what was coming. I cannot believe that this is the fault of the British Secret Service. . . . I wonder whether there is not some hand which intervenes and filters down or withholds intelligence from Ministers. Certainly it was so in the case of the German aeroplane preparations four years ago. The facts were not allowed to reach high Ministers of the Crown until they had been so modified that they did not present an alarming impression. It seems to me that Ministers run the most tremendous risks if they allow the information collected by the Intelligence Department, and sent to them, I am sure, in good time, to be sifted and coloured and reduced in consequence and importance, and if they ever get themselves into a mood of attaching importance only to those pieces of information which accord with their earnest and honourable desire that the peace of the world shall remain unbroken.[2]

Alas, much of this represented a delusion. By no stretch of language could the intelligence service of 1939 be described as the best in the world. The references to the unseen hand, which Mr Churchill omitted from *The Gathering Storm*, were widely taken at the time as a thinly-screened attack upon Sir Horace Wilson. Nothing that has come to light in the ensuing forty years lends any weight to this theory, though we understand the more readily why Mr Churchill as Prime Minister insisted that material obtained by the intelligence services should come to him in the shape of 'authentic documents . . . in their original form'. At all events, the purpose of this essay is to make good a little of the missing dimension, to place the secret information in a somewhat broader context, and to ask, first, how well informed were the British about the intentions and capacities of the states which they might have to fight and, secondly, to what degree was the security of Britain's own operations compromised?

Among its other tasks, the Secret Intelligence Service (SIS), under the control of the Foreign Office, was charged to gather information about the military performance and planning of other states. Such information was supplied to the Admiralty, the War Office and the Air Ministry; which also had their own channels. Major Desmond Morton, who worked for SIS in the 1920s, was responsible for building up the Industrial Intelligence Centre, the chief purpose of which was to assess the industrial potential of other powers, with special attention to the manufacture of arms. The IIC had an importance disproportionate to its small size. As the official historian points out, it supplied the economic research and many of the new ideas on which plans for economic warfare were based, and at the beginning of war provided the nucleus of the intelligence department in the Ministry of Economic Warfare;[3] and it was widely believed, not least by Hitler, that the blockade of the First World War had enabled the British inexorably to choke the life out of Germany.

It seems that the intelligence staffs at the three Service departments had little to do with each other. No joint staffs existed. Each of the ministries was estimating separately Germany's strength and intentions. One well-placed observer, then working in the German Intelligence section of the War Office, has remarked on the 'extraordinary disinclination to listen to our reports and much disbelief', nowhere stronger than among military audiences. Too much effort was being devoted in the Service ministries to political intelligence, because officers believed that the Foreign Office was not capable of interpreting political intelligence in terms of military needs. By contrast, the Services themselves were devoting too little effort to technical military advance and scientific innovation in other countries.[4] To complicate the picture still further some of the most significant information reaching the British about Germany came through the private network of contacts maintained by Sir Robert Vansittart (Permanent Under-Secretary of the Foreign Office 1930–37, then Chief Diplomatic Adviser), who records in his memoirs that money for secret intelligence was insufficient, and counter-espionage starved. The head of one section of the intelligence services 'was so short of funds that at times he was reduced to relatives for assistance'.[5]

The British government had no adequate machinery for the collation and assessment of intelligence. In theory, perhaps, the work might have been done by the Committee of Imperial Defence and its sub-committees. In practice, the pressure of other business and the unsuitability of the structure made that impossible. In the nature of the subject, knowledge of the most valuable material had to be kept within a tight circle. The Foreign Office was extremely reluctant to share information or responsibility with the Service departments. So far as the evidence shows, no Prime Minister or Foreign Secretary of the 1930s realised quite how dangerous this position was, at least until 1939.

Even when all these deficiencies are admitted, the broad judgment which the British government formed in 1934 and 1935 was sound. Germany replaced Japan as the most important potential enemy, the one against which the bulk of British preparation would be directed; the armed Services were told to work to a state of readiness by 1939; the near-impossibility of fighting Japan and Germany simultaneously, without an ally stronger than France, was in practice understood. It was correctly anticipated, at least by Chamberlain, that nothing short of an outright attack on American possessions would cause the United States to fight. However, the speed of German rearmament, and therefore the scale of preparation needed on the British side, were not sufficiently understood by ministers or their advisers. The sums which they were solemnly considering in 1934 and 1935 show this clearly, and look almost comic by comparison with the figures of a year or two later. But rearmament on a great scale is a complicated business; if the wrong potential enemy or the wrong date had been chosen, it is likely enough that Britain would not have survived the first twelve months of the war.

The estimates of Germany's capacity to build aircraft, and of her actual construction, varied wildly. Availing himself of statesman's licence, Hitler soon told the British Foreign Secretary to his face that

Germany had already attained parity in the air. What was to become of Baldwin's pledge that in air power Britain should not be inferior to any country within striking distance of its shores? He felt compelled to say that he had been wrong in his estimate of Germany's future building. 'We were completely misled on that subject. . . .'[6] Over the timing and scope of German rearmament in the air, the government had made a serious misjudgment; not exactly the error to which Mr Baldwin confessed, but one which nevertheless was to have most serious political consequences. Fear of the devastation which would be wrought by bombing cut very deep, as anyone who studies the newspapers, debates and official documents of the 1930s knows. German aircraft production soon exceeded British by a very large margin, and it was not until 1939 that the figures became nearly equal again. As the war approached, British estimates of Germany's effective air strength became more accurate, after a period in which they had been much inflated; and the dread of attack from the air undoubtedly played a serious part in the hesitations which beset the British in 1937 and 1938. As Chamberlain was flying back to London from his second meeting with Hitler in September 1938, the aircraft came in low over the sprawl of south-eastern suburbs. He turned to his companion Sir Horace Wilson and said, 'You know, it is a terrible thing to be responsible for the decision as to peace or war, knowing that if it is war there is very little we can do to save all these people.'[7] That Germany had the industrial capacity, the political will, the martial tradition, to produce formidable fighting forces was on the other hand well understood by the British.

It has been remarked that the British government did not possess detailed information about the Italian invasion of Abyssinia in October 1935, the seizure of the Rhineland zone by German troops in March 1936, or the absorption of Austria by Germany two years later. However, all three events had been confidently anticipated; only the method and timing were in doubt. It is improbable that better information would have altered British policy. Everyone believed, after Mussolini had shown himself adamant against compromise in the summer of 1935, that operations against Abyssinia would begin as soon as the rainy season ended. The French had long observed Germany's quiet infractions of the demilitarised status of the zone, and had realised that Germany would try to profit from the tension between Britain, France and Italy. The absorption of Austria had been widely predicted, though many, including Hitler himself, had expected the process to be completed by the rotting away of that state from within, rather than by

outright conquest. A further acceleration of rearmament was announced; but in Eden's time as in Halifax's, Britain did not intend to
oppose by force a German seizure of Austria; and, as Chamberlain
pointed out to Parliament, nothing but force could have made any
difference. Appeasement was not a policy suddenly invented, or
radically changed in its character, during 1937. It is no doubt true that
the policy was more energetically pursued, and given an edge, when
Chamberlain became Prime Minister. That was chiefly because while
the dangers were growing, the day of security in armaments apparently
drew no nearer, to the understandable dismay of ministers; and the
vulnerability of the British on several fronts was as plain to Hitler as to
them. During 1937 one alarming development followed another. In
February, the Foreign Secretary detected as the chief dangers in Europe
'first, Central Europe, and more particularly Czechoslovakia; and
second the chances of some sudden attack by Germany on this country
and France'.[8]

The British had plenty of facts about Germany's striving after
autarchy and search for the synthetic alternatives to raw materials
which she would lack under blockade. They heard a good deal about
the strains in the German economy. Fear that German rearmament
must result either in a foreign adventure or an internal crash was one of
the chief reasons for Eden's apprehensions. In July, Japan resumed her
onslaught upon China. Almost more alarming was the flow of
intelligence from the Mediterranean, the Middle East and North Africa
about Italy's intentions. Quite apart from any general desire to preserve
the peace, Chamberlain had powerful military reasons, constantly
urged upon him by the Secretary of the Cabinet and the Chiefs of Staff,
for trying to purchase better relations with Italy.

The decision to treat Italy as a potential enemy had hardly been
reached when Mussolini gave the order for unrestricted submarine
warfare in the Mediterranean. The British were reading many of Italy's
naval and military cyphers, and a good deal of her diplomatic traffic. In
the next three weeks, the shipping of Britain, Russia, France and the
Spanish government was assailed by submarines, and by aircraft based
in Majorca. After an Italian submarine had tried to torpedo the British
destroyer *Havock*, the Foreign Secretary wished to sink one of General
Franco's cruisers. The Admiralty preferred to concentrate on intense
operations in the areas where British ships had been attacked. Even
before the Nyon conference started, the Foreign Secretary and the First
Sea Lord knew that its purpose was almost certainly achieved. Within a

day or two, the Admiralty learned from the intercepts that Italian submarines had been ordered to break off all offensive action.[9] Groups of destroyers, British and French, patrolled the Western Mediterranean. From time to time, historians have commented with surprise or gratification upon the contrast between the flat and decisive tone which the British adopted in this crisis, and the more normal fumblings. The explanation is not far to seek: unusually, they had hard intelligence in good time; and in deciding to institute the naval patrols, they were exploiting superiority in the only arm in which they enjoyed it. Amidst considerable merriment in Europe, Italy soon asked that her warships should join in the task of hunting her own submarines. Count Ciano in his diary had the hardihood to describe this result as a victory;[10] it is unlikely to have improved the temper of his father-in-law.

So far as we can trace, Sir R. Vansittart's most important source of secret information outside SIS was Group Captain M. G. Christie, who had once been air attaché in Berlin and enjoyed many close contacts in Germany, not least among opponents of Hitler. A good deal of Vansittart's information about the German air force came through Christie, who was acquainted with Goering. It might be imagined that since the British list of probable enemies was increasing, Russia would be looked to as a counterweight. But this was the time of the purges, when the wholesale executions among the higher ranks of the Red Army indicated that Stalin was not expecting to fight a great war in the near future. The British were constantly informed of Russian intrigues and propaganda against the empire;[11] and it is clear that somehow the intelligence services got wind of a possible moving together of Russia and Germany. It may be that the mission to Germany conducted in deep secrecy by David Kandelaki on Stalin's behalf early in 1937[12] reached the ears of the British or French. When Christie saw Goering in February, the latter asked what would be the British attitude towards a German alliance with Russia? When Christie had another long talk with Goering in the summer, this subject did not recur. Nevertheless, the earlier conversation may provide at least part of the reason for which Eden pointed out to his colleagues in December the extreme fluidity of the political situation. If Stalin's reorientation of Russian policy should result in a Moscow–Berlin Axis, he asked, would not this be a more formidable combination than the Rome–Berlin Axis?[13]

By then, the head of Stalin's intelligence service in Western Europe, Walter Krivitsky, had defected. He was interrogated first by the French and later by the American intelligence services. It is probable that he foretold, as he did in the book so opportunely published in the summer of 1939, the making of an agreement between Russia and Germany. It is equally probable that the French intelligence services passed the gist of this to the British; which may explain a reference in a private letter of Chamberlain, just after the seizure of Austria:

> With Franco winning in Spain by the aid of German guns and Italian planes [he wrote], with a French government in which one cannot have the slightest confidence and which I suspect to be in closish touch with our Opposition, with the Russians stealthily and cunningly pulling all the strings behind the scenes to get us involved in war with Germany (our Secret Service doesn't spend all its time looking out of the window), and finally with a Germany flushed with triumph, and all too conscious of her power, the prospect looked black indeed.[14]

Again through the good offices of Christie, Vansittart made considerable efforts to smooth down the worst frictions between the government of Czechoslovakia and the Sudeten Germans before that issue became acute. Goering had said to Christie in the summer of 1937 that Germany intended to become a unified empire: 'England must realise that; in the end it is a question of Czechoslovakia or England.' Christie asked, 'Do you mean you must have both Austria and Czechoslovakia?' Goering replied 'Austria will come into our Reich of its own free will, but if the Czechs remain unyielding we shall have to take Bohemia and Moravia; we do not want the province of Slovakia.' Christie was told by a high official of the German government that these sentiments were undoubtedly those of Hitler as well.[15]

The essential question for British foreign policy in 1938 was to judge whether Germany's demands could and should be opposed; whether Germany would in practice rest content with the absorption of Austria and part of Czechoslovakia. The military intelligence which the Cabinet received was of the most melancholy kind; it encouraged renewed efforts to keep Italy neutral, to retreat before Japanese outrages, and to placate Germany if possible, to postpone war if not. There was nothing to encourage a belief that Britain and France could by guaranteeing Czechoslovakia enable that state to hold out against a

German onslaught, especially after the seizure of Austria had turned the Czech fortifications. Whether this judgment is right is still a matter of dispute among experts; what is certain is that the Prime Minister and Cabinet were much influenced by it. As Chamberlain put it to French ministers, in language equally applicable to the Polish guarantee of 1939, an undertaking to Czechoslovakia would merely constitute an occasion for declaring war on Germany.[16] In sum, the course which the Cabinet followed was that recommended by Cadogan, the new Permanent Under-Secretary of the Foreign Office. Even Vansittart, noting the disastrous effects on British foreign policy of deficiencies in the air, observed sadly, 'For the first time within memory we have been driven from our political course by sheer national helplessness.'[17] In dealing with an opponent as merciless and unscrupulous as Hitler, this left precious little basis for British diplomacy.

It is never possible to recapture in more than a faint manner the atmosphere of a sustained crisis. Whitehall received between the *Anschluss* and Munich a mass of information, much of it stated to spring from the most authoritative sources. Ministers and their advisers knew that the Nazis regarded the planting of false rumour, the steady screwing up of tension and pressure, the threat or fact of mobilisation, as more or less ordinary instruments of diplomacy. In the 'May crisis' of 1938, it was widely believed that Germany had ordered partial mobilisation in order to put pressure upon, or to invade, Czechoslovakia. The Germans vehemently denied it, but as Sir Nevile Henderson pointed out to them, they had equally denied the troop movements immediately before the *Anschluss*. More to the point, expert investigation on the spot by the military attaché of the British embassy in Berlin failed to reveal signs of mobilisation.[18] It is probable that the story was an invention, a wild exaggeration, or a mistake; but the material fact is that the Prime Minister, Vansittart's sources, and SIS, believed it. Chamberlain recorded on 28 May that he had no doubt the German government had made all preparations for a *coup* but in the end decided after British warnings that the risks were too great: 'the incident shows how utterly untrustworthy and dishonest the German government is and it illuminates the difficulties in the way of the peacemaker.'[19]

Small wonder that the head of SIS should admit a little later in the summer that it was especially difficult to interpret the German situation. In addition to the constant flood of facts and opinions received from the embassy in Berlin, numerous other capitals and all the usual sources in London, the Foreign Office was receiving much material through Group Captain Christie. Some of this came from German officials and was heavily depended upon by Vansittart.[20] Many of them pleaded for a clear warning to Hitler, which the Cabinet consistently declined to give. No one could guarantee that a threat would prevent war. Indeed, some of those who asked for it intimated that until a war began, Hitler could not be ousted. All the objections to war at that time and on that issue therefore remained unaltered. Chamberlain and Halifax were never convinced that they could afford a gamble. Some of the reports stated that Hitler's ambitions were limited to the seizure of the Sudetenland or a larger part of Czechoslovakia; others that he had definitely decided to attack Czechoslovakia and then proceed further east. This Chamberlain reported to the King on 13 September, by which time SIS had informed the Prime Minister that all German missions had been notified of a decision to invade Czechoslovakia on 25 September. As he pointed out in the same letter, the British ambassador in Berlin had on the other hand steadily maintained that Hitler had not yet made up his mind to violence.[21]

If we could now show that there was an overwhelming probability of a successful revolt in Germany; that Hitler would have been deterred by a warning; that a diplomatic alignment of Russia, France and Britain would have frightened Hitler into moderation; or that the preparations for war were merely theatrical, a bluff which would be abandoned under pressure; then it might be possible to say that for lack of a sufficient flow of dependable intelligence, or for want of nerve in following its conclusions, the British had thrown away the last and probably the only opportunity to bring down Hitler cheaply. The evidence presently available does not justify so firm a judgment. Whether Hitler's assessments were rational and well founded is beside the point. Much of the secret intelligence conveyed the warning that he was prepared, even keen, to fight. British ministers did not know with certainty whether such orders had been given; but they knew enough of Hitler to realise that it was quite possible, and the policy pursued in September 1938 was not reached because of any failure to understand that issue. During his visits to Germany, Chamberlain came to the conclusion that when Hitler threatened war, he meant what he said.[22] Nothing we have learnt since then disproves it.

Before Daladier went to Munich, the French secret service had advised that Germany was not only ready to attack Czechoslovakia but prepared for a general war.[23] A trusted informant told the counter-espionage section of the intelligence services, MI5, on 28 September that Hitler would order an immediate air attack on London if Britain declared war.[24] In the penultimate stage of the crisis, and rather surprisingly encouraged by Gamelin's account of the French army, Chamberlain did take the step which he had resisted steadfastly for the previous six months, and warned Hitler that if after all the concessions made he insisted on marching against Czechoslovakia, France would fight and be joined by Britain.[25] It was after receiving this message, but before knowing that the Royal Navy had been mobilised, that Hitler softened his terms a little.

The Führer, as we know, was apt to rely more heavily upon his intuition than upon the formal processes of diplomacy. He and his henchmen had however a sharp appreciation of their opponents' weaknesses, philosophical and physical. He was exploiting against the British their own oft-proclaimed principle of self-determination. Because the telephone communications from Prague to Paris and London passed through German territory and were tapped, he could measure, as Benes spoke with Czechoslovakia's representatives in those capitals, the success of this campaign. As Hitler put it to representatives of the German press a few weeks later, he was convinced that slowly but surely the nerves of the gentlemen in Prague would be broken. 'Thank God they can all read German', he exclaimed. For proof, Germany was able to listen to the telephone messages,

> and so we could every day confirm how this was working . . . I have almost every day been able to confirm the effect of our propaganda, especially our Press propaganda . . . Gentlemen, we have actually this time with propaganda in the service of an idea acquired 10 million people with over 100,000 square kilometres. That is something enormous.[26]

The German government made no secret of these intercepts, and indeed used them openly in the final stages of the negotiation. The Germans even supplied the British with copies, which were translated at once in the Foreign Office. They indicated that Masaryk in London and Osusky in Paris had kept in touch with members of the respective oppositions, and had been hopeful that the British and French governments would be pushed by public opinion to support Czechoslovakia more strongly.[27] It is probable that the British government also was tapping the telephones of the Czechoslovak

Legation, for Chamberlain recorded on 9 October that he had found
the four days of debate in the House after Munich a trying ordeal

> especially as I had to fight all the time against the defection of the
> weaker brethren and Winston was carrying on a regular conspiracy
> against me with the aid of Masaryk the Czech Minister. They, of
> course, are totally unaware of my knowledge of their proceedings; I
> had continual information of their doings and sayings which for the
> nth time demonstrated how completely Winston can deceive himself
> when he wants to and how utterly credulous a foreigner can be when
> he is told the thing he wants to hear. In this case the thing was that
> 'Chamberlain's fall was imminent'![28]

We read that the art of decoding messages was highly developed in
Hitler's Germany. The State Secretary, Weizsäcker, estimated that the
German government was reading half the telegrams sent to foreign
diplomats in Berlin and remarked in his memoirs on the disadvantages,
as well as the advantages, of this situation. While it was useful to know in
advance what a diplomat would say before he entered the room, and
easy to check whether he reported the conversations correctly, it was
extremely difficult to hold confidential talks with representatives of
countries whose cyphers the German government had broken; and
clearly this included its Italian partners. The most secret British code
was not known to the Germans. Since the British ambassador,
Henderson, has been stiffly criticised for his indiscretions on the
telephone in the last few days of peace, it is perhaps right to add that he
was careful not to implicate Weizsäcker in telegrams containing delicate
information.[29] Though the British did not read most German diplomatic cyphers, they did intercept some of the traffic; in which, not long
after Munich, the Prime Minister was put out to find disobliging
references to himself.[30]

It is time to consider the most serious known breach of British security in
this period. The efficient Italian intelligence services had recruited
Signor Constantini, a servant in the Chancery at the British embassy in
Rome. He abstracted documents and cyphers, which were taken away,
photographed and returned. Duplicate keys to the safes were apparently possessed by the Italian authorities. These leakages continued

until the declaration of war in 1940.[31] The chain of events reveals an almost incredible carelessness, a sublime confidence in British methods, and incontestable damage to British interests. Moreover, the interests of Greece, Yugoslavia, Austria and other powers were compromised; and Italy was able to use the leakage not only to read British intentions and appraise British weakness, but also as a lever in her relations with Germany, and more surprisingly still, with Soviet Russia. There is only one gleam of comic relief; Signor Constantini had been employed by the British embassy since 1914 and having grown grey in the service, found his loyalties rewarded by an invitation to proceed with his wife, at the expense of the British government, to London for the coronation of 1937. We must trust that his absence interrupted the flow of purloined papers for a week or two.

The late Professor Toscano, who in his capacity as editor of the Italian diplomatic documents had examined much of the original material, stated that a large part of Mussolini's foreign policy must be related, directly or indirectly, to the interceptions and decoding of the intelligence service. These documents, regularly transmitted to him, were the ones which he read most avidly, underlining passages and inscribing abundant marginal notes after the style of the Kaiser Wilhelm II. The fact that the Italian government was reading British documents is, always according to Toscano, essential for an understanding of some of the Duce's attitudes towards England – at times audacious, at others resentful, and at still others inflexible. For instance, Mussolini was defiant when informed by the British ambassador of the movement of the Home Fleet to Gibraltar in 1935, because he had been reading the signals exchanged between the Admiralty and the Mediterranean showing the shortage of ammunition and the Fleet unprepared for immediate action. The same authority believed that Mussolini's policy throughout the Ethiopian campaign was largely based on interceptions of British material.[32] It is only too probable that he read, then and later, unflattering descriptions of himself and of the venality, unscrupulousness and opportunism of Italian policy. Indeed, one of the most powerful advantages of reliable intercepts is that they provide a guide to the fears and expectations of other powers. We are told by the British official historians that reading of some of the Italian cyphers threw a useful light on Italy's policy during the Abyssinian crisis and the Spanish Civil War.[33] However, there can be no question that the advantage lay on the Italian side.

Early in 1936, the new Foreign Secretary, Eden, circulated to the

Cabinet a memorandum entitled 'The German Danger', to which was attached a collection of reports from the embassy at Berlin. They contained, he wrote, clear evidence of the steady and undeviating development of German policy under Hitler; whose ambitions were defined as the militarisation of the whole German nation and economic and territorial expansion so as to absorb all those of German race who were citizens of neighbouring states. He concluded that it was 'vital to hasten and complete our own rearmament', and within a few weeks the Cabinet did indeed agree to a vastly larger programme. Mr Eden suggested that the Cabinet consider whether it would be possible, while this rearmament was pursued, to make some arrangement with Hitler's Germany which would be both honourable and safe and lessen the increasing tension in Europe. The paper concluded with a special plea for secrecy: 'There is evidence that there have been serious leakages of the information obtained by His Majesty's Ambassador at Berlin; and reports have been spread as to the nature of his views. Continuance of these leakages must prejudice his own position and the sources of his information.'[34]

This memorandum was obtained by the Italians. It has often been assumed that once again the leakage took place in Rome. In fact, the paper was almost certainly secured in London.[35] It is not clear how. Of course, it may have been stolen or photographed by an agent. It probably reached the Italian ambassador in London, Count Grandi, in the late summer, about eight months after it was written. That was the period after the failure and withdrawal of sanctions, when the Spanish Civil War had just begun. There were plenty of people in London desperately anxious to repair the breach, and secure Italian neutrality if not active friendship. It is not inconceivable, in other words, that someone let Count Grandi have the document as an act of policy, in the hope that it would provide Italy with food for thought before she aligned herself more closely with Nazi Germany. However, this is mere speculation. To add another strand to the story, we know that at some stage the Italian intelligence services in Rome, or Signor Constantini as an act of private enterprise, started to provide copies of the stolen British material to the Russians.[36] Whether any similar collaboration extended to the activities of the two intelligence services in London we do not know with certainty; if it did, Count Grandi might have secured the memorandum by that method, for the Russians had at least one well-placed agent within the Foreign Office.

Mussolini saw what a serviceable weapon had been placed in his hands. Hating the British for leading the pack against him at Geneva, despising them for their failure and timidity, anxious to prevent Germany and Britain from drawing together, the Duce lost no time in telling a visiting German minister that from Eden's memorandum it was clear that 'England intends to live with Germany only in so far as it will give her time to achieve rearmament'. Count Ciano told the German Foreign Minister that the documents proved Britain's intentions towards Germany; news which caused Neurath no distress, for he was jealous of Ribbentrop's mission to London and remarked that after reading the documents the Führer would be 'able to discard with more peace of mind those remnants of the illusions which Ribbentrop inspired in him, according to which England wished to follow a policy of friendship and sincere collaboration with Germany'. In conversation with Hitler, Ciano said that Germany must have no illusions; British policy was directed as actively against Germany as against Italy, and if there were no positive indications of the fact, that was because England was trying to gain time to complete her rearmament. At this point he handed to Hitler the Cabinet paper. Attached to Mr Eden's pithy memorandum was a telegram from the ambassador in Berlin, Sir Eric Phipps, which characterised the German government as composed of dangerous adventurers. This document, we are told, produced 'a profound impression' on Hitler. When Britain built her empire, he said tartly, she too was led by adventurers; today she was governed merely by incompetents. Germany and Italy must take an active role, go over to the attack against the democracies, and execute this manoeuvre on the tactical field of hostility to Bolshevism. Britain would fight Italy or Germany or both if she could do it with impunity. Both powers represented a threat to Britain's established interests. If England continued to form offensive plans and merely sought to gain time to rearm, the dictatorships would defeat her on her own ground, since their rearmament was proceeding more rapidly than Britain's. Hitler added that he intended to attain such a state of military preparedness as to give absolute assurance of success.[37] Immediately after this meeting, basing himself upon the notes provided by Ciano, Mussolini proclaimed the Rome–Berlin Axis.

It need hardly be argued that the strategy which the British were following – namely, of keeping matters as quiet as possible while Britain gained strength from rearmament – turned to a peculiar degree upon the secrecy of communications, just as the military policy of the British government in this period of heightened danger and strained resources depended upon the ability to create and sustain uncertainty in the mind of the potential enemy. 'We must keep the dictators guessing', as the phrase ran in those days. Chamberlain, and Cadogan, would occasionally retort that all the guessing was done by the British. In this they spoke more truly than they knew.

Despite the theft of Lady Drummond's necklace from a locked red box in the embassy, an investigation which revealed all manner of shortcomings, and a known leakage of remarks made in the strictest confidence by the Prince Regent to the British minister in Belgrade,[38] the Italian penetration of the cyphers and the embassy's safes continued unchecked. At one point, probably early in 1939, Ciano brazenly handed to the Prime Minister of Yugoslavia copies of two despatches sent by Sir Ronald Campbell to Lord Halifax. The Prime Minister showed them to the Prince Regent; who, in the habit of giving Campbell the most secret information, sent for the British minister, and told him to go to London forthwith and inform the Foreign Secretary that the security of the Foreign Office had been penetrated. Prince Paul himself, it appears, wrote to Halifax and sent the letter by messenger. Long afterwards, Campbell informed him that it had taken over a year to unmask the agent 'who had worked in the archives section of the British Foreign Office and had had a Russian mistress. She had delivered the documents to the Russian Embassy [in London] and Soviet Ambassador Maisky had turned them over to Italian Ambassador Grandi to make political mischief as he saw fit.'[39] It is not easy to test the authenticity of this account. That Russia had an agent in the Communications Department of the Foreign Office is certain; but he was unmasked less than a year later, and not as a result of this disclosure. Nor do the published accounts of the agent in the Communications Department fit this description in other important particulars.

This supply of British material was naturally used by Italy as the needs of her own policy required. On Mussolini's instructions, the German government received a copy of a telegram sent by Lord Halifax to the ambassador in Berlin in May 1939, stating that Britain would honour her guarantee to Poland; if there were a war between Poland and Germany, Great Britain and France would certainly intervene and such a war would lead to the destruction of the Nazi regime and the liquidation of the German Reich. Professor Toscano comments that before Italy signed the Pact of Steel with Germany a few days later, the Italian government thus had authoritative guidance. However, the

Duce's thoughtful gesture was on this occasion unnecessary; the telegram had been sent, at the request of the British ambassador in Berlin, in one of the less secure cyphers, so that the Germans would be sure to read it.[40] That summer, Mussolini entertained the King of Greece, and conceived himself to have made a powerful impression. He had, but not in the sense imagined, for the King of Greece while in London expressed himself in unflattering terms about Mussolini. The telegrams went to Rome, of course; they were read as usual by the Italians; Mussolini was furiously resentful; and, unbelievable as it seems, this fact had 'an important influence' on Italy's decision to attack Greece in 1940.[41] If that be so, there was perhaps a certain retributive justice in it. The attack on Greece proved a costly and humiliating fiasco for Italy, damaging to the prestige of the state and the Duce; eventually the situation had to be retrieved by Germany; the diversion contributed to the delay in Germany's invasion of Russia in 1941 and prevented the conquest of Moscow.

We may turn for consolation to a more successful exercise of British diplomacy. A standard account refers innocently to the 'startling accuracy' of information available to the Foreign Office in the winter of 1938–9,[42] when the British were trying to prevent the conversion of the anti-Comintern Pact into a triple alliance between Germany, Italy and Japan. The fact is that in 1937, and almost certainly up to the war, the British were reading some of the Japanese cyphers. Since some of the Italian traffic was also being read, the British were well informed of the relationships between the three powers. The Foreign Office had the text of the secret agreement signed between Germany and Japan when the anti-Comintern Pact was concluded. It knew at the end of 1937 that there was nothing so definite as an alliance between the three powers, though rumours to the contrary frequently appeared.[43] It is likely that the British decided in October 1938 to bring the Anglo-Italian agreement promptly into effect in order to make the conclusion of a three-power military alliance more difficult, and the point was not lost on the Italian Foreign Minister. As is well known, the celebrated Russian spy Richard Sorge, later created a hero of the Soviet Union, had attained a remarkable position in the German embassy in Tokyo and through his German and Japanese contacts was able to send to Moscow intelligence of the highest quality over a long period. Probably relying on this source, Litvinov (still Russian Foreign Minister) told the British ambassador in Moscow in November 1938 of his certain knowledge that the anti-Comintern Pact was to be transformed into an alliance.[44]

With reliable information provided by intercepts, the British moved sure-footedly to take advantage of Japanese hesitations. The ambassador in Tokyo had good sources of his own, one of whom was Shigeru Yoshida, lately returned from the Japanese embassy in London and after the war to be Prime Minister.[45] However, the Foreign Office had still better information. The British government adopted a stiffer attitude towards Japan at the end of 1938 and early in 1939. Meanwhile the *News Chronicle* of London, a journal believed to derive more than occasional inspiration from the Russian embassy, had been publishing articles about the negotiations between the three powers. The account appearing on 17 January 1939 was in essentials true; it explained that the Italian government now desired very early signature of this pact, whereas the Japanese wished to sign only if the alliance were directed against Russia.[46] From a Russian point of view, therefore, the intelligence derived from Sorge, almost certainly supported by material obtained by at least one Russian agent in London, and probably complemented by the leakage in Rome, showed during these months that the Japanese might fight Russia but were not at all anxious to fight Britain and the United States, whereas Germany was trying hard to embroil the Japanese in an obligation against Britain. This would give plausibility to German protestations that an attack against Russia was not intended. Already by January 1939 these were signs of some thaw in relations between Soviet Russia and Nazi Germany. To adapt a phrase of Stalin's, they ceased to heap pails of manure on each other.

For the British, the secret intelligence was comparatively reassuring about Japanese intentions, and most disconcerting about German. It is not difficult to see both strands of British policy at that time and in the ensuing nine months. These transactions were taking place shortly after the visit paid by Chamberlain and Halifax to Rome. An episode arising from that visit would indicate strongly that Russian intelligence, however good in particular subjects, was not comprehensive where Britain was concerned; for the Russian government was given to believe that in conversation with the Duce, Chamberlain had referred with approval to the possibility of German expansion at Russia's expense in the Ukraine. This is quite untrue; and British and Italian records show it clearly.[47] But there is every reason to think that the Russian government swallowed the version which it had been given. It was perhaps the more ready to do so because of the collaboration between the two intelligence services in Rome.

Step by step, sometimes in harmony with his American colleague in Tokyo, the British ambassador pursued his campaign with the Japanese government. The Foreign Secretary, making an oral statement to the Cabinet in mid-February from sources 'of a highly confidential character', correctly surmised that Japan did not wish to do anything which might lead Britain and America to stop selling her the many essential supplies which she must buy from them for the production of munitions. Moreover, Japan did not wish for commitments which might automatically involve her in any distant adventure upon which her allies might embark; whereas Germany no doubt desired to be able to threaten Britain with simultaneous war in the North Sea, the Mediterranean and the Far East.[48] The Japanese Foreign Minister, a day or two later, said that his country had no intention of joining the Rome–Berlin Axis or of assuming obligations in Europe, and if any new agreement were made it would not be directed against British interests.

The most it would be prudent to claim is that these British interventions, supported by an American statement that a three-power alliance would make the worsening of relations between Japan and America irremediable, reinforced Japan's powerful reasons for caution. The negotiations between the three powers dragged on in a desultory way throughout the spring and summer. Germany and Italy, eventually losing patience, signed the Pact of Steel in late May. Failure to make satisfactory terms with Japan had a most important effect on the course pursued by Hitler. Indeed, he claimed in a letter to Mussolini that the Japanese willingness to accept an obligation only against Russia

> would have in the prevailing circumstances only a secondary interest for Germany and in my opinion, for Italy also. She had not, however, agreed to an equally definite obligation against England, and this, from the standpoint not only of Germany but also of Italy, would have been one of the decisive factors.[49]

In the three months after Munich, the British government received most alarming reports about Germany's intentions and power. By mid-

January 1939, there were further serious evidences from secret sources. Their importance derived from two main factors; all the reports were agreed in judging Hitler to be 'barely sane, consumed by an intense hatred of this country, and capable both of ordering an immediate aerial attack on any European country and of having his command instantly obeyed'.[50] Moreover, many of the informants gained credibility because they had forecast Hitler's policy with considerable accuracy in the summer of 1938. There had been a shift of emphasis of the intelligence; whereas in November and December it had seemed most likely that if German expansion continued, it would be to the east, by January it seemed as probable that Germany would attack in the west. Neither the authors of the reports nor those who commented upon them in the Foreign Office pretended to read Hitler's mind with certainty. Though the surviving German evidence is by no means comprehensive, it seems highly probable that the information about plans for an air attack on London or a German descent upon Holland was deliberately planted, with skill and care, by Germans who wished Britain to accelerate her rearmament still further, and pledge herself to a continental commitment. There is no question that the secret information received in December and January did play a substantial part in both policies. On 26 January, Bonnet announced that in a war in which Britain and France were both involved, all the forces of Britain would be at the disposal of France, just as all the forces of France would be at the disposal of Britain. Four days later, Hitler said that if Italy went to war, Germany would march with her. On 6 February Chamberlain announced that the solidarity of interest by which France and Britain were united was such that any threat to the vital interests of France 'from whatever quarter it came, must evoke the immediate co-operation of this country'.

This gloomy mid-winter had one feature lacking in the events of the previous summer. The ambassador at Berlin had then taken a more optimistic view of German policy than that contained in the other reports reaching the Foreign Office. But he was absent from his post from November to the first part of February. Immediately upon his return Henderson reported that the Germans were not contemplating any immediate adventure.[51] The sum of other information at the end of February had become somewhat less alarming. Chamberlain's government would certainly not have gone to war to prevent a German economic, and to a large degree political, dominance over central and south-eastern Europe. What the British feared, and with good reason, was a Germany which by internal subversion or outright conquest would so strengthen herself as to be invincible if she turned westward, or irresistible if she threatened that course. Hence the decision of February 1939, taken well before the seizure of Prague, to plan at last for an army on the continental scale. Hence also the decision, later in the summer, to qualify the pledges given to Australia and New Zealand that an adequate battle fleet would, in the event of war in the Far East, be sent out to Singapore regardless of circumstances in Europe.

By the end of February, information from secret sources suggested that Hitler had for the time being abandoned the idea of precipitating an immediate crisis. However, 'reports have recently reached us pointing to the possibility of a military occupation of Czechoslovakia. Hitler is clearly preparing for every possible eventuality.'

As for Italy, there had been an abnormal amount of military activity but it would be premature to deduce that Mussolini had decided on war in the immediate future; 'in this connection there are reports from sources that cannot be ignored that instead of risking a major war by pressing her demands on France, Italy might seek cheap glory in the annexation of Albania.'[52]

These are not snippets culled from a wide variety of sources in order to show that the British government was well informed. The quotations come from a telegram summarising all the information available to the British government, covering less than two-and-a-half pages in the printed documents and also including a good account – more accurate than anything available to the American government – of the state of negotiations between Germany, Italy and Japan. On the other hand, the information of the American government pointing to a crisis or even a war by the end of March was perhaps more reliable than that of the British.[53]

Henderson's return to Berlin immediately revived the sharp contrast between his own view and Vansittart's. This was not simply a result of the ambassador's desire to look on the bright side. When he sent a despatch to the Foreign Office in early March, anticipating a period of relative calm in the immediate future, the head of the Central Department (whom no one ever accused of undue tenderness towards Germany) minuted: 'This view is supported by our most recent summary of information from other sources.'[54]

It is clear from the notes written on this paper by Cadogan on 11 March and Halifax on 12 March that neither had firm information about an impending German stroke against Czechoslovakia though, as we have seen, they had received warnings of the possibility. Probably influenced by Henderson's despatch and telegrams, and by his own rising confidence in the strength of the western position, the Prime Minister had meanwhile given a cheerful account of affairs to the press. This made Chamberlain himself, and the government, look ridiculous within a few days. Naturally enough, Vansittart criticised Henderson's failure to foresee the occupation of Prague and the extraordinary official optimism which was in consequence being disseminated on the eve of the catastrophe:

> I myself received and transmitted three separate warnings nearly a month before the events happened. I had hoped that sufficient action might be taken in Berlin to serve as a deterrent, although it was clear that Hitler's mind was already made up. But nothing seems any good; it seems as if nobody will listen to or believe me. I shall never know why.[55]

This lamentation does not do justice to all the difficulties. That Vansittart and others had received reports indicating a seizure of Czechoslovakia is true. But even reports from the most authentic sources had pointed to the several choices open to Hitler, and his unpredictability. Moreover, it was clear that on military and political grounds the British were not going to fight if Hitler took the remainder of Czechoslovakia. On the other hand, they were prepared to adopt the advice that a stand must now be taken. There is no doubt that a greater sureness about rearmament, the widespread revulsion at Hitler's tearing up of his own promises, the disappearance of the view, which at earlier stages had been entertained by Vansittart himself and many others in the Foreign Office, that Hitler was essentially concerned with uniting Germans within one Reich, all contributed much to the new mood. Chamberlain denounced Hitler's faithlessness in ringing terms.

Discussions were opened with a number of governments to see how Germany might be confined, quickly confirming the mutual hostility between Poland and Russia. The capture of Memel gave plausibility to rumours that Germany would attack Poland in the near future, rumours which reached London through the embassy at Berlin and from a newspaper correspondent who had close contacts with the German general staff.[56] The reports were wrong. A British guarantee might well have been given to Poland even if such reports had not come, though it would not have been so quickly given or necessarily in the same form. The announcement which Chamberlain made in Parliament on 31 March shows that the British government, though aware of the rumours, did not have hard evidence to support them.[57] The guarantee was not given as a result of military advice, or in defiance of it. It was the kind of step for which many of Britain's German informants had often asked; a warning to Hitler that assault on another country would mean war. Given the British commitment to the Low Countries and France, and the extension of the guarantees during April to Romania, Greece and Turkey, the British government had served notice that a German or Italian aggression would mean a general war. Whether the dictators could be convinced that the guarantees meant what they said, or that the British had the military capacity to make them effective, was another matter.

Britain was less unwilling to fight in 1939 than 1938, and felt that the risk could in the last resort be run. Had ministers guessed that the French army would collapse in 1940, they might well have thought differently. The stream of intelligence about Germany's economic difficulties and shortage of foreign exchange inclined the British to believe in the need for deterrence – since those domestic conditions might well incline Hitler towards war as a diversion – and decreased their reluctance to risk war, since Germany seemed ill-fitted to enter a long struggle. Hence the importance of ensuring that Britain was not so weak that she would be knocked out in the early stages of a war, after which superior economic strength and power of blockade would bring eventual victory; or so the theory said.

The reputation of SIS and the Foreign Office suffered in Whitehall because some of the reports circulated in the spring of 1939 proved misleading. The official historians say that the Foreign Office incautiously circulated such papers.[58] That is perhaps severe. In the atmosphere of crisis, when it was believed that the next aggression might take place at any moment, the Office had little choice but to send round reports which seemed to come from good sources. Early in April, for example, an informant connected with the German war ministry gave news of a plan for an unannounced air attack, but this time against the fleet, not on London. It seems that Admiral Canaris, head of the German military intelligence service, was responsible for planting this false story. This he no doubt did in order to provoke a strong British reaction and show of readiness. Another alarm, to the effect that German submarines were patrolling the Thames estuary, showed how necessary was a recasting of the machinery, for which the service departments had long been anxious and which the Chiefs of Staff were now able to insist upon.[59] The staff of the Foreign Office were naturally anxious that it should remain the main source of political intelligence. Nevertheless, deficiencies in the system were acknowledged. 'I quite see', Cadogan had written a month or two earlier, 'that there is a situation that must be remedied. There are, as is pointed out, a number of sources of information, including our official telegrams and despatches, and SIS reports, copies of all of which are simply flung round, without comment, to the various Departments, who have varying ability to test and appraise them. The result is that they all exercise their ingenuity upon them with, no doubt, conflicting conclusions.'[60]

A representative of the Foreign Office had already begun to attend some meetings of the Joint Intelligence Sub-Committee of the Chiefs of Staff. In April, after the Albanian crisis, a Situation Report Centre was established under the chairmanship of the Foreign Office. The other three members came from the directorates of intelligence of the service departments. Its purpose was to collate information from abroad and issue daily assessments, in order that any emergency measures should be based only on carefully co-ordinated information. The Situation Report Centre and the JIC were merged later in the summer, with the Foreign Office's representative presiding from the beginning. The functions of the new body were enhanced. In addition to preparing daily reports and weekly commentaries, it was charged to consider any further measures which might be thought necessary 'to improve the efficient working of the intelligence organization of the country as a whole.'[61] Here was a development of the first importance to the British war effort.

Clearly this machinery brought a considerable advance. What it could not do was to make good, at least in the short run, deficiencies in the supply, of which perhaps the most remarkable occurred in this summer of 1939. Although the possibility of an agreement between Germany and Russia had not been overlooked, the service departments and the Foreign Office had no authentic evidence of the negotiations actually proceeding. It was suspected that the rumours of *rapprochement* were being exploited as propaganda by Germany to influence Japan and dissuade the western powers from committing themselves too deeply to Poland, and by Russia to induce the British and French to reach agreement on her terms. The 'head of the German secret service' (presumably Admiral Canaris) was reported in late June to have said that negotiations were in progress, that Russia would not support Poland in war but would supply Germany with raw materials. Other reliable sources said the opposite.[62]

On more than one occasion, and presumably through leakage from the Foreign Office, the German embassy in London secured accurate information about their rivals' negotiations at Moscow. It was not until September, and then thanks to the revelations of Krivitsky, that the American government provided evidence pointing to a Russian agent in the Communications Department of the Foreign Office. The offender was tried in secret and sentenced to ten years' imprisonment. We do not know with certainty how long he had been working for Russia, or how much information he had passed over. Since Cadogan's diary describes the revelations of the enquiry as 'awful', we must conclude that this was another serious breach of security. The entire staff of the Communications Department was dismissed or moved.[63]

Krivitsky also pointed to another Russian agent in the British government, coming from a political family, whose work was connected with the Committee of the Imperial Defence (this is not the exact title given in the published accounts, but that is the part of the British government which most nearly fits the title given). This agent has often been identified as Donald Maclean, whose father had been a Liberal Cabinet minister. It is not clear at what date he began to spy for the Russians, though he may well have done so from the moment of his entry into the diplomatic service. He was at this time serving as a secretary in the embassy in Paris, and had access to highly confidential material; but the rest of the description does not fit. Even after recent revelations, we may still have something to learn about Russian penetration of the British government before the war. It is established that the egregious Guy Burgess was collecting information on behalf of Russia from at least one junior official of the Foreign Office in 1939.[64] It does not seem to have been of much value; whether he had more useful sources is obscure.

When Ribbentrop descended upon Moscow, therefore, the British and French ambassadors knew nothing of the purport of Molotov's conversations with the Germans, which had been proceeding fitfully for some months. In London, the House of Commons was hurriedly recalled on 24 August. The Parliamentary Under-Secretary at the Foreign Office, Mr R. A. Butler, not surprisingly found himself asked what 'our intelligence was up to?' The paper drawn up by the Northern Department in reply referred to the notorious difficulty of obtaining reliable information from Soviet sources. Such information as had come thence had tended to show that a political agreement was unlikely; material from German sources had been much more plentiful, but contradictory. Reports from third parties 'usually came from persons of questionable reliability'. The last part of the memorandum expresses admirably the problems of those who, without the unimpeachable evidence of intercepts, are asked to anticipate policies likely to be followed by governments conducting their affairs in the strictest secrecy and adept in clouding their real intentions:

> We find ourselves, when attempting to assess the value of these secret reports, somewhat in the position of the Captain of the Forty Thieves when, having put a chalk mark on Ali Baba's door, he found that Morgiana had put similar marks on all the other doors in the street and had no indication to show which mark was the true one. In this case there were passages . . . in many of our reports which told against the probability of a German–Soviet rapprochement. We had no indications that these statements were in general any less reliable that those in a contrary sense: and from an impartial consideration of Soviet interests, as far as we could estimate them by trying to put ourselves in the position of the Soviet government, it seemed to us likely that they were reliable – at least to the extent that isolation, rather than a rapprochement with Germany, seemed indicated as the probable alternative policy to one of agreement with France and this country.

'The fact remains', Sir O. Sargent noted rather frostily below, 'that we were never told that the Germans and Russians had started negotiations with one another – which was the only thing that mattered.'[65]

Had the British been receiving timely and circumstantial intelligence about the talks between Germany and Russia, at least their tactics might have varied. The substantial points upon which, as Lord Strang describes, the west gave way to Russia might have been conceded more swiftly; the argument of those who said that the west must make terms with Russia because the alternative would be an agreement between Hitler and Stalin would have been greatly strengthened (Chamberlain on 21 May described this reasoning as 'a pretty sinister commentary on Russian reliability');[66] and the British and French would have been more reluctant than ever to hold confidential military discussions with the Russians. The conduct of foreign policy in a parliamentary democracy differs fundamentally from that in a rigid dictatorship. Stalin and Hitler could and did make somersaults which could not be performed by any parliamentary government wishing to survive. It is not clear that even close knowledge of the conversations between Berlin and Moscow would have enabled the west to outbid Germany. Apart from the obligations of the guarantee, it was inconceivable that Britain and France could invite Soviet Russia to take eastern Poland, the Baltic States and Bessarabia, and hard to see how with any lesser offer they could have competed with Hitler. Nevertheless, that is not the end of the matter. Had the British known, for instance, what the American embassy in Moscow knew throughout, they could have exploited the knowledge in their dealings with the Japanese, which reached a point of acute crisis in the summer of 1939; in their manoeuvrings with Italy; and by skilful leakage they might have made it harder for Germany to conclude the agreement. Whether any such tactics would have affected the eventual outcome remains doubtful. It was not an instance where the forces were evenly balanced. No amount of good information would have overcome the fundamental facts: Russia's unfitness to face a great war, to which Stalin's purges had contributed notably; and Britain's weakness on land.

The essential British difficulty in the summer of 1939 was, as the Permanent Under-Secretary at the Foreign Office expressed it, to steer between provocation and an impression of impotence. 'If you are too bellicose, you provoke Dictators into doing something irrevocable. If you are too passive, you encourage them to think they can do anything.'[67] So far as the formal declarations went, the position was clear enough. On the other hand, the British heard repeatedly during the summer of 1939 that their new-found resolution was hardly credited by Hitler and discounted by Ribbentrop. Proposals from German contacts for a show of resolution are generally held to have fallen upon barren soil. That is not entirely so. They came at the moment when Danzig was likely to be the focus of the next crisis and all the information of the British government pointed to a quiet time until about the third week in August. As the Prime Minister remarked, it was nearly always the predicted crisis that did not materialise; 'the curious accident by which we shall have a gigantic fleet exercising in the North Sea all August and September may possibly have some influence in this direction.' And again at the end of the month:

All my information indicates that Hitler now realizes that he can't grab anything else without a major war and has decided therefore to put Danzig into cold storage. On the other hand he would feel that with all these demonstrations here, mobilization of the fleet, territorials and militiamen training, bombers flying up and down France, he must do something to show he is not frightened. I should not be at all surprised therefore to hear of movements of large bodies of troops near the Polish frontier, great flights of bombers, and a crop of stories of ominous preparations . . . That is part of the war of nerves . . . .[68]

The British government tried during 1939 to conduct a policy which did not bring war unnecessarily, was firm but unprovocative and showed Germany and Italy that if they behaved acceptably, their legitimate needs would be met. The dividing line between such flexibility and mere weakness must always be a difficult one to draw. The Prime Minister believed that Hitler did not know whether the British meant to attack him as soon as they were strong enough; for if he did think that, it would naturally be his policy to begin the war when it suited him rather than wait until it suited his opponents. Chamberlain remarked that in various ways he was trying to get the truth on this point conveyed to the only quarter where it mattered;[69] but there are enough recorded remarks of Hitler, from the conversation with Ciano in 1936 to the Hossbach meeting in 1937, his observations to Mussolini after Munich and to his leading military men on 22 August, to indicate that there was force in Chamberlain's reasoning. It may very well be that Hitler more than suspected a determination on the part of his 'hate-inspired antagonists',[70] Britain and France, to fall upon Germany as soon as their rearmament made it convenient. Of course, he may have spoken in this sense simply to rationalise a lust for violence and a determination to go to war as soon as might be. Hitler's assumption was that Germany would expand her territory and economic power substantially by one means or another. He was broadly correct to believe that the balance of armed strength would tilt in Germany's disfavour the longer he delayed. The British, following exactly the same calculation, for the same reason wished to postpone the issue. If Hitler and Mussolini did judge that the democracies would fall upon Italy and Germany as soon as it was militarily feasible for them to do so, each was making a profound mistake which proved fatal for himself and his regime.

This is to stray beyond the immediate issues of 1939. Because of his confidence that the British defences became stronger with every passing month, Chamberlain did his utmost to hold the position, on the grounds that longer war was put off the less likely it was to come at all.[71] By mid-August, that supposition looked a good deal less certain. The sum of information about Hitler's desires seemed to indicate that he wished for the familiar free hand in the east, in which event there was no means of accommodating him.[72] The British had excellent information, which they were shortly to exploit with skill in prising Italy away from the Axis, about the state of play between Mussolini and Hitler. Even before the Foreign Office knew anything of Ribbentrop's impending *coup* with Molotov, Halifax had suggested that the Prime Minister should send a warning in the clearest terms. By the time the terms were agreed, London had news of the Nazi–Soviet pact. Chamberlain was thus able to state that the British would fight if Poland were invaded, and that an agreement between Germany and Russia, whatever its terms might be, would make no difference.[73]

On the night of 27 August Chamberlain recorded in 10 Downing Street, 'I feel like a man driving a clumsy coach over a narrow crooked road along the face of a precipice.'[74] Even when the war had begun, he did not conclude that Hitler had been deliberately practising a deception to the last while he matured his schemes, because the British had good evidence (which we now know to have been correct) that orders for the invasion on 25 August were actually given and then cancelled at the last moment. Chamberlain believed that Hitler had seriously contemplated an agreement with the British and had worked seriously at proposals which 'to his one-track mind seemed almost fabulously generous'. At the last moment, some brainstorm had taken possession of him, perhaps stirred up by Ribbentrop, and once he had set the machine in motion he could not stop it:

> That, as I have always recognised, is the frightful danger of such terrific weapons being in the hands of a paranoiac.
>
> Mussolini's proposals were I think a perfectly genuine attempt to stop war, not for any altruistic reasons, but because Italy was not in a state to go to war and was exceedingly likely to get into trouble if other people did. But it was doomed to failure because Hitler by that time was not prepared to hold his hand unless he could get what he wanted without war. And we weren't prepared to give it to him.[75]

✩

The intelligence services, it is manifest, were starved of resources for too long. The vital function which good intelligence can perform, and the serious errors which may flow from patchy or wrong information, were insufficiently understood until 1939. On the broad plane of military intelligence, inadequate attention had been paid to Italy, Japan, Russia and France. Grave misconceptions prevailed about the excellence of the French army. The ability of the Polish army to hold out against a German onslaught was somewhat overrated, partly because none could measure before the autumn of 1939 the effects of well-directed air power in support of armour.

British information had proved defective about the earlier stages of German naval rearmament, and Germany had been able to sustain a scale of spending on armaments which in the earlier 1930s had been thought impossible. On the other hand, well informed about Germany's economic frailties, the British had made detailed plans for a rigorous blockade and the severance of German exports. Chamberlain always took a close interest in the economic weapon, and attended meetings of the committee which planned economic pressure on Germany. It had been estimated in 1938 that German stocks would not last long after the outbreak of war. By the time of the seizure of Prague, however, the estimates were substantially revised, though Germany still had serious deficiencies in certain crucial commodities. By August 1939, it was thought that Germany might be able to maintain her war effort for as much as fifteen or eighteen months. Material from documents captured after the war indicates that many of these calculations were soundly based.[76] In practice, Germany's swift military successes in 1939 and 1940, which gave her physical possession of a large part of Europe and economic control of practically all, invalidated the assumptions.

It is easy to multiply examples of faulty information or anticipation. Yet in the wider sense of the term 'intelligence', which embraces the understanding as well as the acquisition of facts, the British perhaps judged the prospects at the outbreak of war less badly than did their enemies. They did not make the miscalculations which led Germany to ruin against Russia, or Japan against the United States. They appreciated the mixture of braggadocio, sensitivity and military weakness which made up Mussolini's policy, and the danger which Italy would pose if fighting at the same time as Germany and Japan; the indecision in Tokyo and reluctance of most Japanese leaders to become embroiled in war with Britain; the formidable strength of Germany, a greater power than Britain in population, space, mineral resources and industrial output.

In July 1939, the Government Code and Cypher School said that it could hold out little hope of mastering, even if war came, the sophisticated Enigma machine by then being used for many of the most secret German communications. Later in that month, a momentous meeting took place between the Polish and French experts and the head of GC and CS, its chief cryptanalyst, and Colonel Menzies, soon to succeed Admiral Sinclair as head of SIS. The Poles explained how they had unlocked the secrets of Enigma, though not in its later version. They even produced examples of the machines, giving one to the British and one to the French.[77] Acts of policy commonly generate unintended effects. Had the British not committed themselves to Poland and given the guarantee, it is improbable that the Poles would have made this present of the machine and invaluable technical help. It did not enable the British to read the German traffic at once; but that task was much facilitated and by dint of intense work during the winter, the British began to secure valuable results in April and May 1940, at the time of the campaign in Norway and the battle in France and the Low Countries.

It would exaggerate to say that the possession of good intelligence by itself enables wars to be won. But it is precisely when the resources are stretched and the tasks many, when the forces are evenly matched and the issue trembles in the balance, that good intelligence and sensitive interpretation matter most. We may debate endlessly whether it would have been wise for Britain and France to declare war on Germany in 1938. In that year, Britain did not have the chain of radar stations; the Ultra material, which the mastery of the Enigma machines eventually provided; or the Spitfires and Hurricanes. By 1939 she had two of those assets in part. By 1940 she had two in good measure, and a growing command of the Ultra material. Each of these strengths reinforced the others. When we remember that the margin of survival could hardly have been more narrow in 1940, it is imprudent to say flatly that the decision to postpone war was wrong. Had the British appreciated the magnitude of their peril at an earlier date, had they embarked on an ambitious rearmament programme in 1934 instead of 1936, it might all have turned out otherwise.

8. The Moscow Negotiations, 1939

THE LATE LORD STRANG

EARLY in June 1939, as a junior official of the Foreign Office,[1] I was sent to Moscow to help the British ambassador, Sir William Seeds. The ambassador was at that time engaged, together with his French colleague, M Naggiar, in a negotiation with the Soviet government, represented by the recently appointed People's Commissar for Foreign Affairs, M Molotov.

Although this had been far from the original intention of the British government, the outcome of the negotiations was turning out to be the possible conclusion of a comprehensive mutual assistance agreement with the Soviet government.

Why was this negotiation embarked upon? What was its objective? Why did it fail? What were the consequences of failure?

The answers to these questions, like most others connected with the so-called period of appeasement, are matters of controversy.

There has so far been no comprehensive study of these events by a professional historian. For this, a good deal more research is needed, as well as access to the Foreign Office archives for the years leading up to 1939. The best account we have is still that contained in *The Eve of War, 1939*[2] published for the Royal Institute of International Affairs. But there has been no lack of partisan studies attacking or defending the records of the statesmen responsible for these transactions. The Russians, for example, obsessed by the nightmare of capitalist coalitions, have maintained the thesis that the real object of the hypocritical policy of Great Britain and France was 'to conclude a firm agreement with Germany and "channel" aggression to the East'.

Meanwhile, however, as further documents, especially from the German side, have become available, historians like Mr A. J. P. Taylor and Professor W. N. Medlicott have put forward fresh interpretations of the negotiations, and in particular of the place they hold in the events that led to the outbreak of the Second World War. In the light of all these views, and of what I myself wrote about it in 1956,[3] I propose to take a fresh look at this still puzzling episode.

As with so much in the 1930s, one has to go back to the First World War and to the Treaty of Versailles. What Europe had to face was a revolt by a resurgent and revengeful Germany, now under the demonic leadership of Adolf Hitler, against the provisions of the Treaty. There was an ambition to conquer living space for Germans in Eastern Europe, and to gain for Germany the dominant status of a Great Power in Europe and in the world. Whether Hitler worked upon a specific plan to achieve these results has recently been questioned, and there is much to be said for the view that, within a clear general purpose, he did not look more than one move ahead, but improvised his prospective objectives as events suggested or as his gambler's intuition directed. The state of Europe favoured his success. There was a widespread belief, inculcated by the Germans themselves, that Germany had well-founded grievances, and there was a hope that if these could be redressed Europe could be pacified and got back to business. The two victor European Powers, Great Britain and France, had suffered a failure of strength and of will. A third victor, the United States, was in isolation. Both Italy and Japan were acting side by side with Germany against the established order. The remaining European Great Power, the Soviet Union, defeated in the war, but recovering strength, was held to be outside the concert, something alien, untrustworthy and disruptive, and, since the drastic civilian and military purges of 1936–38, unlikely to be militarily effective.

The independent states created or aggrandised by the peace treaties, lying between Germany and Russia, were exposed to intimidation by Germany. They feared Russian assistance as much as they feared German aggression. Poland, in particular, owed her independence and territorial extent to the simultaneous post-war weakness of Germany and Russia. Her position became precarious when these two neighbours, both of whom had large territorial claims against her, recovered their strength. The difficulties which in the end obstructed the Moscow negotiations arose in great part from the existence of these debatable lands.

Hitler had a further advantage. He could play on the fear of war in the minds of his prospective victims and of his possible adversaries. One way was boastfully to exaggerate the strength of his land and air forces.

In fact, unprepared for a long war, his aim was, if possible, to gain his ends without war, or at the risk of a small or short war. For the democratic governments, a general war, the kind of war which they could remember, with its grim tale of slaughter, and now with the added horror of massive air-bombardment, would be the supreme calamity. They felt that if only a general settlement in Europe, redressing Germany's legitimate grievances, could be achieved without recourse to arms, a new concert among the Great Powers might ensure a peaceful and prosperous future for Europe. This was no doubt a grievous error. Yet they did realise, if too late, that conciliation was not enough, and that in order to hope to keep Germany within peaceful courses, they would have to rearm. But in practice, the drive for conciliation still outran measures of deterrence. Churchill's injunction, 'Arm to parley', was not sufficiently followed. By the spring of 1939, rearmament had made good progress, especially in the air, but even then the surplus of power required to sustain an active political and military role was lacking.

Chamberlain had been conscious of this. Writing to a correspondent in January 1938, well before the Czechoslovak crisis, he said, 'In the absence of a powerful ally, and until our armaments are completed, we must adjust our foreign policy to our circumstances, and even bear with patience and good humour actions which we should like to treat in very different fashion'.[4]

This so-called policy of appeasement has been held to have been, in its origins, humane and rational in conception, if, in the end, tragically disastrous in execution. Its practitioners were, as Arnold Toynbee has said, 'high-minded men who had gone to unusual lengths in putting ethical principles into political practice in the jungle of international power-politics'. That policy has recently come under cool and dispassionate scrutiny by historians. There has been a questioning of the easy gibes about the 'guilty men' and the 'Cliveden set'. Professor Medlicott has said that 'appeasement should now be added to imperialism on the list of words that no scholar uses'. Mr A. J. P. Taylor, in his private opinion at the time a strong anti-appeaser, has said, as a historian, that it is a mistake to write off the appeasers as stupid or as cowards. He sees them as men confronted with real problems doing their best in the circumstances of the time, and as men who recognised that an independent and powerful Germany had somehow to be fitted into Europe; and he suggests that, in this recognition, later experience might indicate that they were right.

But the fact was that, from the end of 1937 onwards, Chamberlain undertook a positive international role for which he had not the necessary military power. With an uncertain France as sole ally, he was setting himself a task beyond his strength. The tragic issue of his Czechoslovak initiative, as it emerged in the final stages at Berchtesgaden, Godesberg and Munich, was the consequence of insufficiently credible military power and political will. I was at all three meetings, and the most powerful impression left on my mind was the imperative need for a massive rearmament programme.

Again, with the British guarantee to Poland, means were not adequate to ends, and Chamberlain was at that time under strong pressure from press and from Parliament to do something about the situation. His new purpose was clearly stated in his speech at the Albert Hall on 11 May 1939: 'We are not prepared to sit by and see the independence of one country after another successively destroyed.'

These were times when Europe was again and again shaken by threat or rumour of war. But in March 1939 matters once more came to a head. The rump of the Czechoslovak state fell apart. On 15 March, Hitler occupied Prague and declared a protectorate over what had been left of Bohemia and Moravia. He also forced Lithuania to surrender Memel. In the same month, Mussolini prepared to move into Albania, and Franco joined the Anti-Comintern Pact. The British press, which had all but unanimously applauded the Munich settlement, now, with similar unanimity, condemned the occupation of Prague and the incorporation of a non-German people.

Hitler had been wooing Poland in order to keep his Eastern frontier quiet while he meditated an attack on the West. He now repeated to Poland the offer of a deal over Danzig and an extra-territorial road- and rail-link across the Corridor, accompanied by proposals for a guarantee of the German–Polish frontier and a hint about a common anti-Soviet policy for the Ukraine. The Poles refused. Hitler changed his tactics and turned the heat on Poland. There was a scare about Romania which turned out to be unfounded. News came to London by way of a British press correspondent from Germany of an impending German invasion of Poland.[5] This was not confirmed and later proved to be untrue; but Chamberlain acted on it.

He obtained the assent of Colonel Beck, the Polish Foreign Minister, to a parliamentary statement, to be made in association with France, Poland's ally, to the effect that if Polish independence were clearly threatened and if the Polish government resisted with their national forces, the British government would at once lend the Polish Government all the support in their power.

Other guarantees were scattered abroad, to Romania, to Turkey, and to Greece. This Polish guarantee was made reciprocal, and towards the end of August it was embodied in a formal treaty. It was in virtue of this that we went to war.

Thus, the direct and explicit guarantee, not afforded to Czechoslovakia in 1938, was given to Poland in 1939, in an area where, even in the days of her strength in the nineteenth century, Great Britain had met with rebuffs. An impressive case can be made against it. It was hastily improvised and issued without adequate examination of its military implications. It carried with it no promise of concrete military assistance, and, when war came, none was available. Its credibility was not enhanced by past British and French behaviour over Czechoslovakia. It tended to stiffen Polish resistance to British suggestions for concessions to Germany. It weakened the British and French bargaining position with the Soviet Union. It encouraged Hitler to decide to attack Poland, and seek an accommodation with Moscow.

One of the aspects of the guarantee was strongly criticised by powerful voices in Parliament immediately after it was proclaimed. Why not have insisted upon Polish consent to the passage of Soviet troops over Polish territory as a price for the British guarantee? But Chamberlain had carried through one Munich and could not face the British public, in its present mood, with another. Having abandoned Czechoslovakia, he could not abandon Poland, however basely Poland had behaved in sharing the spoils of Munich, and even if she was now seen to be standing in the way of the construction of a peace front in Eastern Europe.

But one further crucial step Chamberlain did take in this decisive month of March 1939. The Soviet Union had been left out at Munich. She could no longer be left out now that the crisis had moved to Eastern Europe. Now, albeit with hesitation, he made an approach to Moscow. With hesitation because, as he noted at the time: 'I must confess to a most profound distrust of Russia.'[6]

His first idea was for a joint declaration by the United Kingdom, France, the Soviet Union and Poland in which the four Powers would undertake to consult together immediately for joint resistance to any threat to the independence of any European state.[7] This suggestion for a peace front was accepted by the Soviet Union, provided that both France and Poland joined in. It was rejected by Poland. Colonel Beck would not have any truck with the Russians. He believed that this might drive Hitler into an act of aggression against Poland. With the British guarantee, when it came, he felt strong enough to stand aloof, in independence of both Berlin and Moscow.

For this intransigence, the Poles were to suffer in the war immeasurably more, but to shine more nobly, than the more pliant Czechs. In the end, both Czechs and Poles found themselves held fast in the Soviet orbit, and the Poles lost their non-Polish eastern territories to the Russians. Would the Poles have been worse off than they now are if they had been willing to work with the Russians and had had an agreement to let the Russians in if the Germans attacked? Who can tell? And if one asks oneself whether we did well to go to war for Poland, one comes back to the firm fact that, with the decisive uncovenanted involvement of Russia and the United States, Hitler's regime was destroyed, and Europe was freed from the foul infection of Naziism. These things might have been achieved in other ways. But they might not. Merely to have stopped Hitler at some stage would not necessarily have sufficed to destroy him. In order to do that, perhaps there was no other way but war. The military power of Germany had first to be shattered. Perhaps it was not an unnecessary war after all. Perhaps that, when all is said, is the justification for the guarantee to Poland in March 1939.

If we ponder upon this act, an act, shall we say, almost of desperation, we might recall some words of the nineteenth-century French historian, Albert Sorel. The history of the English, he says, 'is full of alternations between an indifference which makes people think them decadent and a rage which baffles their foes. They are seen . . . turning from peace at any price to war to the death.'

It would be tedious to recount in detail the complex and exasperatingly slow-moving course of the negotiations with the Russians in Moscow, from the first British approach in March 1939 until the suspension of the Anglo-French discussions with Molotov on 2 August.[8] But since there has been a good deal of misunderstanding about this, even among historians who should know better, it may be useful to see what point the negotiations had reached when they were suspended, and what was the content of the draft agreement which had so far been achieved. That content was very considerable. It amounted to an attempt to create a new and comprehensive system of security in Europe, both East and West, in the face of German ambitions.

There was first of all a direct obligation of mutual assistance among the three Powers. If one of them were the victim of aggression by a European Power (that is, Germany), the other two would render all effective assistance.

Secondly, there was an obligation relating to certain other states, chiefly border states, both in the East and in the West. These were states whose independence and neutrality one or more of the three Powers felt obliged to defend. This obligation was a good deal more difficult to define. What the agreement said in effect was that if any such state were the victim of aggression by Germany, and if any of the three Powers became involved in hostilities with Germany in defence of such state, then the other two Powers would again render all assistance.

The states concerned were to be named in a secret protocol. They were Estonia, Latvia, Finland, Poland, Romania, Turkey and Greece, in the East, and Belgium alone in the West. The Soviet government declined to include Holland and Switzerland. Nothing was said in the draft about the consent of the defended state having to be obtained for the receipt by it of military assistance. As to this, the defending state would be the judge. Russia, for example, would be the judge as regards military assistance to the Baltic states; the consent of the Baltic states would not be required to Soviet military action in their defence.

Further, in the case of the named states, the draft agreement provided for the case, not only of direct aggression, but also of what was called 'indirect aggression'. The term 'indirect aggression' was to be defined in the text of the agreement. On this definition, only partial agreement was reached.

Thirdly, there was an all-important article which provided that the three governments would concert together as soon as possible to settle the methods, forms and extent of the military assistance to be rendered by them, with the object of making such assistance as effective as possible.

It was further said that this main political agreement would enter into force simultaneously with the agreement about military assistance. The two agreements would form a single whole.

Here then was the main structure of the draft political agreement, so far as it went, and it went a very long way. Nothing so comprehensive had been negotiated with the Soviet Union before; and not until the war-time conferences from 1943 onwards was anything of like scale to be negotiated in future.

This was the end result of many weeks of discussion. At the start, the two sides had been far apart. The British Government had wanted help from the Soviet Union to build up security in Eastern Europe, in reinforcement of their guarantee to Poland; but they wanted this to be arranged without disregarding the susceptibilities of Poland and Romania. They still hoped to maintain impartiality between Russia and Germany; and they had been anxious not to do anything which might provoke violent action by Germany. As so often, they aimed at objectives which were mutually irreconcilable.

The history of the negotiations for the political agreement is the story of how the British government were driven step by step, under stress of Soviet argument, under pressure from Parliament and the press and public opinion polls, under advice from the ambassador at Moscow, and under persuasion from the French, to move towards the Soviet position. One by one, they yielded points to the Russians. In the end they gave the Russians the main part of what they asked for. Everything in the essential structure of the draft agreement represented a concession to the Russians. Molotov made only three concessions of any substance, the chief of which was the waiver of a direct guarantee by the Western Powers to the Baltic states.

Molotov, though ruthless in his questioning, was, except on a few occasions, patient enough with our continued resistance to his proposals. In a letter to the Deputy Under-Secretary at the Foreign Office, I confessed that on the whole the negotiations had been a humiliating experience. Time after time, we had taken up a position and a week later we had abandoned it; and we had had the feeling that Molotov was convinced from the beginning that we should be forced to abandon it.[9] At our final meeting on 2 August, he expressed strong displeasure at a statement made in the House of Commons by Mr R. A. Butler, the Parliamentary Under-Secretary, which, he said, had grossly misrepresented the Soviet attitude regarding the Baltic states. It was on this bitter note, and on the subject of indirect aggression, that the political conversations were suspended.[10]

The question of defining indirect aggression, raised formally by the Soviet government early in July, became the central theme in our discussions. The conception of indirect aggression, though not in the precise Soviet sense, had already arisen during the Anglo-Polish conversations in March and April. Molotov had put the crux of the problem to Sir William Seeds on 29 May in relation to the Baltic states.

At the end of our negotiations, the point at issue between the two sides might look to be a narrow one. It was agreed by the Western Powers that if, for example, Germany, by threat of force, constrained Latvia to abandon her independence or neutrality in favour of Germany, so that Germany had now, so to speak, a 'borrowed frontier' with the Soviet Union, then, if the Soviet Union, without Latvian consent, intervened in Latvia in order to restore the situation and in consequence became involved in hostilities with Germany, Great Britain and France would render her effective assistance. So much was agreed, at any rate in principle. This was to go very far. But the Soviet government wished to go further. If, they said, Latvia voluntarily, or under persuasion, abandoned her independence or neutrality, even without threat of force from Germany, the Soviet government wished to be free to take the same action in Latvia, and they wished Great Britain and France, in this case also, to accept the same obligation. The French would have agreed to this, but the British government thought it went much too far in the sense of interference in Latvian affairs, and they were unable to agree. Whether or not, if negotiations had been resumed, a compromise formula on this point could have been found, I do not know, but I believe that it could. Alternative drafts were in fact prepared in London, for use later if opportunity offered, but the talks were never resumed.

It was natural enough that the British and Russians could not look at the fate of the Baltic states in the same way. On the Russian side there was a comprehensible, if obsessive, sensitiveness to the threat which could arise to the vulnerable approaches to Leningrad through Latvia or Estonia; while, on the British side, one need only recall that we have even now not recognised *de jure* the absorption of the Baltic states into the Soviet Union.

With the opening of the military conversations on 12 August we leave the sphere of word-spinning and come to realities.[11] The object of these conversations was to settle by agreement the methods, forms and extent of the military assistance to be afforded by both sides. The Soviet government, for their part, held firmly to the view that, if they were to make an agreement with the Western Powers such as that already almost completely drafted, they would need to be satisfied that the military contribution by their partners would be precisely defined and, if it came to war, would be adequate, prompt and effective. They wanted to know in advance how much, how soon, and where: how many divisions, how much artillery, how many tanks, how many aircraft, how many vessels of war. They required us to disclose our military plans to them before it was certain that we were going to be allied by treaty. The French and British delegations did their best to comply; their war-plans were described; but the outcome could not be satisfactory to the Russians. In particular, the Russians, among a whole range of naval measures, wanted us to undertake to despatch a naval force to the Baltic and to secure the use of bases in Finland, Latvia and Estonia. Had this demand been pressed to the point of decision, it is most unlikely that it could have been agreed to. But the breaking point came over Poland. The Russians asked how they were to come to the assistance of France and Great Britain if these two Powers were at war with Germany. The Soviet Union had no common frontier with Germany. The Russians would have to move into and through Poland in order to reach the Germans. They would have to know the Polish military dispositions, and the Poles would have to know theirs.

To these questions there was no satisfactory answer. The Poles, in this as in everything else in the crisis, were adamant in their refusal to comply, in spite of representations from the British and heavy pressure from the French. The Polish Foreign Minister, Colonel Beck, told the French ambassador: 'I cannot admit that in any measure whatever there can be discussions about the use of part of our territory by foreign troops. This is for us a question of principle. We have no military agreement with the Russians. We do not wish to have one.'

By 17 August, the military talks had reached a deadlock, although there were further contacts between the French and the Russians until 22 August.[12] The next day, 23 August, the Nazi–Soviet Pact was signed in Moscow.

When, on 14 August, Marshal Voroshilov put the question to the British and French military delegations whether the Red Army would be allowed to cross Polish and Romanian territory, he said that this was the 'cardinal point to which all other points are subordinate'. Why, one may ask, was so obvious a question not put by the Russians at an earlier stage in the protracted negotiations, but left until so late a date, especially since there was evidence, by June at any rate, that a German attack on Poland was being prepared? The point was a familiar one. It had been raised, for example, by the Russians several times since early 1937 in connection with Czechoslovakia. Is it possible that the Russians thought, in spite of all past evidence, that the British and French, having taken the negotiations thus far, had assured themselves, or had at least good hope, of Polish and Romanian consent? Or did the Russians, well knowing what the Western response would be, hold this decisive point in reserve, to be used as a sure ground for bringing the talks to a halt at any time that suited them? We do not know the answers to these questions. But in their later official statements, the Soviet Government maintained that it had been the attitude of the Western Powers to the question of the entry of Russian troops into Poland which finally convinced them that France and Great Britain were not in earnest in their negotiations for a treaty, and that this left them with no alternative but to come to terms with Germany. Was this a true statement? Or ought one rather to think that the military conversations were, on the Soviet side, little more than a pretence or, in the words of an American historian, 'a shameless deception', for the short time that they lasted? I have never thought so. The Russians may well have said to themselves: 'It is most unlikely that the British and French will come up with satisfactory answers, but let us at any rate make sure.' Indeed, as late as 16 August, Molotov told the United States ambassador that the Soviet government attached great importance to the negotiations with Great Britain and France.[13] These were aimed at specific mutual obligations to counteract aggression. They expected the negotiations to succeed. What the outcome would be depended on others as much as on the Soviet government; but much had already been done towards success, and the negotiations were continuing.

Molotov, we were to find in later times, could on occasion be open and responsive. Was this one such occasion?

All the same, one cannot help suspecting that Stalin himself had for long hankered after an accommodation with Germany, if a way could be found. The failure of the Anglo-French discussions found him that way.

It has been asked why the British and French took so long over the political talks when it took only a few days to conclude the Nazi–Soviet Pact. Although tentative soundings had been going on between Berlin and Moscow intermittently for months past, there was now a new initiative from Germany, and a decisive one.

But it is right to note that the Nazi–Soviet Pact was not a treaty of mutual assistance like the projected treaty with the Western Powers. It was an agreement for non-aggression. The Russians gave no undertaking to afford military assistance to Germany. What they undertook to do was to maintain neutrality, a very different and much less demanding obligation. And in return they received an assurance that the Germans would not encroach on the Soviet sphere of influence in the Baltic states and in the eastern marches of Poland.

The Russians thus secured both present immunity from attack from Germany, and the promise of the free hand, and more than the free hand, which they had vainly sought from the British and French. For the present, they stood in no risk of having to face the Germans alone; and if in future they did have to meet the Germans, they would meet them well in advance of their own borders. At the time, this seemed to them a much better bargain than the Western Powers could offer. Little wonder that they closed with the bargain so soon; or that Hitler, who was in a great hurry to launch an attack on Poland, accepted the Soviet draft of the treaty without reservations as it stood.

I now return to the questions which I asked at the beginning of this paper. Why was the operation embarked upon? What was its objective? Why did it fail? What were the consequences of failure?

I do not propose to spend time on the more extreme conspiracy theories which have been developed on either side. It is hard to believe, as communist writers assert, that Great Britain and France were scheming, by a class-based or an ideologically based conspiracy, to involve the Soviet Union single-handed in war with Germany. Nor, on the other side, are there good grounds for thinking that the Soviet Union was seeking above all to promote a war between the Western Powers and Germany. It is most unlikely, too, as some historians have been inclined to maintain, that the Soviet government intended all along to come to terms with Germany, and used the negotiation solely as a means of attracting favourable offers from Germany; though it must be said that the replacement of Litvinov by Molotov in May 1939 was a pointer in this direction that could not be overlooked.[14] The truth seems to be that none of the three Powers had clear policies for solving the insoluble German problem.

Since the war, neither they nor the Americans have ever known what to do about Germany. They do not know even now. In 1939, the three Powers were groping on unfamiliar ground in a situation of danger and great complexity. While the three-power negotiations were going on in Moscow, both sides had been in contact with the Germans, particularly in the economic sphere. The last thing that any of the three parties wanted was a general war in Europe. They came together in an attempt to establish a deterrent which would save Europe from this. But, to start with, that was the bare extent of their agreement. In the beginning, they differed widely both in the interests they were concerned to serve, and in the method by which the deterrent should be framed.

Great Britain and France were closely leagued in defence of the West. Though grimly aware of the danger they ran, they thought that in the early stages they could hold a German attack, if it came, and impose a state of static warfare as in the First World War. In this, as 1940 was to prove, they were mistaken. But, in the East, other considerations applied. If Germany attacked in the East, she could in time gather strength which would make her dominant in Europe and much more formidable if then she turned on the West. In the hope of deterring the Germans, Great Britain gave guarantees to Poland and to other states; and in order to reinforce such deterrence, she sought at the outset to persuade the Soviet government to undertake to help Poland if Poland were attacked, and if she wanted to be helped. The Western Powers feared for Eastern Europe and in particular for Poland; and the British had aimed originally to bring the Soviet Union in as a subsidiary.

The Soviet government would have none of this. They insisted on equality and reciprocity. They did not fear, as such, for Poland, for whom they had no sympathy and upon whose territory they had wide and strongly held claims. They feared to have to face the Germans alone. They feared for themselves. Had not Hitler made it clear that, reviving earlier German imperial aspirations, he was bent on conquering living space in the plains of Eastern Europe? Sooner or later, his attack would come. The last thing that the Soviet Union wanted was to get imprudently involved in war with Germany through, as the saying went, 'pulling the chestnuts out of the fire' for the Western Powers or for Poland. They had less than no interest in maintaining the inequitable eastern frontier of Poland, which had been imposed upon them by the Treaty of Riga in 1921. Like the British, too, they had grave preoccupations in the Far East, amounting in their case to hostilities with Japan on the Manchurian–Mongolian frontier.[15] As for relations with the Western Powers, the Soviet chargé d'affaires in Berlin confided to a German colleague on 10 August that the negotiations with Great Britain and France had been entered into without enthusiasm, but the Soviet Union had to protect herself against the German threat, and had to accept assistance wherever it might be offered. On this interpretation, the Soviet government would think it worth trying to see whether such help could be found. As we have seen, the arrangement which was attempted was not adequate, either politically or militarily. Their own security, which was what the Russians were intent on, would not be safeguarded by the kind of agreement afforded by the Western Powers. And apart from that, could those Powers be relied upon not to leave the Soviet Union in the lurch, to fight the Germans alone? The course taken by negotiations encouraged Hitler to judge that they would not succeed, and he gambled on this in bringing off his most spectacular *coup* so far, his agreement with the Soviet Union. Once again, as had repeatedly occurred in the last two centuries, there was found to be a common interest between the two countries; and this now in spite of what had been too confidently regarded as an unbridgeable ideological gap.

One ought never to underestimate the national Russian basis of Soviet foreign policy.

As for Hitler, disappointed in his attempt to persuade Japan to enter into a general military alliance with Germany which would have served to neutralise the threatened Anglo-French-Soviet coalition, he had now, as an alternative, to try to break up the threatened coalition by detaching the Soviet Union from it. This he succeeded in doing.

Professor Medlicott has suggested that military considerations may well have been a decisive factor in the abortive discussions of the Western Powers with the Russians.[16] There is a good deal to be said for this. There was little enthusiasm on either side. Each took a sceptical view of the military prospects and political reliability of the other. The British never seem at any time to have seriously relied on the prospect of Russian help. Chamberlain wrote of the Soviet Union on 26 March that he had 'no belief in her ability to maintain an effective offensive, even if she wanted to'.[17] This is what the experts, military and civilian, told him. And indeed, during the military conversations in Moscow, Marshal Voroshilov admitted that the Red Army was not well disposed for offensive operations. On 22 May, a Foreign Office memorandum, while arguing, on balance, in favour of a three-power mutual assistance agreement, stated that 'it has to be considered that the actual material assistance to be expected from the Soviet Union is not very great', and it spoke with distaste of having to collaborate with a 'dishonest and incompetent partner'.[18]

When one thinks of Stalin's root-and-branch purges of the Soviet armed forces in 1937 and 1938 (when, for example, they lost three of their five marshals, and seventy-five out of eighty members of the Military Soviet), when one remembers the poor showing of the Red Army in an offensive role in Finland in 1939 and 1940, when one recalls the reluctance of the Soviet Union to face the prospect of war with Germany in 1941, and the early disasters suffered by the Red Army, even in a defensive role, in that war when it came, there is, in the light of after knowledge, some justification for such scepticism on the Western side. That, in the event, the Western Powers should have been ready to act without Russia in going to war for Poland proved their seriousness of purpose, but it also suggests that they did not set great store by the help that might have been given by the Russians. Indeed they seem to have thought so little of the Soviet Armed Forces that, crazy as it may now seem, they actually contemplated the possibility of getting involved in hostilities with Russia over Finland early in 1940.

On the other side, the British ambassador in Moscow found Litvinov in the spring of 1939 convinced that France was 'practically done for'; and the few British divisions that could immediately be sent to France were, in Soviet eyes, derisory.

In the absence of Soviet documents, we cannot be sure what the Soviet government were thinking, even if documents would reveal this. But, as it happens, there is confirmatory evidence from Stalin's own mouth.

At supper in Moscow on the night of 15–16 August 1942, when Churchill asked Stalin why he had 'double-crossed us at the beginning of the war', Stalin replied that he thought England must be bluffing; he knew we had only two divisions we could mobilise at once, and he thought we must know how bad the French army was and what reliance could be placed on it. He could not imagine that we should enter the war with such weakness. On the other hand, he said he knew Germany was certain ultimately to attack Russia. He was not ready to withstand that attack.[19]

Then again, during the Teheran Conference in November 1943, Stalin told Churchill that in the winter war against Finland, the Soviet Army had shown itself to be very poorly organised and had done very badly; that as a result of the Finnish War, the entire Soviet Army had been reorganised; but, even so, when the Germans attacked in 1941 it could not be said that the Red Army was a first-class fighting force.[20]

If this general diagnosis is correct, then the primary Western objective – not at all a promising one – was to conclude a treaty with the Soviet Union which, by its very existence, and without too hopeful reliance on its military content, whatever that might be, would cause Hitler to pause in his warlike course and be more amenable to the process of peaceful adjustment. And if war came, the treaty would at least ensure that Russia would be involved and would not be neutral or on the other side. For the Soviet Union, on the other hand, if, for purposes of security, the military content of the agreement was inadequate, then it would be dangerous to conclude it. Since that was the final Soviet standpoint, we can see now, though neither side probably wished to see this at the time, that the negotiations were almost certainly doomed to failure from the start.

If Lord Halifax or Mr Eden (as he volunteered to do) had gone to Moscow to take charge of the proceedings, it would, in my view, have made no substantial difference except conceivably in accelerating the tempo of the discussions. In fact, the negotiations foundered, in an immediate sense, over Poland; but in a wider sense they broke over failure to agree upon the 'methods, forms and extent' of the military assistance to be rendered, or perhaps, more widely still, as John Erickson has suggested, 'over the absence from the very beginning of any mutually compatible purposes'.

When Churchill later, in his large and sweeping way, said that 'Britain and France should have accepted the Russian offer, proclaimed the Triple Alliance, and left the method by which it could be made effective in case of war to be adjusted between allies engaged against a common foe', he overlooked that that was precisely what the Soviet government consistently and unalterably declined to contemplate. For them it was essential that the Allied military availabilities and dispositions should be spelled out in detail as an integral part of the treaty itself. Failing that, the treaty fell to the ground.

After that, events took their tragic course. The Nazi–Soviet Pact, the formal Anglo-Polish Treaty, the German attack on Poland, the British and French declarations of war, the Fourth (or was it the Fifth?) Partition of Poland, the absorption of the Baltic states, the German attack on Russia, Churchill's broadcast promising assistance to Russia, Pearl Harbour, the German declaration of war on the United States, and then, after all, and again after difficult negotiations, an Anglo-Soviet Alliance. When Molotov, who had again conducted the negotiations on the Soviet side, came to London to sign the Anglo-Soviet Treaty of May 1942, and I was one of those present on that occasion, he at once recognised me and came up and shook me cordially by the hand and said: 'I am glad to see an old friend. We did our best in 1939, but we failed: we were both at fault.'

During the Anglo-American-Soviet conference in Moscow in the autumn of 1943, the most productive of all the war-time conferences, Stalin gave the usual great banquet. After the feast, we withdrew to the adjoining salons. After a while I was told that Stalin wanted to see me. Having repaired to the corner where the great ones were assembled, I found them in a state of loud hilarity. Stalin was pointing the finger at Molotov as the man who had failed to reach agreement with the Western Powers and had made a deal with Ribbentrop in 1939. Stalin invited me to confirm that all this was Molotov's fault. Remembering

Molotov's remark to me in London the year before, I thought it only right to return courtesy for courtesy, and evaded the summons as best I could by suggesting that in those days everybody had been at fault.

And there I will leave it.

Notes and References

Crown copyright material is reproduced with kind permission of Her Majesty's Stationery Office.

INTRODUCTION *David Dilks*

1. D. N. Dilks, *Curzon in India* (Hart-Davis, 1969) vol. I, p. 220.
2. G. Monger, *The End of Isolation* (Nelson, 1963) p. 69.
3. Lord Newton, *Lord Lansdowne* (Macmillan, 1929) pp. 331–2, 338.
4. G. M. Trevelyan, *Grey of Fallodon* (Longmans, 1937) pp. 127–8.
5. PRO CAB 2/2/1: minutes of 88th meeting of CID (25 May 1906); copy of the minutes held in the Brotherton Library, University of Leeds.
6. CAB 2/2/2: minutes of 100th meeting of CID (22 Oct 1908); Trevelyan, *Grey of Falloden*, pp. 154–5.
7. Ibid., pp. 215–16.
8. CAB 2/2/2: minutes of 111th meeting of CID (26 May 1911).
9. CAB 2/2/2: minutes of 112th meeting of CID (29 May 1911).
10. PRO R/41: H. H. Asquith to King George V (4 July 1911); copy held in the Brotherton Library, University of Leeds.
11. CAB 2/2/3: minutes of 118th meeting of CID (11 July 1912).
12. CAB 37/130/16: memorandum by W. S. Churchill (18 June 1915); microfilm held in the Brotherton Library, University of Leeds.
13. Austen Chamberlain Papers: memorandum and letter, W. S. Churchill to A. Chamberlain (23 Feb 1925); I am indebted to the Birmingham University Library for permission to print material from the Chamberlain papers.
14. *Hansard*, HC, 5th ser., CCCX, 1443.
15. E. L. Woodward and R. d'O. Butler (eds.), *Documents on British Foreign Policy* 3rd Ser., vol. II, p. 550.
16. *Hansard*, HC, 5th ser., CCXLV, 2482.
17. R. A. C. Parker, 'Economics, Rearmament and Foreign Policy: the United Kingdom before 1939 – a preliminary study', *Journal of Contemporary History*, X (1975) pp. 644–5.
18. Neville Chamberlain Papers: Neville Chamberlain to Ida Chamberlain (23 July 1939), Birmingham University Library.

I. BRITISH POWER IN THE EUROPEAN BALANCE 1906–14 *Keith Wilson*

1. Memorandum by Crowe (1 Jan 1907) in G. P. Gooch and H. W. V. Temperley (eds) *British Documents on the Origins of the War 1898–1914* (London 1926–38) iii p. 403, hereafter cited as BD.
2. *Hansard*, 4th Ser., CXXXV, 535–6 (1 June 1904).
3. British Library Add. MSS 50901: C. P. Scott Diary (6–8 Sept, 1 Dec 1911, 29 Sept 1912). Gainford MSS, Nuffield College, Oxford: J. A. Pease Diary (20 July 1910).
4. Grey MSS, PRO FO 800/41: Grey to Cartwright (6 Jan 1909). BD, vol VI, no. 182: to Goschen (9 June 1909).

5. *Hansard*, 5th Ser., XXXII, 60 (27 Nov 1911).

6. J. Lepsius, A. Mendelssohn-Bartholdy and F. Thimme (eds), *Die Grosse Politik des Europaischen Kabinette 1871–1914* (Berlin, 1922–7) vol. XXXIX no. 15612: Lichnowsky to Bethmann Hollweg (3 Dec 1912).

7. *BD*, vol. XI, no. 369: memorandum by Crowe (31 July 1914).

8. *BD*, vol. VI, p. 628: minute by Crowe (14 May 1911).

9. WO 106/46: note by Ommanney on memorandum by Grant-Duff (4 Jan 1907).

10. WO 106/45 El/1: memorandum by Ewart (Mar 1909); Grey MSS, FO 800/102; Ewart MSS., with the Hon. H. Munro: Ewart Diary (12 July 1909, 21 Mar 1910).

11. .CAB 38/19/47: memorandum by Wilson (12 Aug 1911), 'The Military Aspect of the Continental Problem'.

12. CAB 2/2/2: minutes of 114th meeting of CID (23 Aug 1911) p. 5.

13. WO 106/47A and CAB 38/19/50: notes by Wilson (15 Aug 1911) on memorandum by Churchill (13 Aug).

14. Hardinge MSS, vol. 19, Cambridge University Library: Chirol to Hardinge (1 Dec 1910).

15. Roberts MSS, WO 105/45: Wilson to Roberts (17 Apr 1910).

16. Imperial War Museum: Wilson Diary (20 July, 9, 29 Sept 1911).

17. Gainford MSS, Nuffield College, Oxford: J. A. Pease Diary (8 Mar 1911).

18. CAB 2/2/2: minutes of 114th meeting of CID p. 2; CAB 16/5: Proceedings of first meeting of CID sub-committee on the Military Needs of the Empire (3 Dec 1908); see also CAB 38/16/9.

19. WO 106/49: minute by DMO (26 Dec 1911).

20. Imperial War Museum: Wilson Diary (12 Nov 1912); WO 106/49: memorandum on the Development of the Expeditionary Force, unsigned (Sept 1913); ibid.: notes of a conversation with Dewar (Assistant Chief of Staff, Admiralty) on the Recent Trend of Admiralty Policy (11 Oct 1913).

21. K. M. Wilson, 'To the Western Front: British War Plans and the "military entente" with France before the First World War', *British Journal of International Studies*, III, 2 (July 1977) 166.

22. *BD*, vol. III, no. 216: Grey to Bertie (Paris) (15 Jan 1906).

23. CAB 37/94/89: memorandum by Churchill (27 June 1908); for Lloyd George in the same vein, see E. T. S. Dugdale, *German Diplomatic Documents 1871–1914* (London, 1930) vol. III, 286; CAB 2/2/2: minutes of 114th meeting of CID; ADM 116/3474: memorandum by Churchill (16 Oct 1911).

24. Chirol MSS., *The Times* Archives: Chirol to Steed (2 June 1905). *BD*, vol. III, no. 98: Lascelles to Lansdowne (12 June 1905).

25. ADM 116/3486, /1043B part i; Ruddock MacKay, *Fisher of Kilverstone* (Oxford, 1973) p. 370.

26. A. J. Marder, *From the Dreadnought to Scapa Flow* vol. I, (Oxford 1961) p. 379.

27. CAB 16/5: note by Esher (14 Dec 1908), App. VII to Proceedings of sub-committee on the Military Needs of the Empire.

28. Ibid.: memorandum by General Staff (5 Mar 1909), App. VIII (B).

29. Ibid.: Report of CID sub-committee on the Military Needs of the Empire (24 July 1909) para 13 (my italics).

30. *BD*, vol. III, no. 299: minute by Hardinge (23 Feb 1906).

31. *BD*, vol. V, App. V: memorandum by Hardinge (May 1909).

32. Carnock MSS, FO 800/347: Nicolson to Cartwright (23 Jan 1911).

33. Carnock MSS, FO 800/348: Nicolson to Bertie (17 May 1911); *BD*, vol. VI, p. 623: minute by Nicolson (10 May 1911).

34. Imperial War Museum: Wilson Diary (11 Sept, 23 Nov 1911, 11 Jan 1912); Hardinge MSS, vol. 92, Cambridge University Library: Nicolson to Hardinge (18 Apr 1912).

35. CAB 17/61: Report by de Salis, Trench and Heath, forwarded by Goschen (26 Mar 1910); *BD*, vol. vi, no. 405: Goschen to. Nicolson (22 Oct 1910).

36. Ibid., no.446: Goschen to Grey (12 Mar 1911).

37. Carnock MSS, FO 800/349: Goschen to Nicolson (18 Aug 1911).

38. Spring-Rice MSS, 1/20, Churchill College, Cambridge: Spring-Rice to Chirol (13 Apr 1905); note by Chaumié (6 June 1905), *Documents Diplomatiques Français 1871–1914* (Paris, 1929–62) 2nd Ser., vi, Annex i; FO 371/455/18033, /18454: minutes by Spicer (26 May), by Hardinge (29 May 1908); FO 371/1133/2007: minute by Langley (18 Jan 1911); Grey MSS, FO 800/55: memo by Bertie (8 Mar 1914), sent to Tyrrell; Carnock MSS, FO 800/373: Nicolson to Buchanan (7 Apr 1914).

39. Hardinge MSS, vol. 92; Cambridge University Library: Chirol to Hardinge (17 Feb 1911); Carnock MSS, FO 800/360: Bertie to Nicolson (28 Nov 1912).

40. Add. MSS 50901: C.P.Scott Diary (1 Dec 1911, 6, 22 Jan 1912).

41. Carnock MSS., FO 800/367: Watson to Goschen (12 May 1913).

42. *Hansard*, 4th Ser., cxxx, 1405–6 (1 Mar 1904).

43. CAB 2/2/2, /3: minutes of 111th, 117th, 118th meetings of CID (26 May 1911, 4, 11 July 1912); *Hansard*, 5th ser., lix, 2189–90 (18 Mar 1914).

44. Campbell-Bannerman MSS, Add. MSS 41231: note by Tweedmouth (11 Nov 1906).

45. Asquith MSS, vol. 34, Bodleian Library, Oxford. Haldane to Asquith (1 Sep 1922).

46. Campbell-Bannerman MSS, Add. MSS 41210: Asquith to Campbell-Bannerman (30 Dec 1906); Asquith MSS, vol. 10, Bodleian Library, Oxford: Campbell-Bannerman to Asquith (4 Jan 1907).

47. Grey MSS., FO 800/103: Grey to Knollys (28 Mar 1906).

48. Harold Nicolson, *Lord Carnock–A study in the Old Diplomacy* (London, 1930) p. 206.

49. *The Times* (21 Oct 1905); *BD*, vol. iii, no. 299.

50. I. Nish, *The Anglo-Japanese Alliance: The Diplomacy of Two Island Empires 1894–1907* (London 1966) pp. 300–9.

51. Ibid., pp. 354–8.

52. *BD*, vol. iv, no. 135: MacDonald to Lansdowne (15 July 1905).

53. B. Williams, 'The Strategic Background to the Anglo-Russian Entente of August 1907,' *HJ*, ix (1966) 365.

54. Campbell-Bannerman MSS, Add. MSS 41223: Morley to Campbell-Bannerman (6 Jan 1907) CAB 38/13/20; India Office Library MSS, Eur. D 573/2: Morley to Minto (19 Sept 1907).

55. FO 371/371/26042: minutes by Grey and Hardinge (6 Aug 1907) on Spring-Rice to Grey (16 July 1907), (my italics); see Spring-Rice MSS, FO 800/241: Grey to Spring-Rice (30 Nov 1906).

56. India Office Library MSS, Eur. D 573/3: Morley to Minto (20 Mar 1908); Grey MSS, FO 800/100: Grey to Campbell-Bannerman (31 Aug 1907).

57. *BD*, vol. iii, no. 299.

58. FO 371/320/28370: Grey to Nicolson (26 Aug 1907).

59. See D. Dakin, *The Greek Struggle in Macedonia 1897–1913* (Salonika, 1966) p. 349.

60. Carnock MSS, FO 800/340, /341: Hardinge to Nicolson (25 Nov 1907, 7 Jan 1908); *BD*, vol. iv, no. 544: minute by Hardinge (28 Oct 1907).

61. See B. Williams, 'Great Britain and Russia 1905–7' in F. H. Hinsley (ed.), *The Foreign Policy of Sir Edward Grey* (Cambridge, 1977) p. 135.

62. *BD*, vol. v, p. 550: Hardinge to Nicolson (4 Jan 1909).

63. *BD*, vol. vi, no. 575: Nicolson to Goschen (15 Apr 1912); Carnock MSS, FO 800/351, /359: to Barclay (24 Oct 1911), to Buchanan (22 Oct 1912).

64. Carnock MSS, FO 800/365: Nicolson to Buchanan (22 Apr 1913).

65. Ibid. /367: Hardinge to Nicolson (16 May 1913).

66. Ibid. /373: Nicolson to Townley (7 Apr 1914).

67. *BD*, vol. x (2) no. 538: Buchanan to Nicolson (16 Apr 1914).

68. *BD*, vol. vi, no. 361: Grey to Goschen (5 May 1910).

69. Grey MSS, FO 800/89: Grey to Churchill (22 Apr 1909).

70. Bertie MSS, FO 800/171: Grey to Bertie (7 Jan 1909); Grey MSS, FO 800/51: to Bertie (30 Aug 1909); Grey MSS, FO 800/62: to Goschen (26 Oct 1910); Grey MSS, FO 800/53: to Bertie (7 Feb 1912).

71. Gainford MSS, Nuffield College, Oxford: J. A. Pease Diary (20 July 1910).

72. *BD*, vol. x (1), no. 914; Carnock MSS, FO 800/363: Goschen to Nicolson (late Jan 1913).

73. Add. MSS 50901: C. P. Scott Diary (25 July 1911).

74. Hardinge MSS, vol. 92, Cambridge University Library: Grey to Hardinge (28 Jan 1912).

75. *BD*, vol. xi, no. 101.

76. Ibid. no. 490.

77. Ibid. no. 447.

78. Grey MSS, FO 800/94: note by Nicolson for Grey (21 July 1911); Carnock MSS, FO 800/349: Nicolson to Goschen (24 July 1911); FO 371/1123/32100: note by Nicolson (3 Aug 1911).

79. Balfour MSS, Add. MSS. 49747: Mallet to Short (4 May 1912).

2. PUBLICITY AND DIPLOMACY: THE IMPACT OF THE FIRST WORLD WAR UPON FOREIGN OFFICE ATTITUDES TOWARDS THE PRESS   *Philip Taylor*

1. H. Temperley and L. M. Penson, *A Century of Diplomatic Bluebooks, 1814–1914* (Cass, 1938).

2. E. H. Carr, *Propaganda in international politics* (No. 16 in the Oxford pamphlets on world affairs) p. 7.

3. O. J. Hale, *Germany and the Diplomatic Revolution: A Study of Diplomacy and the Press, 1904–06* (Philadelphia: Univ. of Pennsylvania Press, 1931) pp. 1–7.

4. J. A. Spender, *The Public Life*, 2 vols (Cassell, 1925) vol. ii, p. 40.

5. B. Akzin, *Propaganda by Diplomats* (Washington DC: Digest Press, 1936) pp. 1–3.

6. Spender, *Public Life*, ii, p. 40.

7. P. M. Kennedy, 'Imperial cable communications and strategy, 1871–1914', *English Historical Review (EHR)*, LXXXVI (1971) 728–52.

8. Z. Steiner, *The Foreign Office and Foreign Policy, 1898–1914* (Cambridge University Press, 1969) p. 172. My italics.

9. *Cf.* R. Langhorne, 'The Foreign Office before 1914', *Historical Journal (HJ)*, XVI 4 (1973) 857; J. Tilley and S. Gaselee, *The Foreign Office* (Putnam's, 1932) p. 278.

10. K. Jones, *Fleet Street and Downing Street* (Hutchinson, 1920) pp. 98–100.

11. E. M. Carroll, *Germany and the Great Powers, 1866–1914: A Study in Public Opinion and Foreign Policy* (New York: Prentice-Hall, 1938); E. M. Carroll, *French Public Opinion and Foreign Affairs, 1870–1914* (Cass, 1931).

12. O. J. Hale, *Publicity and Diplomacy – with Special Reference to England and Germany, 1890–1914* (Gloucester, Massachusetts: Peter Smith, 1964) p. 40.

13. P. G. Lauren, *Diplomats and Bureaucrats: the First Institutional Responses to Twentieth Century Diplomacy in France and Germany* (Stanford: Hoover Institution Press, 1976) p. 181.

14. Carr, *Propaganda in international politics*, p. 9.

15. J. A. Spender, *Life, Journalism and Politics*, 2 vols (Cassell, 1926) vol. i, p. 186.

16. Steiner, *The Foreign Office and Foreign Policy*, pp. 172–91; Hale, *Publicity and Diplomacy*, pp. 38–40.

17. J. A. Spender, *Fifty Years of Europe* (Cassell, 1933) p. 239.

18. S. B. Fay, *The Origins of the First World War*, 2 vols (Macmillan, 1928) vol. I, pp. 47–9.

19. Jones, *Fleet Street and Downing Street*, p. 97.

20. CAB 38/28/3: Enquiry regarding press and postal censorship in time of war, Report (31 Jan 1913).

21. FO 800/329, Pp/21/1: memorandum by W. Tyrrell (10 Dec 1921).

22. M. L. Sanders, 'Wellington House and British propaganda during the first world war', *HJ*, XVIII (1975) 119–46.

23. J. D. Squires, *British Propaganda at Home and in the United States from 1914 to 1917* (Cambridge, Massachusetts: Harvard University Press, 1935).

24. Sanders, 'Wellington House and British propaganda . . .'.

25. Sir E. Cook, *The Press in Wartime* (Macmillan, 1920).

26. A. G. Marquis, 'Words as weapons: propaganda in Britain and Germany during the first world war', *JCH*, XIII (1978) 478ff.

27. Willert MS, *The Times* Archives: G. Robinson to A. Willert (1 Oct 1914).

28. INF 4/4A: H. O. Lee, 'British propaganda during the Great War'.

29. Ibid.

30. CAB 37/136/34: memorandum by J. A. Simon (27 Oct 1915).

31. P. Knightley, *The First Casualty: the War Correspondent as Hero, Propagandist and Mythmaker from the Crimea to Vietnam* (Deutsch, 1975) pp. 80–112; N. Lytton, *The Press and the General Staff* (Collins, 1921) p. viii.

32. INF 4/4A: H. O. Lee, 'British propaganda during the Great War'.

33. CAB 24/3, G.102: Foreign Office memorandum, 'British propaganda in Allied and Neutral countries' (20 Dec 1916).

34. INF 4/4A: H. O. Lee, 'British propaganda during the Great War'.

35. Ibid.

36. INF 4/9: Lord Robert Cecil at a conference at the Home Office (26 Jan 1916).

37. CAB 24/3, G. 102: Foreign Office memorandum (20 Dec 1916).

38. INF 4/4B: Robert Donald to Lloyd George (9 Jan 1917).

39. CAB 24/3, G. 102: Foreign Office memorandum (20 Dec 1916).

40. Ibid. My italics.

41. CAB 24/6, GT26: memorandum by C. H. Montgomery (14 Feb 1917).

42. *Hansard*, 5th Ser., CIII, 656 ff.

43. A.C. 15/7/7: Austen Chamberlain to Lords Milner and Curzon (21 Feb 1918).

44. CAB 24/67, GT 6007: memorandum by Lord Beaverbrook (16 Oct 1918).

45. D. M. Smith, *The Great Departure: The United States and World War One, 1914–20* (New York, 1965) pp. 119–20.

46. R. Coggeshall, 'Peace Conference Publicity: lessons of 1919', *Journalism Quarterly*, XIX (1942) 2.

47. D. Lloyd George, *Memoirs of the Peace Conference*, 2 vols (New Haven: Yale University Press, 1939) vol. I, p. 136.

48. Lord Riddell, *An Intimate Diary of the Peace Conference and After, 1918–23* (Gollancz, 1923). Entry for 23 January 1919.

49. Ibid. Entry for 24 March 1919.

50. Ibid. Entry for 29 March 1919.

51. Ibid. Entry for 3 May 1919.

52. 'The History of *The Times*', *The 150th Anniversary and Beyond* (PHS, 1954) Part I, pp. 270–8.

53. H. A. Taylor, *Robert Donald* (Stanley Paul, undated) pp. 187–90.

54. CAB 24/77, GT 7062; CAB 23/11, 594 (5): 16 July 1919.

55. FO 395/301, 00409: memorandum by G. B. Beak, 'Policy and propaganda' (2 Dec 1918).

56. FO 395/301, 00409: memorandum by S. A. Guest (24 Jan 1919).

57. A. J. P. Taylor, *The Trouble Makers: Dissent over Foreign Policy, 1792–1939* (Panther edition, 1969) chs 5 and 6.

58. CAB 24/78, GT 7154: memorandum by R. S. Horne (28 Apr 1919).

59. CAB 24/78, GT 7160: memorandum by the Home Secretary (30 Apr 1919).

60. *Hansard*, 5th Ser., CIX, 947–1035.

61. CAB 23/10, 561(1): (1 May 1919).

62. T 162/42, E2862: Treasury memorandum on publicity (28 July 1923).

63. FO 366/1029, X 3097/431/504: 'Publicity services in government departments' (April 1938).

64. FO 366/787, 32759: memorandum by Lord Curzon (26 Mar 1919).

65. FO 800/151: Curzon to Lord Burnham (1 Oct 1919).

66. FO 366/783, 5: memorandum by P. A. Koppel (10 Feb 1922).

67. FO 366/790, 2800: C. H. Montgomery to Treasury (16 Nov 1920).

68. FO 371/4382, 619: memorandum by J. W. Headlam-Morley, (28 Oct 1919), enclosed in Headlam-Morley to Tyrrell (28 Oct 1919).

69. FO 371/4382, 619: minutes by Hardinge and Curzon (31 Oct 1919).

70. The immediate post-war decisions relating to the News Department must be considered in the broader context of Foreign Office reconstruction. For further details see Z. Steiner and M. L. Dockrill, 'The Foreign Office Reforms, 1919–21', *HJ*, XVII (1974) 131–56.

71. Lord Vansittart, *The Mist Procession* (Hutchinson, 1958) p. 249.

72. Jones, *Fleet Street and Downing Street*, p. 341.

73. FO 800/329, Pp/21/1: memorandum by Tyrrell (10 Dec 1921).

74. Lord Hankey, *Diplomacy by conference* (London: Allen and Unwin, 1946); A. Willert, *Washington and other memories* (Boston: Houghton, Mifflin and Co., 1972).

75. FO 366/783: memorandum by J. D. Gregory (21 Feb 1925).

76. P. M. Taylor, 'Cultural diplomacy and the British Council, 1934–1939', *British Journal of International Studies*, IV (1978) 3, 244–265.

77. *Hansard*, 5th Ser., CCCXLIII, 1825 (15 Feb 1939).

3. THE FOREIGN OFFICE, THE DOMINIONS AND THE DIPLOMATIC UNITY OF THE EMPIRE, 1925–29 *Norman Hillmer*

1. Philip G. Wigley, *Canada and the Transition to Commonwealth* (Cambridge University Press, 1977) chs 6–8, especially pp. 240–4, 249–55.

2. FO 372/2198/13684: minute (22 Nov 1926).

3. FO 372/2198/T14837: minute (10 Nov 1926).

4. FO 372/2197/T5885: memorandum (16 Jan 1926), and *passim*.

5. CAB 32/47: Imperial Conference, 1926, Documents Committee, minutes (7 July 1926).

6. FO 372/2216/T12079: minute (23 July 1926).

7. CAB 32/57: Imperial Conference, 1926, Committee on Inter-Imperial Relations, Treaty Procedure Sub-Committee, minutes (6, 8 Nov 1926).

8. Cmd 2769, pp. 17–20.

9. CAB 32/57: Imperial Conference, 1926, Committee on Inter-Imperial Relations, Treaty Procedure Sub-Committee, minutes (9, 16 Nov 1926), and *passim*. The memoranda and minutes on the 'central panel' issue are collected in CAB 32/42 and FO 372/2215–16. See also H. Duncan Hall, *Commonwealth: A History of the British Commonwealth of Nations* (Van Nostrand Reinhold, 1971) pp. 661–74.

10. CAB 32/56: Imperial Conference, 1926, Committee on Inter-Imperial Relations, minutes (7, 4 Nov 1926).

11. David Dilks, 'Baldwin and Chamberlain' in Lord Butler (ed.), *The Conservatives: A History from their Origins to 1965* (George Allen and Unwin, 1977) p. 301.

12. FO 372/2444/T12916: minute (7 Dec 1928).

13. FO 372/2442/T2193: minute (25 Feb 1928). See also Norman Hillmer, 'A British High Commissioner for Canada, 1927–28', *Journal of Imperial and Commonwealth History*, 1 3 (May 1973) 339–56.

14. A. B. Keith (ed.), *Speeches and Documents on the British Dominions 1918–1931* (Oxford University Press, 1966) pp. 349–50. See also CAB 24/197, CP285(28).

15. FO 371/12828/A1108: memorandum by Chamberlain (15 Feb 1928); A. I. Inglis (ed.), *Documents on Canadian External Relations* (Ottawa: Information Canada, 1971) vol. IV, 1926–30, p. 42: telegram, King to Skelton (16 Aug 1928); PAC, King Papers: Diary (26 Aug 1928); DO 35/55/D10117: Price to Batterbee (22 Sep 1928), minute of Price (28 Sep 1928).

16. Max Beloff, 'The Commonwealth as History', *Journal of Imperial and Commonwealth History*, I, 1 (October 1972) 111.

17. CAB 24/193, CP 87(28), and the minutes on FO 372/2445/T2429; CAB 23/57, Cabinet 15 (28) (21 Mar 1928), Conclusion 3. See also FO 627/1/U45: minute by Orde (25 Jan 1929).

18. CAB 23/59, Cabinet 54(28) (5 Dec 1928), Conclusion 6; PAC, King Papers, J4/88/663/C67845–61: memorandum by King (10 Nov 1928).

19. CAB 24/201, CP 22(29) Appendix A: Amery to the Dominions (21 Dec 1928).

20. PAC, Papers of the Department of External Affairs, vol. 792: memorandum by Skelton (2 Jan 1929); CAB 24/201, CP 22(29) Appendix B: Secretary of State for External Affairs, Irish Free State, to Amery (31 Dec 1928).

21. FO 627/1/U4: minute by Orde (8 Jan 1929); CAB 23/60, Cabinet 4(29) (6 Feb 1929), Conclusion 3.

22. CAB 24/201, CP 22(29); FO 627/1/U31: Batterbee to Montgomery (17 Jan 1929); interviews with former Dominions Office officials, Sir Harry Batterbee (11 Feb 1970), and Sir Charles Dixon (30 June 1971).

23. FO 627/2/U160: telegram, King to Amery (20 Mar 1929). My italics.

24. FO 371/14103: Hurst to Chamberlain (27 Mar 1929); FO 371/14104: Committee of Jurists on the Statute of the Permanent Court of International Justice, minutes (11–19 Mar 1929) pp. 70–72.

25. FO 627/2/U179: telegram, Amery to King (23 Mar 1929).

26. FO 627/2/U181: telegram, Hertzog to Amery (21 Mar 1929); FO 627/2/U182: telegram, Clifford to Hardinge (22 Mar 1929); FO 627/3/U391: memorandum of Dominions Information Department (20 June 1929).

27. FO 627/2/U242: telegram, King to Amery (20 Apr 1929).

28. FO 627/3/U267: minute (3 May 1929). Malkin's reservation was understood, although not stated, when final agreement was reached a month later.

29. PAC, Papers of the Department of External Affairs, vol. 792: telegram, Amery to King (11 May 1929); FO 627/3/U251: Murphy to Amery (15 Apr 1929); FO 627/2/U223: minute by Dixon (9 Apr 1929); FO 627/3/U391: memorandum of Dominions Information Department (20 June 1929).

30. Keith, *Speeches and Documents on the British Dominions*, pp. 446–7. The new formula was used for well over a decade after 1929 and never formally abrogated. See Hall, *Commonwealth*, pp. 420–1.

31. FO 627/3/U391: memorandum of Dominions Information Department (20 June 1929).

32. Ibid.

33. British Museum, Balfour Papers, Add. 48775: Amery to Balfour (1 Nov 1926).

34. FO 627/3/U267: minute (3 May 1929), and other minutes on this file.

35. FO 627/13/U559: Malkin to Batterbee (15 Sep 1929).

36. Canada, House of Commons *Debates* (31 Mar 1939), pp. 2466–7.

4. BRITAIN AND GERMANY: THE SEARCH FOR AGREEMENT, 1930-37
Norton Medlicott

1. The substance of this paper was delivered to the University of London as the Creighton lecture for 1968.

2. *Hansard*, HL, CXXXI, 363 (29 Mar 1944); he elaborated the argument on 25 January 1945 (ibid., CXXXIV, 727-30). *Cf.* Sir Walford Selby, *Diplomatic Twilight, 1930-1940* (London, 1953) pp. 17, 136-8, 183-4, and Sir Horace Rumbold's comment: Hugh Dalton, *The Fateful Years* (London, 1957) p. 244.

3. Lord Vansittart, *The Mist Procession* (London, 1958) pp. 305, 550.

4. Winston S. Churchill, *The Gathering Storm* (London, 1948) p. 155.

5. Woodward, Butler (eds) *Documents on British Foreign Policy*, hereafter *BD*, 2nd Ser., vol. XV, no. 455. Many of the Foreign Office documents referred to in the notes to this paper are being published in volumes XVI-XVIII of this series.

6. *Cf.*, *The Ribbentrop Memoirs* (London, 1954) p. 47: 'Vansittart and the Foreign Office opposed any kind of agreement with Germany and advocated rigid adherence to the system of Versailles.'

7. *Cf. BD*, 2nd Ser., vol. I, nos 344, 346; Vansittart, *The Mist Procession*, pp. 404-5.

8. C7752/55/18 (FO 371/18851): Sargent-Wigram joint memorandum (21 Nov 1935).

9. Vansittart, *The Mist Procession*, p. 507.

10. Martin Gilbert, *The Roots of Appeasement* (London, 1966) p. 132, quotes this proposal and others from the Sargent papers in favour of concessions to Germany in 1931-2, but is guessing wrongly when he says later: 'The Foreign Office, in particular, showed little enthusiasm from 1933-6 for Anglo-German rapprochement' (p. 149).

11. Valentine Lawford, *Bound for Diplomacy* (London, 1963) p. 258.

12. F. T. A. Ashton-Gwatkin, *The British Foreign Service* (Syracuse, 1950) pp. 26-31.

13. Selby, *Diplomatic Twilight* pp. 4-7, 10-11.

14. *Cf.* Ashton-Gwatkin, *The British Foreign Service* p. 72.

15. C5448/29/18 (FO 371/17709): minute by Vansittart (12 Aug 1934).

16. *BD* 2nd Ser., vol. V, no. 229. It should be noted that this, and not, as is sometimes assumed, his despatch no. 425 of 26 April 1933 (ibid., no. 36), is Rumbold's real 'final despatch'. Sargent told Phipps in October 1933 that no. 642 was 'our Bible' on Nazi policy.

17. *BD* 2nd Ser., vol. V, no. 492.

18. C8045/20/18 (FO 371/17696).

19. Outstanding among Phipps' masterly despatches is his famous 'bison despatch' of 13 June 1934 (*BD* 2nd Ser., vol. VI, no. 452), which had the usual fairly wide circulation to the Cabinet, and which was believed to have 'leaked' in Berlin. A similarly devastating despatch, no. 285 of 22 March 1935 (C2626/2626/18), describing Goering's wedding, was kept in the Foreign Office on Sargent's instructions in order to prevent any further indiscretion.

20. C8045/20/18 (FO 371/17696).

21. Vansittart, *The Mist Procession*, p. 455.

22. C7114/20/18 (FO 371/17695).

23. *BD* 2nd Ser., vol. VI, no. 322. Lord Avon, *Facing the Dictators* (London, 1962), gives a somewhat different account of this interview.

24. C5004/55/18 (FO 371/18847): Phipps to Wigram (18 June 1935).

25. C4583/20/18 (FO 371/17695).

26. C8045/20/18 (FO 371/17696).

27. Simon vaguely describes and defends his German policy in his disappointingly meagre memoirs, *Retrospect* (London, 1952) pp. 197-204. He mentions Vansittart once, misspells Wigram's name, and omits Sargent altogether.

28. *BD* 2nd Ser., vol. VI, no. 363.

29. This was in accordance with the recommendation of the Defence Requirements Committee of which Vansittart was a member along with Sir Maurice Hankey, Sir Warren Fisher, and the Chiefs of Staff.

30. In a minute of 28 May 1935. C4174/55/18 (FO 371/18842).

31. CAB[inet] CON[clusions] 28(34), C4532/3279/4: (11 July 1934).

32. See C7281/90/18 (FO 371/17736); C8738/90/18 (FO 371/17738).

33. *Cf.* CAB CON 42(34), 26 Nov 1934.

34. C8654/20/18 (FO 371/17697): Simon to Clerk (20 Dec 1934).

35. C435/55/18 (FO 371/18823).

36. Vansittart commented (4 Feb), 'Lord Lothian is, I fear, an incurably superficial Johnny-Know-All'. C785/55/18 (FO 371/18824). The interview is referred to in J. R. M. Butler, *Lord Lothian* (London, 1960) pp. 202–4; the text is in Appendix III (a).

37. C600/55/18 (FO 371/18823).

38. *Cf.* C1506/55/18 (FO 371/18827).

39. C655/55/18 (FO 371/18823): Simon's instructions to Clerk, telegram no. 17 (25 January 1935).

40. CP34(35): C892/55/18; C893/55/18 (FO 371/18824).

41. This was the substance of the Anglo-French Declaration of 3 February, published next day, following the discussions in London, 1–3 February. The minutes are in C893/55/18 (FO 371/18824).

42. *Documents on German Foreign Policy 1919–1939*, hereafter *GD*, Ser. C, vol. III, no. 490.

43. C907/55/18 (FO 371/18824); C922/55/18 (FO 371/18825).

44. *Cf.*, C1471/55/18: Sargent's comments (7 Feb 1935); and C1040/55/18) (FO 371/18827): Chilston to Simon, telegram no. 11 (7 Feb 1935).

45. Sargent initiated this discussion with a paper of 28 Jan, C962/55/18.

46. N880/135/38.

47. C1467/55/18 (FO 371/18827): Phipps to Simon, telegram no. 67 (22 Feb 1935).

48. C1834/55/18 (FO 371/18828): Phipps to Simon, unnumbered telegram (23 Feb 1935).

49. C1374/55/18 (FO 371/18826): minute by Wigram (21 Feb 1935).

50. C1834/55/18 (FO 371/18828): letter from Vansittart to Phipps (5 Mar 1935).

51. *GD* Ser. C, vol. III, no. 542.

52. Cmd 4848 (1935); telegram no. 208, C2214/55/18; *cf.* Simon, *Retrospect* pp. 202–3.

53. Telegram nos 48, 49, FO 371/18826, and telegram no. 119, C2130/55/18 (FO 371/18830).

54. *GD* Ser. C, vol. III, no. 555; the British account, C2580/55/18, is fuller.

55. C4336/55/18 (FO 371/18843): Simon to Phipps, despatch no. 571 (29 May 1935).

56. *Cf.*, C4104/55/18 (FO 371/18841): minute by M.J.Cresswell (23 May 1935).

57. C4659/55/18 (FO 371/18845). After the Franco-Russian pact, which greatly dimmed the prospects of the eastern pact, the air pact had become in British eyes the most vital element in the comprehensive programme.

58. J4768/1/1: Hoare to Foreign Office (11 Sep 1935). *Cf.* C6516/55/18 (FO 371/18850).

59. *GD* Ser. C, vol. III, nos 234, 249, 252, 253, 281. C5592, C5708, C5823, C5839/55/18.

60. *Hansard*, HC, cccxxx, 1832 (21 Dec 1937).

61. 18 November: this was a comment on Phipps's despatch no. 1160, 13 November 1935, which quoted von Blomberg's remark to him in October that if Germany were not allowed to expand 'the kettle would someday burst'. C7647/55/18 (FO 371/18851).

62. C7854/4/18 (FO 371/19914).

63. C7752/55/18 (FO 371/18851).

64. Ibid.: 'Annex. Note by Mr [F.T.A.Ashton-] Gwatkin on Germany's economic position.'

65. C8523/55/18 (FO 371/18852).

66. C8524/55/18 (FO 371/18852): minute by Vansittart (1 Dec 1935).

67. CP13(36): C454/4/18. The Cabinet discussed the paper on 29 January: C614/4/18 (FO 371/19884). *Cf.*, Avon, *Facing the Dictators*, p. 315, a brief reference.

68. C807/4/18, signed by F. Ashton-Gwatkin and Gladwyn Jebb. It initiated a debate with numerous ramifications among the officials. Phipps (despatch no. 286, 7 March) did not agree that prosperity would end Naziism. 'Hitlerism is no longer the symptom, but the disease itself.'

69. C997/4/18 Para. 38 (FO 371/19885).

70. G36(3): C1027/4/18 (FO 371/19885).

71. C998/4/18 (FO 371/19885).

72. G(36) 1st Meeting: C1028/4/18 (FO 371/19885).

73. C850/4/18, C1014/4/18 (FO 371/19884); *GD* Ser. C, vol. III, nos 562, 563, 568, 583, 594.

74. C1450/4/18 (FO 371/19887).

75. *Cf.*, E.M.Robertson, *Hitler's Pre-War Policy* (London, 1963) pp. 70–81, for a good survey of the German background.

76. C8375/55/18 (FO 371/18852).

77. *GD* Ser. C, vol. III, nos 589, 596, 601.

78. *Paris-Midi* (28 Feb 1936); C1267/4/18 (FO 371/19886).

79. C1814/4/18 (FO 371/19891).

80. C1769/4/18 (FO 371/19890). *Cf.*, Avon, *Facing the Dictators* p. 338.

81. CP73(36), CAB 24/261: memorandum by the Secretary of State for Foreign Affairs (extract in FO 371/19889).

82. *GD* Ser. C, vol. v, no. 242.

83. C2850/4/18; C3101/4/18 (FO 371/19902–3).

84. CAB CON 31(36), C3301/4/18 (FO 371/19904): (29 Apr 1936).

85. CAB CON 32(36) and 34(36), FO 371/19904–5: (30 Apr and 6 May 1936). On 30 April Duff Cooper, Secretary of State for War, disagreed with a suggestion made on the previous day that 'we ought to reach agreement with Germany even if it could not endure'. C3421/4/18: Eden's despatch no. 541 to Phipps (6 May 1936). *Cf.*, *GD* Ser. C, vol. v, no. 313.

86. C3662–3/4/18 (FO 371/19905): Phipps telegram nos 175, 176. *Cf.*, *GD* Ser. C., vol. v, no. 326.

87. Vansittart's long account of his Berlin visit has been printed for the first time in *BD* 2nd Ser., vol. XVII, app. I, under the title 'A Busman's Holiday'.

88. A copy of the report, dated 9 June 1936 and printed for the CID, is on C4275/97/18 (FO 371/19927), with extensive minutes by Foreign Office officials. See *BD* 2nd Ser., vol. XVI, app. III.

89. C5822/97/18 (FO 371/19928): minutes of Cabinet Committee on Foreign Policy (27 July 1936).

90. C7626/5740/18 (FO 371/19948): 'Papers Relating to Dr.Schacht's Visit to Paris in August 1936'.

91. *GD* Ser. C, vol. v, no. 624. *Cf.*, G. Meinck, *Hitler und die deutsche Aufrüstung, 1933–1939* (Wiesbaden, 1959) pp. 157–62.

92. *GD* Ser. C, vol. v, no. 624. *Ciano's Diplomatic Papers* (London, 1948) pp. 52–61. *Cf.*, Robertson, *Hitler's Pre-War Policy*, pp. 96–7.

93. C5449, 5450/4/18 (FO 371/19910).

94. C6431/4/18 (FO 371/19912); *BD* (2) 2nd Ser., vol. XVII, no. 186.

95. C6554/4/18 (FO 371/19912).

96. C7247/4/18: C7251/4/18; C7325/4/18 (FO 371/19913).

97. C8792/4/18 (FO 371/19916): Eden to Phipps, despatch no. 1370 (8 Dec 1936).
98. *Cf.*, Churchill, *The Gathering Storm*, pp. 174–5, and *The Ribbentrop Memoirs*, pp. 65, 92.
99. C9152/4/18 (FO 371/19916).
100. C8998/8998/18 (FO 371/19949).
101. *BD* (2) 2nd Ser., vol. XVIII, nos. 134, 670 (note 6).

5. BRITISH MILITARY PREPARATIONS FOR THE SECOND WORLD WAR
   Michael Howard

1. CID 1A, CAB 3/1/1A.
2. CID 313C (COS 298), CAB 53/22.
3. See Arthur Marder, 'The Royal Navy and the Ethiopian Crisis of 1935–6', *American Historical Review*, XXV, 5 (1970). Also DPR 21, CAB 16/138: Chiefs of Staff Report to the Defence Policy Requirements Committee (16 Sep 1935).
4. COS 41, CAB 53/12: Chiefs of Staff Sub-Committee Review of Imperial Defence (22 June 1926).
5. See George H. Quester, *Deterrence before Hiroshima* (New York and London: John Wiley, 1966).
6. CID 106A, CAB 3/3: Committee of Imperial Defence Sub-Committee on Continental Air Menace Report (26 Apr 1922).
7. Richard M. Tittmuss, *Problems of Social Policy* (UK Official History of the Second World War, Civil Series, W. K. Hancock (ed.): HMSO, 1950) pp. 4–6.
8. Basil Collier, *The Defence of the United Kingdom* (UK Official History of the Second World War, Military Series, J. R. M. Butler (ed.): HMSO, 1957) app. XXX.
9. Since this paper was presented, two important works have appeared which considerably amplify what is written here, and these should be consulted. They are G. C. Peden, *British Rearmament and the Treasury 1932–1939* (Edinburgh, 1979) and Robert P. Shay, *British Rearmament in the Thirties: Politics and Profits* (Princeton, 1977).
10. DC(M)(32) 214.
11. DRC(12), CAB 16/109.
12. W. K. Hancock and M. M. Gowing, *British War Economy* (UK Official History of the Second World War, Civil Series: HMSO, 1949) pp. 115–16.
13. CP24(38), CAB 24/274: (8 Feb 1938).
14. COS 310, CAB 53/23: Chiefs of Staff Annual Review of Defence Policy (12 Oct 1933).
15. CP218(36), CAB 24/263: (1 Sep 1936).
16. DRC 14, CAB 16/109: Defence Requirements Sub-Committee Report (28 Feb 1934).
17. Baldwin and MacDonald believed that the results of this notorious by-election indicated strong public hostility to rearmament. Not all their colleagues shared this view, and subsequent research has suggested that the election was fought very largely on local issues. See Richard Heller, 'East Fulham Revisited', the *Journal of Contemporary History*, VI 3 (1971), and C. T. Stannage, 'The East Fulham By-Election, 25 October 1933', *HJ*, XIV 1 (1971).
18. Liddell Hart's *The British Way in Warfare* was published in 1932. For a critique, see the present writer's *The British Way in Warfare: A Reappraisal* (Neale Lecture in English History: Jonathan Cape, 1974).
19. DC(M)(32) 41st Conclusions.
20. DRC 37, CAB 16/112. Defence Requirements Committee, Third Report (21 Nov 1935).
21. For an appreciation of the debate see K. Middlemas and John Barnes, *Baldwin: A*

Biography (Weidenfeld and Nicolson, 1969) pp. 912–3.

22. CP26(38), CAB 24/274: (10 Feb 1938).

23. DP (P) 22, CAB 16/183A: Chiefs of Staff Report on the Military Implications of German Aggression against Czechoslovakia (28 Mar 1938).

24. DP (P) 32, CAB 16/183A: Appreciation by the Chiefs of Staff of the Situation in the Event of War against Germany (4 Oct 1938).

25. For a statement of the case that Britain would still have been better advised to go to war with Germany in September 1938 rather than have delayed for a further year, see Telford Taylor, *Munich: the Price of Peace* (New York: Doubleday, 1979) p. 984 ff.

26. DP(P)44, CAB 16/183A: European Appreciation by the Chiefs of Staff Committee (20 Feb 1939).

27. DP(P)61, CAB 16/183A: Note on the Despatch of a Fleet to the Far East (24 June 1939).

28. DP(P)56 CAB 16/183A: Report on First Stage of Anglo-French Staff Conversations (11 Apr 1939).

6. THE HOARE–LAVAL PACT RECONSIDERED   *Norton Medlicott*

1. British documents on the Ethiopian crisis have been published in vols. xiv, xv and xvi of the Second Series of *BD*. Volumes covering the crisis in the comparable French and Italian series have not yet been published, although isolated documents and much varied information have appeared in the press and other sources.

2. G. Rochet, *Militari e politici nella preparazione della campagna d'Ethiopia* (Milan, 1971).

3. Rochat, *Militari e politici nella preparazione della campagna d'Ethiopia*, pp. 376–9; the directive was first printed, however, by the former Minister for the Colonies, Alessandro Lessona, in his *Memorie* (Florence, 1958) pp. 165–71.

4. Frank Hardie, *The Abyssinian Crisis* (1974) gives an up-to-date sketch of the whole crisis, using Foreign Office material. The best available study of Mussolini's imperial aspirations is E. M. Robertson, *Striving for Empire: Italy between the Powers* (1978).

5. General M. Gamelin, *Servir* vol. ii (*Le Prologue du Drame*) (Paris, 1946) pp. 167–71; *cf.* M. Toscano, *Pagine di Storia Diplomatica Contemporanea* (Milan, 1963) pp. 138–9, 145; *BD* 2nd Ser., vol. xiv, no. 487.

6. Ibid., vol. xiv, no. 143; *cf.* no. 145.

7. Ibid., pp. 141–2.

8. Ibid., no. 318.

9. For his approaches to the British Government: ibid., pp. 1–22.

10. Geoffrey Warner, *Pierre Laval and the eclipse of France* (1968) chs 2 and 3, gives a good survey of this phase of Laval's foreign policy. Franklin D. Laurens, *France and the Italo-Ethiopian crisis 1935–1936* (The Hague, 1967), is strongest on domestic aspects of the crisis.

11. *BD* 2nd Ser., vol. xvi, no. 326.

12. J. A. Cross, *Sir Samuel Hoare, a political biography* (London, 1977), is a well-informed and rather sympathetic study; Hoare's own memoir, *Nine Troubled Years* (London 1954) Part ii, gives a frank and not too apologetic account of his problems.

13. *BD* 2nd Ser., vol. xiv, no. 301.

14. Ibid., nos 306, 308, 309, 312, 314, 320; *cf.* Vansittart, *The Mist Procession* pp. 530–1.

15. Ibid., No. 465.

16. Ibid., nos 593, 599, 607.

17. K. Middlemas and J. Barnes, *Baldwin* (1969) pp. 851–5. The naval situation is examined by Professor Arthur Marder in his authoritative article, 'The Royal Navy and the Ethiopian Crisis of 1935–36', *American Historical Review*, (July 1970).

18. *BD* 2nd Ser., vol. xiv, no. 376.

19. Ibid., no. 554; vol. xv, p. 1.

20. The full text of the speech is printed in Ibid., vol. xv, app. iv. See Hoare, *Nine Troubled Years* p. 168.

21. *Cf.* Rosaria Quartararo, 'Imperial Defence in the Mediterranean on the eve of the Ethiopian crisis (July–October 1935)', *HJ*, xx, 1 (1977) 185–220; *BD* 2nd Ser., vol. xv, nos 160, 161, 188, 206, 210.

22. Ibid., nos 71, 178; Hoare, *Nine Troubled Years* pp. 160–1.

23. Avon, *Facing the Dictators* p. 310; *BD* (2) 2nd Ser., vol. xvi, No. 16.

24. H. Feis, *Three International Episodes* (New York, 1947) pp. 315–18.

25. *BD* 2nd Ser., vol. xv, nos 86, 87 (especially note 2).

26. Ibid., nos 91, 95, 115.

27. Ibid., no. 108.

28. Ibid., nos 215, 222, 224, 227.

29. Ibid., no. 251.

30. Ibid., no. 283.,

31. Ibid., no. 274, note 5.

32. Vansittart, *The Mist Procession*, pp. 538–9.

33. Hoare, *Nine Troubled Years*, p. 178.

34. *BD* 2nd Ser., vol. xv, pp. 360–1; no. 293.

35. Ibid., p. 363.

36. Vansittart, *The Mist Procession* p. 539.

37. *BD* 2nd Ser., vol. xv, nos 334, 336, 337, 338.

38. Ibid., p. 754.

39. Laurens, *France and the Italo-Ethiopian Crisis*, pp. 276–7.

40. *BD* 2nd Ser., vol. xv, app. iii (b).

41. Ibid., app. iv (b) *cf.* p. 92 above.

42. Ibid., vol. xvi, chs 1 and 2.

7. APPEASEMENT AND 'INTELLIGENCE' *David Dilks*

1. Austen Chamberlain papers, Birmingham University Library: W. S. Churchill to A. Chamberlain (22 Nov 1924).

2. *Hansard*, HC, 5th Ser.; cccxlvi, 33–4.

3. W. N. Medlicott, *The Economic Blockade* (HMSO, 1952) vol. i, p. 13.

4. Sir K. Strong, *Intelligence at the Top* (Cassell, 1968) pp. 16, 18.

5. Lord Vansittart, *The Mist Procession* (Hutchinson, 1958) p. 398.

6. *Hansard*, HC, 5th Ser., cccii, 367.

7. Sir Horace Wilson recounted this to the author in May 1964.

8. F.O. 954/4: A. Eden to Sir T. Inskip (25 Feb 1937); microfilm in the Brotherton Library, University of Leeds.

9. Vice-Admiral Sir P. Gretton, 'The Nyon Conference – the naval aspect', *EHR*, xc (1975) 103–12.

10. G. Ciano, *Ciano's Diary 1937–1938* (Methuen, 1952) p. 15.

11. Lord Avon, *Facing the Dictators* (Cassell, 1965) p. 520.

12. J. Erickson, *The Soviet High Command* (Macmillan, 1962) p. 432.

13. Christie papers 1/5, Churchill College, Cambridge: Christie's record of a conversation with Goering (3 Feb 1937); Avon, *Facing the Dictators*, p. 520.

14. N.C.: Neville Chamberlain to Ida Chamberlain (20 Mar 1938).

15. Christie papers 1/5, Churchill College, Cambridge: Christie's record of a talk with Goering (28 July 1937).

16. *BD* 3rd Ser., vol. i, pp. 220–1.

17. D. N. Dilks (ed.), *The Diaries of Sir Alexander Cadogan* (Cassell, 1971) pp. 69–70; FO

371/21710: note by Sir R. Vansittart for Lord Halifax (24 Apr 1938).

18. *BD* 3rd Ser., vol. I, pp. 323, 344, 358; Sir K. Strong, *Intelligence at the Top* (Cassell, 1968) p. 33.

19. FO 371/21723,/21736: memoranda by Vansittart (1 June and 9 Aug 1938); N.C.: Neville Chamberlain to Ida Chamberlain (28 May 1938).

20. F. H. Hinsley and others, *British Intelligence in the Second World War* (HMSO, 1979) vol. I, p. 56; Ismay papers, King's College, London, 2/14/1263/2: FO 371/21727, 21729: affidavit by E. von Selzam (8 Apr 1948); memoranda by Vansittart to Halifax (12 and 22 July 1938).

21. A. Duff Cooper, *Old Men Forget* (Hart-Davis, 1953) p. 228; J. W. Wheeler-Bennett, *King George VI: His Life and Reign* (Macmillan, 1958) pp. 346–7.

22. See, for instance, his statement to Parliament on 28 September: 'I have no doubt whatever . . . that my visit alone prevented an invasion, for which everything was ready.' *Hansard*, HC, 5th Ser., CCCXXXIX, 15.

23. Sir K. Strong, *Men of Intelligence* (Cassell, 1970) p. 49.

24. Hinsley and others, *British Intelligence in the Second World War*, vol. I, p. 82.

25. *BD* 3rd Ser., vol. II, p. 550.

26. W.Treue, 'Rede Hitlers vor der Deutschen Presse', *Vierteljahrshefte für Zeitgeschichte*, VI (1958) pp. 183–4.

27. The translations, with a note by F.K.Roberts, are in FO 371/21742.

28. N.C.: Neville Chamberlain to Ida Chamberlain (9 Oct 1938).

29. E.von. Weizsäcker, *Memoirs of Ernst von Weizsäcker* (Gollancz, 1951) p. 165.

30. Templewood papers, Cambridge University Library, XIX, i (B)5: notes of conversation between Lord Templewood and Lord Halifax (5 Dec 1951).

31. *BD* 2nd Ser., vol. XV, p. 693.

32. M.Toscano, *Designs in Diplomacy* (Baltimore: The John Hopkins Press, 1970) pp. 412–13, and *The History of Treaties and International Politics* (Baltimore: The John Hopkins Press, 1966) pp. 29–30.

33. Hinsley and others, *British Intelligence in the Second World War*, vol. I, pp. 52–3.

34. *BD* 2nd Ser., vol. XV, pp. 569–70.

35. M.Muggeridge (ed.), *Ciano's Diplomatic Papers* (Odhams Press, 1948) p. 46, f. 1.

36. Toscano, *Designs in Diplomacy*, p. 409.

37. Muggeridge, *Ciano's Diplomatic Papers* pp. 46, 53, 56–8.

38. FO 371/21198: Sir R.Campbell to the Foreign Office, telegram no. 41 (10 Mar 1937).

39. J.B.Hoptner, *Yugoslavia in Crisis 1934–1941* (Columbia University Press, 1962) p. 125.

40. M.Toscano, *The Origins of the Pact of Steel* (Baltimore: The John Hopkins Press, 1967) pp. 360–1; *BD* 3rd Ser., vol. V, pp. 478, 489–90.

41. M. Toscano, *The History of Treaties* p. 30.

42. Ibid., p. 213.

43. FO 371/21028: minutes by N.Ronald (18 Nov and 2 Dec 1937), and telegram from Foreign Office to Washington (24 Nov 1937).

44. *BD* 3rd Ser., vol. III, p. 280.

45. FO 371/23555: Sir R. Craigie to R.G.Howe (6 Mar 1939).

46. Toscano, *The Origins of the Pact of Steel*, p. 132.

47. Toscano, *Designs in Diplomacy*, pp. 56, 58–60.

48. FO 371/22944: notes by N.Ronald for Lord Halifax's use at the Cabinet (15 Feb 1939).

49. *GD* Ser. D, vol. VII, p. 281.

50. CAB 27/627: memorandum by G.Jebb (19 Jan 1939).

51. FO 800/294: Sir N. Henderson to Sir A.Cadogan (16 Feb 1939).

52. *BD* 3rd Ser., vol. IV, pp. 160–1.

53. S.Aster, *1939: The Making of the Second World War* (Deutsch, 1973) p. 53.

54. FO 371/22966: Sir N.Henderson to Lord Halifax (28 Feb 1939), and minute by W.Strang (7 Mar 1939).

55. Ibid.: minutes by Sir A.Cadogan and Lord Halifax (11 and 12 Mar 1939); I.Colvin, *Vansittart in Office* (Gollancz, 1965) pp. 295–6.

56. Ibid., pp. 298–311; D.N.Dilks (ed.), *The Diaries of Sir Alexander Cadogan* (Cassell, 1971) pp. 162–5.

57. *Hansard*, HC, 5th Ser., CCCXLV, 2343, 2415.

58. Hinsley and others, *British Intelligence in the Second World War*, vol. I, p. 42.

59. Ibid., p. 41.

60. FO 371/23994: minute by Sir A.Cadogan (14 Feb 1939), on a letter of 12 January from Brig-Gen.F.Beaumont-Nesbitt to Sir L.Oliphant.

61. Hinsley and others, *British Intelligence in the Second World War*, vol. I, p. 43.

62. FO 371/23686: memorandum by M12, War Office (4 July 1939), enclosed in Major J.M.Kirkman to L.Collier, Foreign Office (10 July 1939).

63. Dilks, *Cadogan*, pp. 207–8, 227–8, 235; the episode is described, but wrongly dated, in Earl of Birkenhead, *Halifax* (Hamish Hamilton, 1965) p. 419.

64. G.Brook-Shepherd, *The Storm Petrels* (Collins, 1977) pp. 173, 183–4; the junior official of the Foreign Office was Mr J.Cairncross, an account of whose activities appeared in The *Daily Telegraph* (24 Dec 1979) pp. 1, 24.

65. FO 371/23686: minutes by R.A.Butler (25 Aug 1939), L.Collier (26 Aug), Sir O.Sargent (3 Sep).

66. N.C.: Neville Chamberlain to Ida Chamberlain (21 May 1939).

67. Dilks, *Cadogan*, p. 171.

68. N.C.: Neville Chamberlain to Hilda Chamberlain (15 and 30 July 1939).

69. N.C.: Neville Chamberlain to Hilda Chamberlain (15 July 1939).

70. This is the expression which Hitler used in the 'Hossbach' conference of 5 November 1937; *GD* Ser. D, vol. I, p. 32.

71. N.C.: Neville Chamberlain to Ida Chamberlain (23 July 1939).

72. FO 800/316: Lord Halifax to Chamberlain (14 Aug 1939).

73. FO 800/316: Lord Halifax to Chamberlain (19 Aug 1939); *BD* 3rd Ser., vol. VII, p. 127.

74. N.C.: Neville Chamberlain to Hilda Chamberlain (27 Aug 1939).

75. N.C.: Neville Chamberlain to Ida Chamberlain (10 Sep 1939).

76. W.N.Medlicott, *The Economic Blockade* (HMSO, 1952) vol. I, pp. 24–7.

77. Hinsley and others, *British Intelligence in the Second World War*, p. 54; R.Lewin, *Ultra goes to War* (Hutchinson, 1978) pp. 42–5.

8. THE MOSCOW NEGOTIATIONS, 1939 *The late Lord Strang*

The publishers are grateful to Professor Colin Strang for permission to reproduce this essay.

1. Mr (later Sir William, later Lord) Strang had been head of the Central Department of the Foreign Office since January 1937.

2. Arnold and Veronica M. Toynbee (eds), *Survey of International Affairs 1939–1946* (OUP, 1958) vol. II. A more recent study, incorporating much new material, is S. Aster's *1939: The Making of the Second War* (Deutsch, 1973). See also I. Maisky, *Who Helped Hitler?* (Hutchinson, 1964).

3. Lord Strang, *Home and Abroad* (Deutsch, 1956) ch. 5..

4. K. G. Feiling, *The Life of Neville Chamberlain* (Macmillan, 1946) p. 324.

5. This was Ian Colvin, a correspondent in Berlin of the *News Chronicle*. For his visits to

Halifax and Chamberlain, and for other factors, see S. Newman, *March 1939: The British Guarantee of Poland* (Oxford, 1976) p. 182; D. N. Dilks (ed.) *The Diaries of Sir Alexander Cadogan* (Cassell, 1971) pp. 162–5; I. Colvin, *Vansittart in Office* (Gollancz, 1965) pp. 303–11.

6. Feiling, *The Life of Neville Chamberlain*, p. 403.

7. *BD* 3rd Ser., vol. IV, no. 446.

8. *BD* 3rd Ser., vols V and VI give a full documentation; for some of the Russian records, see Ministry of Foreign Affairs of the USSR, *Soviet Peace Efforts on the Eve of World War Two*, 2 vols (Moscow: Novosti Press Agency Publishing House, 1973). The fuller collection of Russian documents *Dokumenty Vneshney Politiki SSSR* has not yet covered 1939.

9. *BD* 3rd Ser., vol. VI, no. 376.

10. Ibid., no. 525.

11. Ibid., no. 636; *cf. Soviet Peace Efforts* vol. II, nos 411, 415.

12. *BD* 3rd Ser., vol. VI, nos 40, 45, 109, 122, 160, 218; *cf. Soviet Peace Efforts* vol. II, nos 432, 440.

13. For the Russian record, ibid., no. 427.

14. Molotov succeeded Litvinov on 3 May. D. C. Watt, in 'The Initiation of the Negotiations leading to the Nazi–Soviet Pact' in C. Abramsky (ed.), *Essays in Honour of E. H. Carr* (Macmillan, 1974) p. 164, offers some evidence that the Russian decision to seek agreement with Germany followed the recall of the ambassador in Berlin, Alexei Merekalov, on 19 April 1939.

15. Russian anxiety on this score emerges clearly in *Soviet Peace Efforts*; see nos 111, 128, 346, 350, 354, 364, 374, 380, 387, 401, 449.

16. W. N. Medlicott, *The Coming of War in 1939* (The Historical Association, 1963) pp. 23–26.

17. Feiling, *The Life of Neville Chamberlain*, p. 403.

18. *BD* 3rd Ser., vol. V, no. 589.

19. A. Bryant, *The Turn of the Tide* (Collins, 1957) p. 472.

20. Department of State, *Foreign Relations of the United States: The Conferences at Cairo and Teheran 1943* (Washington, 1961) pp. 553, 836–7.

For other accounts of the military negotiations, see General A. Beaufre, *1940: The Fall of France* (Cassell, 1967); Admiral Sir R. P. E-E-Drax, 'Mission to Moscow', *The Naval Review*, XL, XLI (1952–3); 'Negotiations between the Military Missions of the USSR, Britain and France in August 1939', *International Affairs*, vols 2–3 (Moscow, Feb–March 1959). C. E. Bohlen, *Witness to History 1929–1969* (Weidenfeld and Nicolson, 1973), shows how information about the German–Russian talks reached the US embassy in Moscow.

List of Contributors

DR KEITH WILSON has been Lecturer in International History at the University of Leeds since 1969. He is the author of articles on British foreign policy before the First World War, and is currently completing a monograph on that subject.

DR PHILIP TAYLOR is Lecturer in International History at the University of Leeds and is co-author of a book to be published shortly on British propaganda during the First World War; he is also writing a volume on the projection of Britain between the wars.

DR NORMAN HILLMER is an official historian at the Department of National Defence, Ottawa, and holds a part-time appointment at Carleton University. He was visiting Professor of Modern Commonwealth History at Leeds, 1978–9, and is English-language Secretary of the Canadian Historical Association.

PROFESSOR W. N. MEDLICOTT is Senior Editor of *Documents on British Foreign Policy*, and the author of books and articles on the history of the nineteenth and twentieth centuries. He held the Stevenson chair of International History at London University from 1953 to 1967, and wrote the official history of *The Economic Blockade*.

PROFESSOR MICHAEL HOWARD is Regius Professor of Modern History at the University of Oxford, having previously held the Chichele chair of the History of War at All Souls' College, Oxford, and Professor of War Studies at London. His numerous books and articles include *The Continental Commitment* and the official history *Grand Strategy*, vol. IV.

THE LATE LORD STRANG served in the Foreign Office from 1919 to 1953 (as head of the Central Department, 1937–9; British representative on the European Advisory Commission, 1943–5; Permanent Under-Secretary, 1949–53). He wrote *Britain in World Affairs* and *Home and Abroad*.

PROFESSOR DAVID DILKS has held the chair of International History at the University of Leeds since 1970. He is engaged upon a biography of Neville Chamberlain.

Index

Abyssinia   16, 17, 89, 90, 93, 96,
    103, 111, 118–28, 130, 132, 133,
    135, 136, 137, 138, 143, 151
Acland, F. D.   49
Admiralty *see* Britain, Royal Navy
Admiralty War Staff   27
Afghanistan   2
Agadir crisis *see* Moroccan crisis
    (1911)
Aitken, M. *see* Beaverbrook, Lord
Albania   140, 159, 162, 173
Algeciras Conference *see* Moroccan
    crisis (1905–6)
Allen, Lord (of Hurtwood)   86
Amery, L. C. M. S.   65, 70, 72, 73,
    76
Anglo-French agreement (1904)   4,
    6, 21, 25, 29, 32–3, 37, 39, 40
Anglo-Japanese alliance (1902)   3,
    35
Anglo-Russian agreement
    (1907)   5, 6, 25, 34–7, 38, 39
Anschluss   18, 91, 113, 139, 143, 144,
    146, 147
Air Force *see* Britain, RAF
Army *see* Britain, British Army
Asquith, H. H. (Earl of Oxford and
    Asquith)   7, 27, 30, 34, 35, 46
Assab   122, 135
Ashton-Gwatkin, F. T. A.   80
Australia   64, 67, 72, 75, 76, 77, 103,
    159
Austria: –1914   2, 8, 23, 26, 37, 40;
    1914–18   8, 9, 12; 1919–39   119,
    151; *see also* Anschluss

Badoglio, Marshal P.   119, 128, 138
Baldwin, S. (Earl Baldwin of
    Bewdley)   85, 86, 127, 131, 133,
    134, 143
Balfour, A. J. (Earl of Balfour)   40,
    76
Balkan Wars (1912–13)   22–3, 27
Balkans   8, 22–3, 27, 37, 38, 116,
    176
Baltic States   165, 176, 177, 178,
    180, 185
BBC   62
Beak, G.   57
Beaverbrook, Lord   48, 49, 52, 53,
    56, 58, 61
Beck, J.   173, 174, 175, 179
Belgium   2, 8, 13, 19, 23, 26, 27, 67,
    95, 98, 109, 161, 169, 176
Belisha, L. Hore *see* Hore-Belisha,
    Leslie
Beneš, E.   149
Berchtesgaden   173
Berlin Congress (1878)   1
Bessarabia   165
Bismarck, O. von   4, 44
Blomberg, W. von   83
Blum, L.   96, 97
Blunden, E.   110
Boer War   3
Bonnet, G.   158
Bono, Marshal E. de   119
Bowles, T. G.   22
Brett, R. *see* Esher, Lord
Britain: –1914   1–8, 21–41, 43–8;
    1914–18   1, 8–11, 42–3, 48–56;

1919–29   11–13, 14–16, 56–63, 64–76, 137; 1930–9   1, 11, 13, 16–20, 77, 78–101, 102–17, 119–38, 139–69, 170–84; 1939–45   14, 105, 107, 168; 169, 184–6; British Army   8, 9, 23–8, 30–2, 88, 93, 104, 105, 109, 110, 115, 119, 129, 171, 180, 181–2, 183, 184; British Council   63; British Empire: –1919   2, 3, 13, 23, 28, 35, 37, 40, 41, 102, 153; 1919–   13–14, 16, 18, 19, 62, 64–77, 86, 93, 102, 103, 108, 109, 111, 112, 113, 116, 121–3, 125, 145; British Expeditionary Force (BEF):   –1918   24–6, 27, 109; 1919–   104, 109, 110, 111, 112, 113. 115; RAF   14, 85, 89, 93, 94, 95, 104–5, 109, 110, 111, 112, 113, 114, 115, 116, 119, 128, 140, 142, 143, 145, 147, 149, 161, 166, 168, 169, 171, 172; Royal Navy   1, 2, 3, 4, 5, 6, 7, 8, 9, 12, 13, 14, 17, 24, 28–32, 33, 34, 80, 89, 94, 102, 103, 104, 107, 109, 110, 111, 115, 116, 120, 122, 124, 127, 128, 129, 131, 135, 137, 140, 144–5, 149, 151, 161, 165, 166, 168, 177

Bruce, S. (Lord Bruce)   76
Brüning, Dr H.   81
Buchan, J. (Lord Tweedsmuir)   52
Buchanan, Sir G.   39, 40
Burgess, G. de M.   163
Butler, R. A. (Lord Butler)   163, 177
Burma   103, 104

Cadogan, Sir, A.   139, 147, 154, 159, 161, 163, 165
Cambon, P.   38
Cameroons   97
Campbell, Sir R. H.   154
Campbell-Bannerman, Sir H.   33

Canada   2, 12, 65, 66, 67, 68, 69, 70, 71, 72, 73, 74, 75, 76
Canaris, Admiral W.   161, 162
Cartwright, Sir F.   22
Chamberlain, Sir J. A.   15, 18, 52, 55, 65, 67, 70, 71, 137
Chamberlain, A. N.   15, 18, 81, 99, 101, 106, 109, 110, 112, 114, 137, 142, 143, 144, 146, 147, 148, 149, 150, 154, 156, 158, 160, 161, 164, 167, 168, 172, 173, 174, 183
Chatfield, Admiral Sir E. (Lord Chatfield)   103, 128, 144
Chilston, Lord   156, 163
China   13, 16, 102, 144
Christie, Group-Capt M. G.   145, 146, 148
Churchill, Sir W. L. S.   9, 14, 15, 28, 39, 78, 79, 90, 130, 140, 141, 150, 172, 184, 185
Ciano, Count G.   98, 145, 154, 166
Clerk, Sir G. R.   119
Clifford, Sir B.   73
Coates, J.   76
Code and Cypher School   109
Collier, Sir L.   87, 91
Colonies: British see British Empire;
French   97–8;
German   7, 92, 93, 97, 98, 137;
Italian   118–37
Committee of Imperial Defence (CID):   –1919   5, 25, 28–30, 31, 32, 33, 35, 47, 97; 1919–   97, 105, 142
Commonwealth see British Empire
Conservative Party   13, 62, 90, 133
Constantini, S.   150, 151, 152
Corbin, C.   86
Cook, Sir E.   48
Craigie, Sir R. L.   156, 157
Cranborne, Lord (5th Marquess of Salisbury)   93

Crewe, Marquess of 30
Crewe House (Enemy Propaganda,
Department of) 48, 55
Crowe, Sir Eyre 21, 23, 40, 79
Czechoslovak Crisis (1938) 18, 91,
114, 140, 147, 148, 149, 150, 172,
174
Czechoslovakia 91, 99, 113, 114,
115, 144, 146, 159, 160, 168, 173,
175, 179; see also Czechoslovak
Crisis (1938)

Daily Chronicle 56
Daily Mail 44
Daily Telegraph 46
Dalziel, J. 61
Danakil 132, 135, 136
Danzig 165, 166, 173
Defence expenditure 33–4, 106–7,
109, 111, 115, 116; see also Air
Force, Army, Navy
Derby, Lord (15th Earl of) 45
Dieckhoff, H. 96
Dillon, E. J. 46
Disarmament Conference (League of
Nations) 82
Dollfuss, Dr E. 85
Donald, R. 48, 51, 56
Douglas, J. 36
Drummond, Sir E. (later Earl of
Perth) 124
Drummond, Lady 154

Economic crisis (1929–39) 16, 106
Economic Warfare, Ministry
of 141
Eden, Sir Anthony (later Earl of
Avon) 19, 83, 88, 89, 92, 93, 94,
95, 96, 97, 98, 99, 101, 124, 126,
127, 130, 131, 133, 135, 137, 138,
143, 144, 145, 151, 153, 185

Egypt 2, 100, 102, 113, 121
Eire see Irish Free State
Empire see British Empire
Enemy Propaganda, Department of
see Crewe House
Enigma machine 169
Eritrea 119, 122, 132, 135
Esher, Lord 28, 29
Estonia 176, 179
Ethiopia see Abyssinia
Evening News 44
Ewart, General Sir J. 24, 25

Far East 3, 12, 13, 14, 16, 17, 103,
104, 105, 107, 108, 109, 112, 116,
128, 157, 159, 182
Finland 176, 179, 183, 184
First World War 9–11; causes 8,
40, 47; intelligence and 139;
press and 48–56
Fisher, Admiral Sir J. (Lord Fisher of
Kilverstone) 4, 7, 29
Fisher, Sir W. 80, 106, 108, 124
Flandin, P-E. 137, 138
Foreign Office: dominions
and 64–77; intelligence
and 139–69; press and 43–63;
see also under countries and areas
which are the subjects of British
diplomacy.
Franco, General F. 144, 146
France: –1914 2, 3, 4, 5, 6, 7, 8,
21, 22, 23, 25, 26, 27, 28, 29, 30, 32,
33, 34, 37, 38, 39, 40;
1914–18 8–10; 1919–29 12, 14,
15, 16, 67, 69, 75, 105, 116;
1930–9 11, 13, 17, 18, 19, 80, 84,
85, 86, 87, 88, 89, 90, 91, 93, 94, 95,
96, 97, 98, 99, 100, 109, 114, 115,
119, 120, 122–3, 124, 128–9, 130,
133, 135, 137–8, 142, 143, 144, 145,
146, 147, 148, 149, 154, 158, 161,

163, 164, 165, 166, 168, 169, 170, 171, 173, 174, 175, 177, 178, 179, 180, 181, 183, 184, 185; 1939–45   117, 169, 184
French, Field Marshal Sir J. (Earl of Ypres)   26

Galla   132
Gamelin, General M.   119, 138, 149
Garibaldi, General E.   133, 134
General Staff: British   23–4, 27, 29, 31, 35, 108, 115; French   26, 115; German   160; Italian   119
George II (King of Greece)   155
George V   134
Germany: –1914   2, 3, 4, 5, 6, 7, 8, 22, 23, 25, 26, 28, 29, 30, 31, 32, 34, 37, 38, 39, 40, 47; 1914–18   8–11, 12, 57; 1919–29   14, 15, 67, 108; 1930–9   17, 18, 19, 20, 78–101, 103, 105, 107, 109, 111, 112, 113–14, 115, 116, 117, 119, 120, 123, 124, 125, 128, 129, 138, 139, 140, 141, 142–3, 144, 145, 146, 147, 148, 149, 150, 151, 152, 153, 154, 155, 156, 157, 158, 159, 160, 161, 162, 163, 164, 165, 166, 167, 168, 169, 171, 172, 173, 174, 175, 176, 177, 178, 179, 180, 181, 182, 183; 1939–45   105, 117, 155, 165, 168, 169, 184, 185
Gibraltar   127, 151
Godesberg   173
Goebbels, Dr J.   83
Goering, Field Marshal H.   83, 89, 90, 145, 146
Goschen, Sir E.   31
Grandi, Count D.   119, 134, 135, 137, 152, 154
Graves, R.   110
Great Britain see Britain
Greece   18, 116, 151, 155, 161, 174, 176

Gregory, J. D.   62
Grey, Sir E. (Lord Grey of Fallodon)   5, 6, 7, 8, 22, 25, 27, 31, 32, 33, 34, 35, 36, 37, 38, 39, 40, 46, 78
Guest, S. A.   57

Haile Selassie, Emperor of Ethiopia   121, 122, 126, 127, 130, 132, 133, 136, 138
Haldane, R. B. (Lord Haldane of Cloan)   23, 26, 27, 30, 32, 35
Halifax, Earl of   97, 144, 148, 154, 156, 157, 159, 167, 185
Hall, Admiral Sir R.   50
Hankey, M. P. A. (Lord Hankey)   84, 89, 90, 109, 124
Hardinge, Sir C. (Lord Hardinge of Penshurst)   30, 31, 36, 37, 38, 39, 60
Harlech, Lord (4th Baron)   137
Harmsworth, Alfred see Northcliffe, Lord
Harmsworth, Harold see Rothermere, Lord
Hart, Capt B. H. Liddell   110
Havas news agency   45
Headlam-Morley, Sir J. W.   59, 60
Hearst press   51
Henderson, Sir N.   139, 147, 150, 155, 158, 159, 160
Herat   36
Hertzog, General J.   73, 76
Hitler, A.   16, 17, 19, 78, 80, 81, 82, 83, 84, 85, 86, 88, 89, 90, 93, 94, 95, 96, 98, 100, 101, 110, 115, 123, 129, 130, 139, 142, 143, 145, 147, 148, 149, 152, 153, 157, 158, 159, 160, 161, 164, 165, 166, 167, 171, 173, 174, 175, 181, 182, 183, 184
Hoare, Sir S. J. G. (Lord Templewood)   89, 90, 92, 124,

125, 126, 129, 130, 131, 133, 134, 135, 136, 137
Hoare–Laval Pact 92, 118, 125, 130, 133, 134, 135–6
Hoesch, L. von 88, 89, 90
Hore-Belisha, L. (Lord Hore-Belisha) 113
Hossbach memorandum 166
Howard, Sir E. (Lord Howard of Penrith) 70
Hurst, Sir C. 66

Imperial Conference (1926) 65–7, 76
India 2, 4, 5, 13, 14, 35–6, 37, 39, 102, 103, 104
Indian Ocean 12, 103
Industrial Intelligence Centre 141
Information, Ministry of 43, 48, 52, 53, 54, 55
Inskip, Sir T. W. H. (Lord Caldecote) 107, 112
Intelligence: British 139–42, 144–69;
British Armed Services 141–2, 162;
French 146, 148, 169;
German 149, 150, 161;
Italian 150–5, 157;
Polish 169;
Soviet 152, 154, 155, 156, 157, 163; US 146, 159
International Court of Justice 65
Iran see Persia
Ireland, Northern 113
Irish Free State 64, 65, 66, 68, 69, 70, 71, 72, 74, 75, 76
Italy: –1914 23; 1919–29 14, 15; 1930–9 17, 18, 20, 87, 89, 93, 96, 98, 100, 103, 107, 111, 114, 116, 117, 118–38, 139, 140, 143, 144, 145, 146, 150, 151, 152, 153, 154,

155, 156, 157, 158, 159, 161, 165, 166, 167, 168, 171; 1939–45 117, 155.

Japan: –1914 3, 4, 5, 9, 33, 34, 35; 1919–29 12, 16, 69, 70, 73, 75; 1930–9 17, 18, 102, 103, 107, 109, 112, 113, 114, 116, 123, 124, 125, 128, 139, 142, 144, 146, 155, 156, 157, 159, 162, 165, 168, 171, 182, 183
Jews, national home for 13, 113
Jones, K. 44, 47, 60
Jones, T. 94
Jouvenel, B. de 94

Kabul 35
Kandahar 35
Kandelaki, David 145
Kenya 121, 122
Keynes, J. M. (Lord Keynes) 106
King, W. L. Mackenzie 69, 70, 71, 73, 74, 76, 77
Kerr, Philip see Lothian, Lord
Knollys, Lord 34
Koppell, P. 65, 68
Krivitsky, W. 146, 163

Labour Party 13, 111, 112
Lansdowne, 5th Marquess of 5, 33
Laval, P. 86, 89, 92, 119, 122, 127, 128, 129, 131, 132, 133, 134, 135, 136, 137, 138; see also Hoare–Laval Pact
Latvia 176, 177–8, 179
League of Nations 11, 16, 17, 53, 65, 66, 67, 82, 87, 92, 93, 95, 99, 108, 112, 118, 123, 124, 125, 127, 128, 129, 130, 131, 132, 133, 134, 136, 138, 153

Léger, A. St L. 127
Leith-Ross, Sir F. 80, 85
Liberal Party 34, 35, 112
Lithuania 173
Litvinov, M. 156, 181, 184
Lloyd-George, D. (Earl Lloyd-George) 11, 52, 53, 55, 56
Locarno Agreements 15, 16, 64, 66, 67, 87, 92, 95, 98, 99, 104, 108
Locock, G. 49
Londonderry, 7th Marquess of 78, 80
Loraine, Sir P. 139
Loreburn, Lord 22, 32, 37
Lothian, 11th Marquess of 86

MacDonald, J. R. 85, 93, 109
McKenna, R. 7, 26, 30
Maclean, D. 163
Maffey, Sir J. (Lord Rugby) 120
Mair, G. 48
Maisky, I. 154
Malaya 102, 103
Malkin, Sir W. 74, 76
Mallett, Sir L. 40
Malta 127
Manchuria 13, 16, 182
Masaryk, J. 149, 150
Masterman, C. F. G. 48
Matsuoka, Y. 157
Maurice, General Sir F. 50
Mediterranean 13, 17, 40, 103, 111, 112, 115, 116, 120, 127, 128, 131, 144, 145, 157
Mein Kampf 78, 82, 94, 99
Memel 91, 160, 173
Menzies, Maj.-Gen. Sir S. 169
Metternich, Count W. von 22, 23, 39
Middle East 13, 39, 113, 116, 144
Milner, Lord 52
Molotov, V. 163, 167, 170, 175,

177, 180, 181, 185, 186; see also Nazi–Soviet Pact
Mongolia 182
Monroe doctrine 10
Montgomery, Sir H. 66
Morley, Lord 32, 34, 35, 36, 37, 39
Morning Post 46
Morocco crisis (1905–6) 5, 34
Morocco crisis (1911) 7, 22, 39
Morton, Major D. 141
Moscow Conference (1943) 185
Munich Conference 18, 114, 147, 148, 150, 157, 166, 173, 174
Mussolini, B. 17, 83, 85, 93, 96, 111, 118, 119, 120, 123, 126, 127, 128, 129, 130, 131, 132, 133, 134, 136, 137, 138, 139, 143, 145, 151, 152, 154, 155, 156, 157, 159, 166, 167, 168, 173

Naggiar, P. E. 163, 170, 179
Navy, see Britain, Royal Navy
Nazi–Soviet Pact (1939) 163–5, 167, 179, 180–1, 185
Netherlands 2, 19, 93, 109, 158, 161, 169, 176
Neuve Chapelle 9
Neurath, Baron K. von 83, 89, 90, 153
New Zealand 64, 66, 67, 72, 75, 76, 77, 102, 103, 159
Newfoundland 76
News Chronicle 156
Newton, Lord 51
Nicolson, Sir A. (Lord Carnock) 31, 34, 38, 40
Nicholas II (Tsar of Russia) 40
Norway 169
Northcliffe, Lord 48, 49, 52, 53, 55, 56, 58, 60, 61
Nyon Conference 144

Ogaden 121, 122, 125, 126, 127, 132, 135, 136
Olympic Games (Berlin 1936) 96
Ommanney, Capt. R. 23, 24
Ormsby-Gore, W., see Harlech, Lord 137
Osusky, S. 149
Ottley, Admiral Sir C. 28

Pacific 7
Palestine 13, 113
Palmerston, Lord 45
Papacy 75, 132
Paris Peace Treaties (1919–20) see Versailles Settlement
Paul (Prince Regent of Yugoslavia) 154
Persia 2, 36–7
Persian Gulf 2, 103
Peterson, Sir M. 132, 133
Phipps, Sir E. 82, 83, 84, 86, 87, 88, 89, 94, 96, 123, 152, 153
Plymouth, Earl of 97
Press Bureau 48, 49, 56, 58
Poland 10, 18, 99, 147, 154, 160, 163, 165, 167, 168, 171, 173, 174, 175, 176, 177, 179, 180, 181, 182, 183, 185

RAF see Britain, RAF
Reid, Sir R. see Loreburn, Lord
Reuters 45
Ribbentrop, J. von 83, 86, 96, 98, 99, 153, 163, 165, 167, 185: see also Nazi-Soviet Pact
Rhine 13, 64
Rhineland 17, 18, 67, 78, 79, 92, 94, 138, 143
Riddell, Lord 54, 55, 61
Riga, Treaty of (1921) 182
Rome-Berlin Axis 145, 153, 154, 157

Rosenberg, A. 91
Rothermere, Lord 61
Romania 18, 161, 173, 174, 176, 177, 179
Ruhr 67
Rumbold, Sir H. 79, 82
Runciman, Lord 93
Russia: –1914 2, 3, 4, 5, 6, 7, 8, 22, 23, 25, 30, 33, 34–41; 1914–17 9–10, 11; 1917– see Soviet Union

Saar 86
Salisbury, 3rd Marquis of 1, 3
Salisbury, 5th Marquis of see Cranborne, Lord
Sargent, Sir O. G. 80, 84, 87, 90, 91, 99, 100, 164, 177
Sassoon, S. 110
Schacht, H. 85, 97, 98
Secret Intelligence Service see Intelligence, British
Secret Service see Intelligence
Seeds, Sir W. 170, 177, 184
Selby, Sir W. H. M. 80, 82
Shortt, E. 58
Simon, Sir J. A. (Lord Simon) 18, 80, 84, 87, 88, 89, 119, 120, 124
Singapore 12, 13, 16, 103, 104, 107, 108, 109, 115, 116, 159
Skelton, O. D. 71
SIS see Intelligence, British
Slade, Admiral Sir E. 29
Somaliland: British 121, 122, 125, 126; French 127, 135, 138; Italian 121, 135
Sorge, R. 155, 156
South Africa 64, 65, 66, 67, 69, 71, 72, 73, 75, 76, 77
Soviet Union: –1917 see Russia; 1917–29 11, 15, 16, 58, 62; 1930–9 17, 87, 88, 89, 90, 91, 94,

99, 100, 115, 139, 145, 146, 148,
151, 152, 154, 155, 156, 157, 160,
162, 163, 164, 165, 167, 168, 170,
171, 173, 174–84; 1939–45   155,
183, 184–6
Spain   96, 99, 144
Spanish Civil War   151, 152
Spender, J. A.   46, 47
Stalin, J.   139, 145, 146, 156, 164,
165, 180, 183, 184, 185
Steed, W.   46
Stoyadinovich, M.   154
Strang, Sir W. (Lord Strang)   100,
159, 164, 170, 177, 185–6
Stresa Conference   89, 123, 138
Sudan   2, 121, 122
Sudetenland see Czechoslovakian
crisis (1938)
Swettenham, Sir F.   48
Switzerland   57, 92, 134, 176

Tabouis, Mme G.   136
Tallents, Sir S.   63
Tanganyika   12, 18, 116, 161, 174,
176
Templewood, Lord see Hoare,
Sir S. J. G.
Teheran Conference (1943)   184
The Times   45, 46, 52
Tibet   2
Tirpitz, Admiral A. von   6
Togoland   97
Toynbee, A.   94, 172
Triple Alliance   41
Turkey   12, 18, 116, 161, 174, 176
Tweedmouth, 3rd Baron   33
Tyrrell, Sir W. (Lord Tyrrell)   46,
47, 49, 54, 59, 60, 61, 64

Uganda   121
Ukraine   91, 156, 173

United Kingdom see Britain
United Nations   11
United States of
America: –1914   2, 3;
1914–18   10–11, 12, 51, 53;
1919–29   11, 12, 13, 16, 53–4, 68,
71; 1930–9   17, 19, 103, 107, 111,
124, 128, 131, 142, 156, 157, 159,
163, 165, 168, 171, 175, 185;
1939–45   168, 185
USSR see Soviet Union

Vansittart, Sir R. G. (Lord
Vansittart)   60, 78, 79, 80, 81, 82,
83, 85, 86, 87, 88, 89, 90, 91, 92, 96,
97, 99, 101, 108, 120, 121, 124, 125,
126, 127, 129, 131, 132, 133, 134,
135, 136, 137, 142, 146, 147, 148,
159, 160
Venezuela   131
Versailles Settlement   11, 53–4, 80,
84, 85, 125, 171
Voroshilov, Marshal K.   179, 183

Walwal incident   118, 121, 122,
124, 136
Washington Conference
(1921–2)   61
Weizsäcker, E. von   150
Wellesley, Sir V.   80
Wells, H. G.   44
Westminster, Statute of (1931)   77
Wigram, R.   78, 79, 80, 81, 85, 86,
88, 90, 91, 93, 96, 100
Wilkinson, S.   46
Willert, Sir A.   61
William II (German Emperor)   4,
5, 6, 31, 32
Wilson, Admiral Sir A. K.   28, 29
Wilson, Field Marshal Sir H.   25,
26, 27, 31

Wilson, Sir H. J.   141, 143
Wilson, President W.   11, 52
Wood, Edward *see* Halifax, Earl of
Wolff news agency   45

Yoshida, S.   156
Yugoslavia   116, 151, 154

Zeila   122, 125, 126, 127, 135